Prue's New
COUNTRY COOKING

Prue Coats

Prue's New Country Cooking

Prue Coats

with photographs by
Matthew Lloyd

Merlin Unwin Books

First published as Prue's New Country Kitchen by Colt Books in 1997
This revised edition published as Prue's New Country Cooking
by Merlin Unwin Books, 2004

ISBN 1 873674 78 3

Merlin Unwin Books
Palmers House
7 Corve Street
Ludlow
Shropshire SY8 1DB
U.K.
books@merlinunwin.co.uk
www.countrybooksdirect.com

Designed & Typeset by Jo Dovey at Think Graphic Design, Ludlow, Shropshire.
Printed in Great Britain by Cambridge University Press

This book is dedicated to the memory of
'Old Archie', gourmet, great sportsman and countryman,
and to his grandson 'Young Archie,' in the hopes that
he will follow in his grandfather's footsteps,
and to Tabitha, his granddaughter, already
a chip off the old block.

ACKNOWLEDGEMENTS

I should like to thank all the people who have helped me with this book, especially my daughter Lucy for her support and advice throughout, and Merlin and Karen Unwin, my publishers, who have been so patient and helpful. To all my friends who have contributed ideas or recipes, my heartfelt thanks and especially to *Shooting Times* and *The Field* for allowing me to include some of my game recipes which were first published in those magazines. The all-important 'tasting panel' have been invaluable with their objective comments.

ABOUT THE AUTHOR

Prue Coats was born in Scotland and grew up in Buckinghamshire, surrounded by horses. During the war she worked for the Free French and afterwards for the British Bloodstock Agency. In 1952 she married Archie Coats, the famous wood pigeon shooter. Their life together was filled with good sport which led to the pleasures of the table and many convivial friendships. All this reflected in her varied and excellent recipes.

Prue Coats is a well-known contributor to *Shooting Times* and *The Field*. Her first book, *Prue's Country Kitchen* (1988) was instantly popular. *The Poacher's Cookbook* (1993) has been described as the best book on game.

She is also the author of *Simply Salmon and other Gourmet Food* (1995)

Contents

FOREWORD by Colin Willock............... xi

INTRODUCTION xiii

SOUPS 1-16
Hot Meat Soups............................. 2
Hot Vegetable Soups............................ 5
Cold Vegetable Soups.................... 7
Fish Soups.................................. 11
Rib-Sticking Soups 12
Stocks and Thickeners 15

STARTERS 19-36
Cold Starters.............................. 20
Hot Starters 24
Pâtés, Terrines and Raised Pies 29
Fish Pâtés 35
Vegetarian Pâté 36

FISH 39-47

GAME 49-67
Game Seasons............................. 51
Roasting Times............................. 51
Accompaniments for Game................. 51
Feathered Game 52
'Furred' Game.............................. 61
Venison.................................... 64

MEAT 69-82
Beef....................................... 70
Lamb 75
Pork....................................... 78
Ham....................................... 80
Offal 81

POULTRY 85-95

FAMILY FARE 97-101

VEGETABLES 103-108

FUNGI 111-114

SALADS 117-123

SAUCES 125-136
Roux-based Sauces and Variations..... 126
Short Sauces 128
Butter Sauces 129
Other Hot Sauces 130
Warm Sauces 132
Cold Sauces 134
Fruit-based Sauces 136

BASIC KITCHEN EQUIPMENT 137

STORE CUPBOARD FLAVOURINGS 138

HERBS, HERB VINEGARS, OILS AND CONDIMENTS 139-147
Herbs, Garden 140
Herbs, Seasonal Wild 142
Herb Vinegars, Oils & Condiments ... 144

PUDDINGS 149-163
Hot Puddings 150
Cold Puddings........................... 155
Ice Creams and Sorbets.................. 160

BREAD, CAKES AND BISCUITS 165-171

PRESERVES AND BOTTLING 173-187
Jellies 174
Jams...................................... 177
Chutney 180
Pickled Fruit and Vegetables............. 184
Bottling 185

DRINKS 189-198
Non-alcoholic Drinks..................... 190
Alcoholic Drinks 192

INDEX 202

Foreword

When I wrote the foreword to *Prue's Country Kitchen* in 1987, I felt sure this would not be the last time we would hear of this remarkable cooking lady. Since then, she has produced *The Poacher's Cookbook* and *Simply Salmon,* apart from being a regular and popular contributor to *The Field* and *Shooting Times.* Now with *Prue's New Country Cooking*, she has brought all this together in a major new statement of her philosophy of the kitchen.

Many of the game and pigeon recipes that made the original book required reading for cooks with country tastes are, of course, still included. But Prue has widened the dimensions of her country kitchen greatly, while still retaining the basis of her cookery philosophy, that much good food can be bought by visiting vegetable markets, local butchers and farm shops, pick-your-own fruit farms, and the like. Do not always, she is saying, take the supermarket's word for it. Look at the labels. See where it came from and remember that much of the best meat, fruit and vegetables in the world are grown in British meadows, orchards and farms.

Though I have known Prue for many years, it came as something of a surprise to learn when talking to her abut this book that she did not really become serious about cooking until she married the late Archie Coats. The 'Master', as he was known to the shooting world, made his living as a professional pigeon shooter. Among the many other good things he brought into Prue's life were two items which had a profound influence on her then-dormant cooking talents. Archie loved good food. In fact he held a certificate from an exclusive school of cookery in Paris attesting to his skill as a cooker of fine meats and blender of sauces. The second influence was introduced by the endless stream of pigeons, and game, and all manner of country produce, that Archie and his shooting companions and friends brought into the household. At one stage the 'Master' was accounting for 25,000 wood pigeon a year. Most of these were sold to earn a living but there was inevitably a surplus to be disposed of. Prue began to invent recipes for cooking this most appetising and delicious bird. It was inevitable that this taste for experiment and invention, encouraged by Archie, should spread to other forms of cooking.

Once the cooking juices had, so to speak, started flowing, there was no stopping Prue. She was perhaps happiest when trying something new on friends and even happier when they approved. 'Cooks,' she says, 'are a bit like actors and painters. They yearn for their work to be appreciated and, if possible, applauded. The best cookery audiences are friends. They will tell you honestly if they think a dish is marvellous and will be equally frank if it isn't.'

She declares that cooking is the perfect antidote to stress. Though she works on a word processor, she finds, like many others, that staring at the letters dancing on the screen for too long can be stressful. When this happens, she switches the wretched thing off, goes into her country kitchen and just cooks something or perhaps tries out a new recipe. Many of these, praise be, have found a permanent home in this book. I'd hate her to get too stressed but I'd like the recipes to keep coming.

Colin Willock
September 2004

KEY TO SYMBOLS

F Freebie

Q Quickie

V Vegetarian

Introduction

Things have changed in the last few years and people have become much more aware of where their food comes from. Farmers' markets, farm shops and regional food festivals have grown beyond recognition, as have the number of small producers. Mail-order has become a big thing and has probably saved many of them from going under.

Another sign of the times is the increasingly hectic pace at which we live and the number of people who juggle careers and family. In order to cater for this new trend I have removed from the earlier editions of this book a lot of the outdated and time-consuming recipes and replaced them with what I call 'Quickies'. However I have still kept some of my favourite traditional dishes for those special occasions. Anyway, for many people cooking can be a therapy and there is nothing nicer than knocking up some fabulous dish for a family get-together or social event.

Wherever possible I have used and mentioned local producers. Britain produces some of the best meat, fish, vegetables and fruit in the world, so let's keep them going. As I have said in the cheese section of this book, our cheeses can face the toughest competition and still come out on top.

Here's to Great Britain's great food and produce! So get cooking and, wherever possible, forget those 'ready-meals.'

Prue Coats
September 2004

Illustration by William Garfit

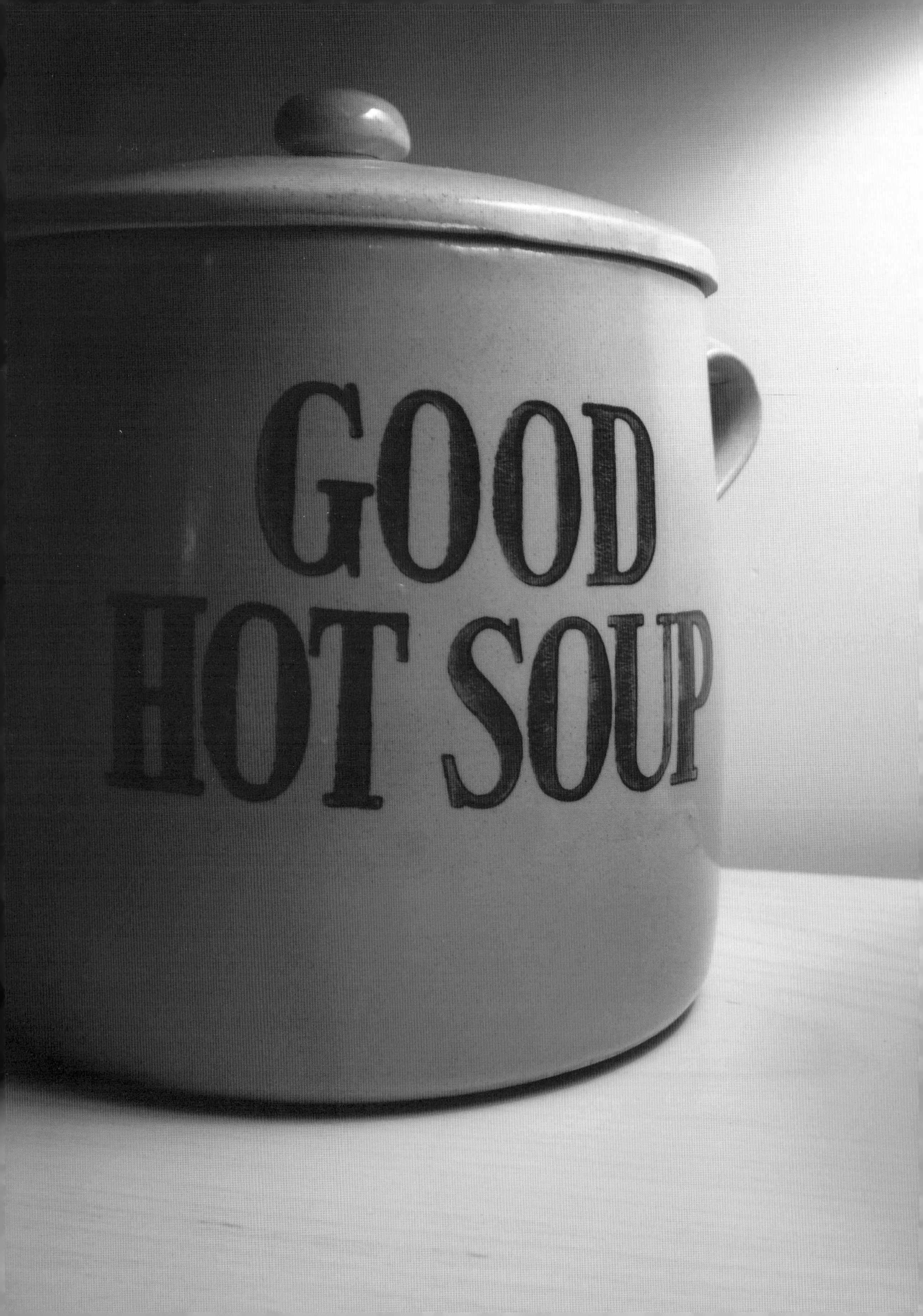
GOOD
HOT SOUP

SOUPS

Sensuous and even sexy, soup runs the gamut of the culinary experience. It ranges from delicate cream of sorrel, precursor to a gourmet repast, to the all-time comfort of a rib-sticking soup, subliminal successor to the poacher's pot which contained everything available in season. Contrary to received wisdom, soup can be one of the quickest dishes to make and, therefore, perfect for the working person. Soups are also wonderful for using up odds and ends in the fridge though, of course, one can never repeat these spontaneous delights. One of the best I ever concocted contained a wedge of apple pie! Vegetable soups take as little as 15–20 minutes from start to finish and, by not overcooking them, you retain the fresh taste. One hostess told me with pride that her vegetable soup had been cooking for 3 hours. All I can say is that it looked like khaki sludge and the smell was reminiscent of school dinners. Stock-based and meat soups are another tale altogether, and the former is one of my culinary 'musts'. No carcass or bone goes into the bin without first having been made into stock, which can then be frozen as a basis for soups or sauces (see page 15).

Chicken and Barley Broth

SERVES 6–8

This simple and delicious broth has its origins in the days when there were such things as boiling fowls. These were 2–3 year old hens which had ceased to lay many eggs, or a rooster whose sex life was deemed by the farmer to have come to an end. In both cases, the meat would have been too stringy to eat on its own.

This is real comfort food and has been used for centuries as convalescent fare by Jewish matriarchs.

You can, if you wish, use a cooked chicken carcass but the taste is best when this soup is made with uncooked poultry. You could also substitute 6 chicken drumsticks for the chicken.

1 chicken, weighing about 1 kg/2.2 lb
2 onions, peeled and cut up
2.25 litres/4 pints water
110 g/4 oz pearl barley
strip of lemon zest
salt and pepper

TO GARNISH
1 hard-boiled egg, finely chopped
2 tablespoons chopped fresh parsley

Place all the ingredients, except the egg and parsley, in a large saucepan and bring slowly to the boil. Turn the heat down and simmer slowly for 2 hours.

Remove the lemon zest and as many of the bones as possible, chop any large bits of meat and serve in bowls, with a garnish of chopped hard-boiled egg and parsley.

Duck Soup, with Wild Mushrooms and Madeira

SERVES 4–6

This can be made with duck, goose or wild duck. It is rich and, as the French would say, unctuous. You can use any kind of wild mushroom, either garnered from field or hedgerow or bought fresh or dried wild mushrooms. This is a real dinner-party offering and should be followed by a light main course.

1 duck carcass, cooked
1 onion
1 carrot
1 celery stalk
1.2 litres/2 pints chicken stock
pinch of dried sage
25 g/1 oz butter
1 shallot, peeled and finely chopped
110 g/4 oz fresh wild mushrooms, sliced thinly, or 40 g/1½ oz dried porcini
25 g/1 oz plain flour
150 ml/¼ pint Madeira
2–3 drops balsamic vinegar
salt and pepper

Place the duck carcass in a saucepan, with the vegetables, stock and sage, and simmer for 2 hours. Melt the butter in a clean pan and cook the shallot and fresh mushrooms for a few minutes, until soft. Sprinkle in the flour and pour in the strained duck liquor, stirring until it thickens. Add the Madeira and balsamic vinegar and season well.

If you have to use dried porcini, soak them in a little warm water for 20 minutes. Strain, reserving the soaking liquor, and proceed as above, adding the soaking liquor to the soup.

Game Consommé

SERVES 6

Do not be deterred from making this by the thought of clarifying the soup. A crystal clear consommé is, visually, a culinary triumph, but the taste remains the same even if it is cloudy. The process by which clarity is achieved is not difficult, and, once you have done it, you will wonder what all the fuss was about. Stock made from pheasant, partridge, pigeon, hare or venison will do, or even a mixture, but the secret is to have a really well flavoured liquid. Obviously this recipe can also be used for making beef consommé.

1 litre/1³/₄ pints game stock (see page 15)
1 onion
1 carrot
1 leek
1 celery stalk
1 glass red wine
1 bouquet garni
6 juniper berries, crushed
salt and pepper
2 egg whites, plus shells

Heat the stock, vegetables, wine, bouquet garni, juniper and seasonings and simmer for 1 hour. Strain and blot off any fat with kitchen paper. Beat the egg whites in a large pan with 275 ml/1½ pint of the stock, until frothy. Pour in the rest of the hot, but not boiling, stock, in a steady stream, and add the egg shells. Agitate gently with a wire whisk over a low flame until it begins to simmer. Now let it 'shiver' for an hour, without stirring, then let it rest for 15 minutes. Scald a clean tea-towel and lay it over a colander or sieve. With a clean ladle, scoop the soup carefully into the colander and let it drain. You should now have a sparkling, clear, golden consommé.

If you wish to serve it jellied, add a split pig's trotter when you make the initial stock.

Oxtail soup

SERVES 6–8

One of the most delicious, rich soups imaginable, and it is ideal for an informal lunch or supper when that unexpected guest drops by; that is, providing you have had the foresight to make and put some in the freezer. If not, just throw together the 'Trick of the trade' and nobody should be any the wiser. It is very rich, so serve it with plenty of hot french bread, a full-bodied red wine and some kind of a salad to follow.

1 oxtail

plain flour, for dredging

oil, for frying

1 unpeeled onion, stuck with cloves

1 carrot, chopped

1 leek, trimmed and chopped

1 celery stalk, chopped

$1/2$ swede, peeled and chopped

2 garlic cloves, peeled and chopped

1.2 litres/2 pints water

$1/2$ bottle of cheap red wine

1 tablespoon tomato purée

1 dessertspoon redcurrant jelly

$1/2$ teaspoon dried mixed herbs

1 glass of sherry or port

salt and pepper

Trim the fat off the oxtail, roll in flour and brown in some oil. Transfer to a large saucepan, with all the other ingredients, except the sherry. Cover and simmer on top of the stove for 4–5 hours, or overnight in the simmering oven of an AGA.

Strain and blot the fat from the cooking liquid with squares of kitchen paper. Return the stock and meat to the pan, re-heat and add the sherry.

Trick of the trade

SERVES 6–8

1 packet oxtail soup

1.2 litres/2 pints water or stock

$1/2$ teaspoon ground bay leaves

1 garlic clove, crushed

1 dessertspoon redcurrant jelly

1 glass of sherry or port

salt and pepper

Heat the stock or water. Mix the contents of the packet with the port or sherry and add, with all the other ingredients. Simmer for 15 minutes and serve with a smug smile.

Broad bean soup, with herbs and diced ham

SERVES 4–6

This takes care of those ancient beans with leather overcoats, and, combined with the herbs and diced ham, makes an unusual and truly delicious soup. You can omit the ham, or use very finely chopped Parma ham and add greek yoghurt. It can be served chilled in the summer and your guests will rave about it.

450 g/1 lb broad beans, shelled

300 ml/¹/₂ pint vegetable stock or water

1 dessertspoon finely chopped fresh thyme, marjoram and savory

milk, to thin

1 tablespoon finely diced ham

salt and pepper

Bring the stock or water to the boil, tip in the beans and herbs, and cook for 10–15 minutes. Have ready a slotted spoon and remove as many of the 'overcoats' which have floated to the top as possible. Blend the soup until smooth in a food processor. Thin with milk to the correct consistency, adjust the seasoning and stir in the ham. You can add a few drops of herb oil (see page 146), if you think it needs more flavour.

Celeriac, apple and walnut soup

SERVES 4–6

Celeriac has a delicious, nutty flavour; it's rounder and smoother than celery and is one of the 'quickies' for soup that I mentioned as it takes no time at all to soften. Teaming it with apple and walnut takes it into the gourmet range. It is also brilliant for those following a low-carbohydrate diet. This comes into the real 'quickie' class.

1 celeriac, peeled and chopped

110 g/ 4 oz cooking apple, peeled and chopped

1 dessertspoon sunflower oil

1 shallot, peeled and finely chopped

300 ml/¹/₂ pint chicken or vegetable stock

squeeze of lemon juice

milk, to thin if necessary

salt and pepper

TO SERVE

Walnut oil

Heat the oil in a saucepan and soften the shallot. Then add the celeriac, apple and stock. Simmer until soft (about 20 minutes) then blend until really creamy, adding a little milk if it is too thick. Season well and add a small squeeze of lemon juice. Drizzle walnut oil over each serving.

SOUPS HOT VEGETABLE

SOUPS HOT VEGETABLE

Pumpkin, tomato and basil soup

SERVES 6–8

At last, pumpkin is emerging from the straitjacket of the Halloween scene and different varieties can be bought for most of the year in supermarkets. Better still, try farm shops, where you can see great mounds of glowing golden globes just waiting for your culinary expertise to turn them into one of the best 'comfort' soups on the scene. Grown in your own garden, they do tend to take up rather a lot of space but 1 plant will produce 2 pumpkins – enough to make soup for a normal family. One spin-off are the seeds. Don't, under any circumstances, throw these away. Wash and dry them, mix them with some oil, sprinkle with salt and dry in a low oven or overnight in the simmering oven of an AGA and you have delicious cocktail nibbles, (if you can keep them long enough!)

1 kg/2 lb pumpkin, peeled and cut up
110 g/4 oz onion, peeled and cut up
110 g/4 oz potato, peeled and diced
2 tablespoons olive or basil oil (see page 146)
2 or more garlic cloves, peeled and chopped
2 bacon rashers, chopped
4 tomatoes, peeled, de-seeded and chopped
1 dessertspoon sugar
300 ml/½ pint vegetable stock
1 tablespoon chopped fresh or dried basil
salt and ground black pepper

Heat the oil in a saucepan and 'sweat' the onion and potato until they are transparent. Add everything else except the basil (unless it is the dried variety). Cook until soft. Squash with a potato masher and add the fresh basil.

Serve with croûtons of fried bread.

If you want a smoother and more delicate soup, omit the potato and bacon and thicken with 1 teaspoon of cornflour, mixed with a little milk. Process until really smooth. Add some cream to each soup cup and garnish with a basil leaf.

Swede soup, with nutmeg croûtons

SERVES 6–8

Many people are ambivalent about swede and some positively dislike it, perhaps with childhood memories of watery offerings at school. Made into a rich, creamy soup, well flavoured with nutmeg, I defy anyone even to know what they are eating and your guests may even ask with bated breath what delicate ingredients you have used. Swede soup is also cheap and very easy to make.

450 g/1 lb swede, peeled and cubed
110 g/4 oz potato, peeled and cubed
1 shallot, peeled and chopped
1 tablespoon demerara sugar
1 teaspoon salt
water to cover
milk
freshly ground black pepper

TO SERVE
freshly grated nutmeg
fried bread croûtons
single cream

Put the swede, potato, shallot, sugar and salt into a saucepan, cover with water and cook over a low heat, until soft. Drain and process until really smooth. Add enough milk to make it the right consistency and stir in some cream. Season with the pepper and more salt if necessary. Grate the nutmeg over the croûtons and mix well. Add a swirl of cream to each cup and sprinkle over a spoonful of croûtons.

Beetroot and cranberry bortsch

SERVES 6–8

Real Russian bortsch is served hot and is quite time-consuming to make, necessitating a long list of ingredients, including marrowbones, which are now under EU interdict. To be really authentic, it should be served with pirozhki, a kind of filled pastry puff. Mine is a simpler, summer, vegetarian variety and the combination with cranberries makes it delicate and delicious. Don't despair if, in summer, you can't find cranberries; just use some cranberry juice and sprinkle a few soaked, dried cranberries into each cup.

450 g/1 lb beetroot, cooked and cut up

50 g/2 oz onion, peeled and chopped

110 g/4 oz white cabbage, chopped

600 ml/1 pint cranberry juice

1–2 tablespoons wine vinegar

sugar, to taste

150 ml/^{1}/$_4$ pint soured cream

2 hard-boiled eggs, chopped

salt and pepper

TO SERVE

25 g/1 oz fresh or dried cranberries

1 tablespoon chopped fresh chives

Cook the onion and cabbage in the cranberry juice until soft then blend in the food processor with the beetroot, until really smooth. Add the vinegar, sugar to taste and the soured cream and season. Stir in the hard-boiled egg, cool and chill.

If using fresh cranberries, cook in a little water until soft. Dried ones can be soaked in boiling water and then drained. Garnish each cup with 2 or 3 cranberries and sprinkle on a few chives.

Trick of the trade

SERVES 4–6

225 g/8 oz pack cooked beetroot

tin of beef consommé

vinegar, to taste

salt and pepper

TO SERVE

soured cream

snipped fresh dill

Blend together the beetroot and consommé. Add vinegar, to taste, and season. Serve in cups, with a blob of soured cream on top and some snipped fresh dill. This is not vegetarian.

SOUPS COLD VEGETABLE

SOUPS COLD VEGETABLE

Courgette and dill soup with fromage frais

This is a brilliant way of using up those mini courgettes that you left growing in your garden one weekend and which, when you returned, were on their way to marrowdom. Otherwise, you can buy from any supermarket or greengrocer – they seem to be in season all the year round, so, in winter, serve this soup hot. This is really one of those 'quickies' that only takes 15 minutes from start to finish – 'Honest Guv'!

700 g/1¹/₂ lb courgettes
1 shallot, peeled and chopped
150 ml/¹/₄ pint water
1 tablespoon chopped fresh dill
2 tablespoons fromage frais
or greek yoghurt
salt and pepper
chopped fresh dill, to garnish

Cut the courgettes into slices, skin and all, and put the slices into a saucepan, with the shallot, water and dill. Bring to the boil and cook for 5–6 minutes. Liquidise, season and add the fromage frais. Cool and refrigerate and serve with a garnish of dill fronds. This freezes well.

Fennel, white bean and Pernod soup

The combination of fennel, white beans and pernod makes this a gourmet dinner party soup which is equally good hot or cold.

salt and 3 fennel bulbs, chopped
1 onion, chopped
2 garlic bulbs, choppoed
1 tablespoon olive oil
150 ml/¹/₄ pint water
1 can haricot beans
1 tablespoon pernod
2 tablspoons crème fraîche
salt and pepper

Soften the onion in the heated oil and then add the fennel and garlic. Cover and cook on a low heat for a few minutes and then add the water. Cook until soft and then tip in the haricot beans and their juice. Heat thoroughly and then blend until really smooth. Add the pernod and season to taste then stir in the cream. Decorate each bowl with a frond of fennel.

Lettuce and sorrel soup

SERVES 4–6

This is another of my favourites. The delicate, lemony tang of the sorrel takes it into gastronomic realms. If you can find the pointed-leaved, wild 'freebie' variety it is even better. On one holiday that my late husband, Archie, and I spent in a caravan on the edge of Loch Awe, wild sorrel was growing all around, so, to precede the main course of freshly caught, grilled trout, with bacon and oatcake, we had wild sorrel soup: a gourmet feast which sticks in my memory. The lettuce part of it uses up the ones which are 'bolting' in your garden or the outside leaves of bought ones.

1 lettuce, roughly shredded
50 g/2 oz sorrel, shredded
25 g/1 oz onion, peeled and chopped
110 g/4 oz potato, diced
25 g/1 oz butter
300 ml/½ pint vegetable stock
300 ml/½ pint milk
1 dessertspoon sugar
salt and pepper
2 tablespoons low-fat crème fraîche, to serve

Cook the onion and potato, in the butter, until transparent. Add the lettuce and sorrel and stir until limp. Add the stock, milk, sugar and seasoning, cover and cook for 20 minutes. Process until smooth and adjust the seasoning. Cool and refrigerate. Just before serving, stir in the crème fraîche, so that the soup looks marbled.

Nettle soup

SERVES 4–6

Another lovely summery soup which is equally good hot or cold.

2 good bunches of young nettle tips
2 shallots, peeled and chopped
225 g/8 oz potato peeled and chopped
25 g/1 oz butter
600 ml/1 pint milk
1 teaspoon sugar
50 g/2 oz cream cheese
salt and pepper

Soften the shallot and potato in the butter then add the well-washed nettle tips and cook for a minute or two. Add the milk and simmer until tender. Season well and add the cream cheese then blend until really smooth. Serve hot or cold.

SOUPS COLD VEGETABLE

Carrot, coriander seed and orange soup

SERVES 6 - 8

At a loss for a starter when friends arrived unexpectedly one day, I foraged in the fridge and all I could find were some carrots, onion, an orange and the remains of some double cream. I made a soup which, though I say it myself exceeded all expectations and everyone wanted the recipe. The secret is the ground coriander seeds which make a perfect partnership with the other ingredients.

450 g/1 lb carrots, roughly chopped

25 g/1 oz onion, roughly chopped

900 ml/1½ pints vegetable stock

3 tablespoons orange juice

1 heaped teaspoon orange zest

1 heaped teaspoon ground coriander seeds

2-3 tablespoons cream

salt and pepper to taste

Place the carrots and onion in a saucepan with the vegetable stock and cook until soft - about 20 - 30 minutes. Place about a dessertspoon of coriander seeds in a mortar and grind with the pestle or do it in the small container of a food mixer. Better still use a coffee grinder. Shake over the soup with a sieve to get rid of the husks.

If possible don't use the ready-ground stuff as it doesn't have the 'zing'.

Blitz the carrots until smooth and then add the rest of the ingredients.

Pour into bowls and garnish with chopped coriander or parsley and a swirl of cream. Serve hot or cold.

Creamy fresh tomato soup, with diced onion and basil

SERVES 6

This is one of my all-time favourite soups and bears absolutely no relation to the commercial 'cream of tomato'. The zingy freshness comes from using fresh, not tinned, tomatoes and it is ideal for using up the summer glut in garden or grow-bag. Skinning and de-seeding isn't much of a hassle and the big 'beefsteak' variety, or plum tomatoes, make it really quite easy. If it is to be frozen, do so before the addition of the onion.

900 g/2 lb tomatoes

1 dessertspoon olive oil or basil oil (see page 146)

600 ml/1 pint vegetable stock

1 teaspoon sugar

salt and pepper

1 teaspoon cornflour (optional)

2 tablespoons diced Spanish or mild onion

150 ml/¼ pint single cream

1 tablespoon torn fresh basil leaves, plus 6 fresh sprigs, to garnish

Make a cross with a sharp knife at the stem end of the tomatoes, cover with boiling water for 2 minutes and then peel. Alternatively hold over a gas flame on a fork for a few seconds or use a blowtorch.

Discard the seeds and chop the flesh roughly. Heat the oil and then add the tomatoes and sugar and cook for a few minutes. Pour in the stock, season, cover and simmer for a short while, until soft. Liquidise until smooth and return to the pan.

If it seems too thin, add the cornflour, mixed with a little water. Cook until it thickens. Place the diced onion in a strainer and pour over a kettle-full of boiling water. Add to the soup and let it cook for 5 minutes, before adding the cream. Cool and refrigerate. Just before serving, stir in the torn basil and decorate each bowl with a sprig.

This is equally good hot.

Salmon bisque, with diced fennel

SERVES 6–8

A smooth and creamy soup which is easy to make and ideal for dinner parties, if you want something hot and fishy and don't want to be actually cooking fish when your guests are there. Fennel is a natural enhancer of fish and the slight crunchiness offsets any hint of blandness.

450 g/1 lb salmon
1.2 litres/2 pints fish stock (see page 16)
strip of lemon zest
1 tablespoon finely diced fennel
25 g/1 oz beurre manié (see page 15)
1 tablespoon cream
1 dessertspoon dry vermouth
salt and pepper

Bring the stock to the boil, with the lemon zest, and throw in the fennel. Cook for 4 minutes and then strain and set the fennel aside. Return the stock to the pan and simmer the salmon for 10 minutes. Take it out and remove the skin and bones. Process the flesh, with some of the stock, until smooth and return to the pan. Drop little bits of the beurre manié into the simmering soup, whisking constantly until it is smooth. Remove lemon. Add the cream and alcohol of your choice and garnish with the fennel.

Smoked haddock chowder

SERVES 6–8

In Scotland, this is known as cullen skink; in Old Scots, cullen meant fish; and skink, stew. This satisfying soup is more commonly known as chowder, which derives from the French chaudière or 'meal in a dish', and is supposed to have been dreamed up by Breton fishermen. Whatever its provenance, the main ingredients are fish, onion, potato and carrot, with the addition of diced bacon or ham. The smoked haddock gives it a nice lift but you can use any fish you fancy, or even a mixture.

450 g/1 lb smoked haddock
1.2 litres/2 pints fish stock (see page 16) or water
300 ml/1 pint milk
225 g/8 oz potatoes, peeled and chopped
1 onion, peeled and chopped
1 carrot, peeled and chopped
50 g/2 oz bacon, diced
salt and freshly ground black pepper
1 tablespoon chopped fresh parsley, to garnish

Cook the vegetables and bacon in the stock or water, until soft. Meanwhile, skin and de-bone the haddock and cook in the milk. Fork it into flakes and add to the soup, with the milk; season well. Sprinkle the chopped parsley on top.

Serve with warm wholemeal baps or oatcakes.

SOUPS HOT FISH

Christmas soup

SERVES 6–8

The ultimate mixture of rich ingredients but, as it uses up all the festive season leftovers, appeals to the thrifty housewife lurking in most of us. As it can't be repeated at other times of the year, it is much looked forward to by my family and you will know that the magic moment has arrived when the cry goes up 'Oh! not cold turkey again!' You can add any leftover vegetables but only put in brussels sprouts if you are going to eat the soup instantly. Make it, serve it in bowls in front of the fire for supper and then indulge in all the forbidden chocolates you didn't have room for on Christmas Day.

1 turkey carcass

surplus stuffing, including chestnuts, if possible

bread sauce

left-over sausages, and bacon rolls

cranberry sauce

salt and pepper

Remove any bits of meat from the carcass and chop them finely. Cover the carcass with water and simmer for 2 hours.

Strain and blot off any grease with kitchen paper. Add all the other ingredients and heat through; then whizz up in the food processor. Return to the pan, tip in the chopped turkey meat and adjust the seasoning.

Lamb broth

SERVES 4–6

You can make this with cheap cuts of stewing lamb or with the remains of a roast leg or shoulder of lamb. This is one of those soups where long and slow cooking is the order of the day and, if you want a bit of crunch, add some of the vegetables just before the end of the cooking time. I have just given a guideline of vegetables as it all depends on what you have in your fridge that needs to be used up.

STOCK

700 g/1½ lb neck of lamb or remains of joint

1.2 litres/2 pints water

1 lamb stock cube

1 onion, peeled

1 carrot

110 g/4 oz pearl barley

TO FINISH

1 onion, chopped

1 carrot, chopped

1 leek, chopped

1 celery stalk, chopped

2 tablespoons frozen peas

salt and pepper

If using remains of joint, cut off the meat and cube it. Put the meat, bones, onion, carrot and pearl barley into a saucepan with the water and stock cube and simmer gently for 2 hours.

Remove the bones, onion and carrot. Tip in the chopped vegetables and cook for 15–20 minutes. Season well, add the peas and cook for a further 6–8 minutes.

Serve with thick slices of Granary bread and farmhouse butter.

Main-course minestrone

SERVES 6–8

This is my version of that classic Italian peasant soup, for which, even in Italy, there are no hard and fast rules: it varies regionally, according to the local produce. Mine is more on the lines of a rich vegetable broth, made more substantial by the addition of pasta. Now that seed catalogues have a wider selection of interesting vegetables for us to grow in our gardens, and there is such a variety to choose from in supermarkets, there is no excuse for not experimenting.

1.75 litres/3 pints vegetable stock

110 g/4 oz pasta shells

1 bunch of spring onions, peeled and chopped

1 garlic clove, peeled and chopped

1 carrot, peeled and chopped

1 celery stalk, scraped and chopped

1 leek, chopped

50 g/2 oz savoy cabbage, shredded, or cavolo nero

50 g/2 oz celeriac, peeled and diced

50 g/2 oz fennel bulb, trimmed and diced

50 g/2 oz mange-tout or sugar-snap peas

50 g/2 oz fine french beans, chopped

50 g/2 oz courgette, squash or pumpkin, chopped

110 g/4 oz tomato, peeled, de-seeded and diced

1 tablespoon chopped fresh thyme, oregano and parsley

salt and pepper

Bring the stock to the boil and throw in all the other ingredients. Simmer until the pasta is done, by which time the vegetables will be cooked. Season well.

Serve with hot ciabatta bread and a bowl of grated parmesan or cheddar cheese, for everyone to help themselves. The ingredients I have given are only a guide, so don't give up if you haven't got them all; just substitute something else or leave out.

Tuscan bean soup

A traditional peasant soup from Tuscany which makes a good 'rib-sticker' to ward off the winter winds. Before the advent of freezers, dried beans were staple country fare for regional dishes both in this country and abroad. You can make this soup with any kind of beans: flageolet, haricot or butter beans would be just as good but the flavour comes from the ham or bacon and the garlic. You must use a good olive oil or, even better, a Provençal herb or Basil oil (see page 146). For a quick cheat, you can use tinned beans.

225 g/8 oz dried or 1 tin of cannellini, borlotti or butter beans

1 ham or bacon bone or 225 g/8 oz unsmoked bacon

1 onion, peeled and cut up

2 garlic cloves, peeled

1.5 litres/2½ pints water

1 teaspoon each dried thyme and oregano

salt and pepper

TO SERVE

4 tablespoons best olive oil

2 garlic cloves, peeled and chopped

6–8 rounds of french bread

grated parmesan cheese

Soak the beans overnight in cold water. Drain and put into a saucepan. Add the ham bone or bacon, onion, garlic and water. Sprinkle in the herbs and simmer slowly for 2 hours or overnight in the simmering oven of an AGA.

Remove the bone or bacon and process half the beans. Tip back into the pan and season well. Heat the oil and fry the chopped garlic until golden, then tip into the soup. Place a round of bread in the bottom of each bowl and pour over the soup, which must be very hot. Sprinkle a little parmesan on top.

STOCKS

Stock is one of the culinary basics and no bone should be left un-boiled. A few cartons of different varieties in the freezer are essential and can be a life-saver when making soups or casseroles.

Brown stock

2 tablespoons olive oil
1 onion, peeled and chopped
2 carrots, peeled and chopped
1 leek, trimmed and sliced
1 celery stalk, chopped
bones of beef, pork, lamb, chicken, or game
1 pig's trotter, split (optional)
1 sprig each fresh thyme, marjoram, and parsley
1 bay leaf
6 peppercorns
1.75 litres/3 pints water

Pre-heat the oven to 230°C/450°F/gas mark 8. Heat the oil in a roasting pan on top of the stove and brown the vegetables and bones; then transfer to the oven and roast for 30 minutes. Remove and pour in the water, stir round well to incorporate any brown bits and transfer to a saucepan. Add the rest of the ingredients, cover and bring to the boil. Simmer for 1½ - 2 hours, skimming periodically.

Strain through a colander. Blot off any fat with kitchen paper. If not intended for immediate use, cool, pour into cartons, label and freeze. If you use a pig's trotter, gelatine will not be needed for any cold dish.

Trick of the trade

Boil down rapidly until the stock looks syrupy and tastes concentrated. Pour into ice-cube trays and freeze. Ideal for quick flavouring of soups and sauces. You can also freeze small remnants of wine in the same way. 275 ml/½ pint makes 14 cubes, i.e. a large ice-cube tray.

White stock

This is what I make if the recipe does not call for a rich stock. It is suitable for soups, stews and sauces. Use all the ingredients listed for brown stock but omit the olive oil and do not roast. Place in a large saucepan, bring to the boil and simmer for 1½–2 hours.

Thickeners

Potato: Added as an ingredient when cooking vegetable soup, potato will thicken it when blended.

Beurre manié (kneaded butter): Equal quantities of softened butter and plain flour, kneaded together, and then dropped bit by bit into boiling soups or stews, whisking continuously until it is thick enough.

Cornflour or potato flour: Mix the required quantity in a small amount, usually 1–2 teaspoons in cold liquid and then add to the boiling soup or stew and stir until it thickens.

SOUPS STOCKS AND THICKENERS

Court bouillon

Court bouillon, translated, means 'short boiling'. It is a flavoured liquid used for poaching fish, game or poultry where a delicate flavour is required.

3 onions and 3 shallots, peeled

2 garlic cloves, peeled (optional)

1 leek, cleaned and trimmed

1 carrot, scraped

2 bay leaves

1 sprig each fresh thyme, parsley, tarragon and chervil

300 ml/½ pint white wine

2.25 litres/4 pints water

1 tablespoon white-wine vinegar

salt and pepper

Bring all the ingredients slowly to the boil and simmer, uncovered, for 30 minutes. Allow to cool before use, unless the recipe states otherwise. Strain when cold.

Variation: For a more exotic and slightly oriental flavour, include the following ingredients: 4 pink peppercorns, 1 star anise, zests of lemon or orange and ½ teaspoon coriander seeds.

Fish stock or fumet

Roughly translated, fumet means 'flavour', of meat or fish. It is, therefore, the fishy equivalent of concentrated or rich stock

25 g/1 oz butter

fish trimmings

1 carrot, onion, leek and 1 celery stick, peeled, cleaned and trimmed

110 g/4 oz button mushrooms or trimmings

1 sprig each fresh parsley, thyme, marjoram and tarragon (or a sachet of bouquet garni)

4 white peppercorns

600 ml/1 pint white wine

600 ml/1 pint water

½ teaspoon salt

Melt the butter in a saucepan and add the fish bones, vegetables, herbs and peppercorns. Cover and cook over a very gentle heat for 15 minutes; do not allow to brown. Add the wine, water and salt and simmer gently for 30 minutes. Cool and strain.

STARTERS

A meal should well balanced. Soon after I was married, we gave a dinner party and invited a rather intimidating lady and her husband. When we had left the men to their port, she informed me that, although my dinner had been excellent, I had committed the cardinal gastronomic sin of using the same ingredient in two courses – I had put cream in the first course and the pudding! Sadly, she is no longer with us but she would be pleased to know that her strictures have remained firmly embedded in my mind ever since. In the same way it is best, if possible, to avoid serving courses that are all the same colour. This happened to my father and mother before the war, when they dined with the late Lord Rosebery. The entire dinner was served on gold plates and all six courses were beige!

If you are having game or a substantial main dish, it is best to have something light as a starter, the object being to set your taste-buds alight and raring for more. In the same way, a rich pâté is best followed by fish or poultry. It also helps the cook-hostess to have a cold beginning and end, or a hot beginning and cold middle, to avoid having to keep disappearing into the kitchen.

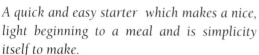

Avocado with feta cheese and salami, in raspberry vinaigrette

Q

SERVES 6

2 avocados, peeled, stoned and diced
50 g/2 oz feta cheese, diced
50 g/2 oz salami, Parma ham or smoked meat, diced
1 dessertspoon sugar
1 dessertspoon whole-grain mustard
1 dessertspoon raspberry vinegar
3 tablespoons sunflower oil
salt and pepper

Place the cheese and salami or other meat in a bowl. Place the sugar, mustard, and salt and pepper in a small jug. Mix well with the vinegar and then slowly pour in the oil, stirring constantly. Pour over the other ingredients and mix well. Spoon into little ramekins and serve with pumpernickel or rye bread.

Purple-sprouting broccoli with hazelnut oil dressing

V Q

SERVES 4

A quick and easy starter which makes a nice, light beginning to a meal and is simplicity itself to make.

24 purple-sprouting broccoli spears
25 g/1 oz hazelnut pieces, toasted

DRESSING

½ teaspoon grated lemon zest
1 teaspoon Dijon mustard
½ teaspoon sugar
1 teaspoon lemon juice
1 tablespoon hazelnut oil
salt and pepper

Trim the purple-sprouting broccoli spears. Cook in boiling, salted water for 2–3 minutes – they should be *al dente*. Drain and cool. Divide between 4 ramekins and scatter with the chopped hazelnuts. Mix the dressing ingredients, whisk well and pour over.

Avocados sauce gribiche

V

SERVES 6

Sauce gribiche is a winner; it goes with all sorts of summer salads.

2 avocados, peeled, stoned and diced
6 tablespoons sauce gribiche (see page 135)

Mix the avocados with the sauce and divide among 6 small ramekins. Serve with thin brown bread and butter.

Chervil-stuffed eggs, with lemon mayonnaise

V

SERVES 4–6

Delicious as a summer starter, this is lovely made with bantam eggs, but, sadly, these are

very difficult to get hold of nowadays. We used to keep bantams when my daughter, Lucy, was little. She had a pet bird, called Rowena, who was so tame that she used to sit on Lucy's shoulder in the car on the school run. The only disadvantage to keeping bantams is that they tend to lay their eggs in unpredictable places and, if you have a cock, you may suddenly find your best laying hen has vanished. Just as you have given up hope and fear she has been eaten by a fox she re-appears, plus a large brood of chicks.

If you increase the number of eggs, you can turn it into a light salad, served on a bed of lettuce. In winter, when you cannot get chervil, use parsley, chives or cress instead.

4–6 hard-boiled eggs

10 g/1/2 oz butter, softened

1 tablespoon crème fraîche

1 tablespoon chopped fresh chervil

300 ml/1/2 pint lemon mayonnaise (see page 134)

salt and pepper

Cut the eggs in half lengthways and scoop out the yolks. Blend the yolks with the butter, crème fraîche and chopped chervil. Season well and replace in the egg halves. Place on small plates and spoon over the mayonnaise.

Serve with brown bread and butter.

Smoked eel with dill and gherkin sauce

SERVES 4–6

The common eel lives in rivers and estuaries and the Fens and is the main ingredient of the famed East End dish of 'pie and mash'. They are highly appreciated on the continent to which many of our native eels are exported though they are becoming increasingly popular over here and can be obtained from several mail-order companies. Some of the best I ever had were with a Dutch friend on the Biesbosch wetland. As we approached, a faint plume of smoke rose from the trees; this turned out to be an old keeper smoking eels in a home-made contraption. Eaten in the fingers and washed down with copious swigs of Dutch gin they were delicious. This makes a really quick last minute starter.

---

450 g/1 lb smoked eels

2 teaspoons sugar

white wine vinegar

salt and pepper

1/2 cucumber

DILL AND GHERKIN SAUCE

25 g/1 oz pickled gherkins

25 g/1 oz capers

1 tablespoon chopped fresh dill or fennel

2 teaspoons Dijon mustard

Divide the eels among 6 plates and garnish with thin slices of cucumber and fronds of dill. Chop the gherkins and capers coarsely and mix with the remaining ingredients. Just before serving drizzle over the eel and hand round buttered pumpernickel bread. To be really authentic serve small 'shots' of 'schnapps' or aquavit (obtainable at any supermarket). Smoked eel is available by mail order - see page 199.

STARTERS COLD

Spicy 'hot-smoked' salmon moulds

SERVES 6–8

450 g/1 lb salmon
1 small carton Greek yoghurt
2 tablespoons Hellman's mayonnaise
2 tablespoons crème fraîche
juice of $\frac{1}{2}$ lemon
1–2 teaspoons honey
10 g/$\frac{1}{2}$ oz fresh ginger, finely grated
1 pinch Chinese 5 spice powder
1 sachet gelatine
salt and pepper

To smoke the salmon yourself: Line a wok or stir-fry pan with foil. Sprinkle 2 handfuls of hickory chips (obtainable at fishing tackle shops) on the bottom. Fold a small square of chicken netting and place on top or use something similar so that the smoke will seep round the fish. Place the salmon on a double piece of foil and bend the edges in so that the juice does not leak out. Sprinkle with salt and spread with honey. Place a lid on top or a sheet of foil and place over a high heat. When it starts to smoke reduce heat and continue for about 20 minutes or until the fish is cooked. When it is done remove salmon taking care not to spill the juice and tip everything into a bowl. Remove the skin and bones (if any) and flake. Beat in the yoghurt, mayonnaise, lemon juice and the flavourings. Finally add the gelatine which you have dissolved in a little warm water. Pour into oiled ramekins and allow to set. To serve turn out and decorate with sprigs of coriander and very finely sliced rounds of ginger or pickled sushi ginger. The latter is important as it gives a nice spicy crunch which contrasts well with the creamy texture

of the mould. If the improvised home-smoking puts you off just order 'SAVU' food smoker bags from Lakeland (see page 200).

Basic smoked haddock mousse and variations

SERVES 6–8

When I suggested to friends that maybe mousses were rather 'Eighties' and that they should be omitted there was an outcry, so I have kept them. To save the hassle of handing round a dish you can always serve them in individual ramekins. Once you have mastered the basic recipe, the sky is your limit, for the variations are endless. The original recipe that I was given evolved during wartime rationing and was made with tinned crab; tinned condensed milk replaced the cream. I'm not sure the latter didn't give a particularly good flavour but I now use cream. If making a spinach mousse or similar, for vegetarians, be sure to use a vegetarian setting agent containing carragheen moss, such as Gelozone or similar. This is obtainable at health-food shops.

225 g/8 oz smoked haddock, cooked, skinned and flaked
150 ml/$\frac{1}{4}$ pint milk
1 bay leaf
1 onion ring
pinch of dried mixed herbs
6 peppercorns
small piece of garlic
3 eggs, separated
1 sachet gelatine
1 tablespoon water
2 tablespoons mayonnaise

300 ml/¹/₂ pint cream, whipped

pinch of cayenne pepper

salt and pepper

Bring the milk to the boil, with the bay leaf, onion ring, herbs, peppercorns and garlic. Allow to sit for 10 minutes or so. Strain and pour into a small bowl. Beat in the egg yolks, place over a pan of boiling water and stir until the mixture is thick enough to coat the back of a spoon. Tip the gelatine into a small jug, add the water and allow to become spongy. Then place in a pan of hot water and stir until it dissolves. Mix together the haddock, flavoured custard, mayonnaise and gelatine and season to taste. Fold in the whipped cream. Whisk the egg whites to stiff peaks and, when the mixture is quite cold and beginning to set, fold in the whites of egg. Spoon into a soufflé dish or ramekins and allow to set. Serve with a watercress salad. Will freeze.

Trick of the trade

Before folding in the whisked egg whites, cool the haddock mixture in the fridge.

Cheese mousse: Stir 225 g/8 oz grated mature Cheddar cheese into the 'custard' mixture, which should be flavoured with mustard instead of the herbs. For a change, try using 'Y Fenni' Abergavenny cheese instead of cheddar, which is made with beer and whole-grain mustard.

Spinach, ham and cheese mousse: Add 225g/8oz cooked spinach, puréed, 110g/4oz finely diced ham, 25g/1oz grated parmesan cheese to the custard.

Salmon or smoked salmon mousse: As for smoked haddock mousse, using 225 g/8 oz flaked, cooked salmon but flavour with lemon juice and a little creamed horseradish. Serve with tartare sauce (see page 134).

Ten minute mackerel mousse

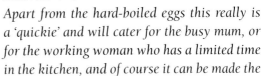

SERVES 4–6

Apart from the hard-boiled eggs this really is a 'quickie' and will cater for the busy mum, or for the working woman who has a limited time in the kitchen, and of course it can be made the day before and refrigerated.

1 sachet gelatine

50 ml/2 fl oz water

3 hard-boiled eggs

1 x 200g Philadelphia cream cheese

4 oz smoked mackerel or similar

1 teaspoon each of Anchovy essence, Worcester Sauce & Harvey's Sauce

1 dessertspoon sherry

juice of ¹/₂ lemon

Schwartz seasoned salt

Schwartz seasoned pepper

Pinch cayenne

Dissolve the gelatine in the water. Remove the white from one of the eggs and place the yolk and rest of the ingredients in a blender. Add the dissolved gelatine and blend until smooth. Finally mix in the roughly chopped white of egg and spoon into ramekins. Garnish with chopped chives. If you make it with smoked salmon, garnish with a blob of sour cream and lumpfish caviar and serve with buttered whole-grain bread and a shot of Lemon Vodka (see page 195)

STARTERS COLD

Asparagus with Lucy's sauce

SERVES 6–8

Asparagus is one of the gems of the culinary world. It requires the patience of Job if you are going to grow it, as the ground has to be very carefully prepared and well manured and then once you have planted the 'crowns' you have to refrain from cutting them until their third year. The pleasure of seeing the fat little spears thrusting their way through the earth is almost orgasmic. Then you have to decide whether to be greedy and eat them all yourself or share them with someone else. They must not be overcooked and should still be bright green and slightly crunchy. Not like those cooked by Lucy for the redoubtable Cousin Constance. Lucy was about to take them out of the pan when she was told firmly that they needed 'at least another 15 minutes', by which time they were of course khaki coloured and, as Lucy removed them, the tips dropped off!

2 bunches of asparagus

Lucy's asparagus sauce (see page 131)

Wash and trim the ends off the asparagus (they can be used for soup). Tie in bundles and stand upright in fast-boiling, salted water, with a lid on the saucepan, for 5–6 minutes, or until just cooked. They can also be steamed. Serve with the sauce separately.

If the asparagus are to be eaten with melted butter, dish up on individual plates accompanied by a small ramekin or egg-cupful of melted butter, into which your guests can dip their spears. This is Gina Garfit's brilliant idea and saves all that wasted butter left on plates.

Samphire with melted butter

SERVES 4–6

A bonus if you are holidaying on a stretch of wild coastland in self-catering accommodation. Otherwise you will have to beg your fishmonger on bended knees to get you some. It makes a delicious 'mini-starter' as a pre-quel to a heavy main course or as an accompaniment to fish.

1–2 bunches samphire

boiling water

melted butter

lemon juice

Wash the samphire well under running water then blanch it in fast-boiling water for 2 minutes. Remove and arrange a small bunch on each plate. Melt the butter, add a squeeze of lemon juice and divide amongst 6 ramekins. Place one ramekin on each plate and wait for the ecstatic grins.

Eggs and Swiss chard with cream

SERVES 4–6

This is my version of 'Oeufs Florentine'. I use Swiss chard which is a kind of spinach with larger leaves and large white stems which give a nice crunch. The variety Bright Lights makes a wonderfully colourful dish but you will probably have to grow it yourself. The seeds are obtainable from Thompson & Morgan. The stems of the plants are red, purple, orange, yellow or green. Ordinary chard can probably be found in your local greengrocer or farm shop. Otherwise you will just have to use spinach and 'jazz' it up with a tiny bit of grated, cooked beetroot.

450 g/1 lb swiss chard

butter

1 tablespoon cooked grated beetroot

4–6 eggs, poached

cream

salt and pepper

parmesan cheese

Chop the chard by cutting across the stems and leaves. The chunks should be roughly 1 cm/1 inch. Melt the butter in a pan and toss the chard in it until it starts to 'wilt'. At this point gently fold in the grated beetroot if using. Spoon onto individual plates, place an egg on top. Melt some butter in a small pan and when foaming add 150 ml/¼ pint cream until it bubbles then spoon over the eggs. Sprinkle a little parmesan over each one.

Henry VIII's poached eggs Ⓥ Ⓠ

SERVES 6

This is an ample version of the slender French King, Henri IV's Oeufs Pochés. Provided you have eggs and smoked salmon and a packet of crispbakes in your cupboard you have the ingredients for a starter or for a main course for a 'girls' get-together'. The mayonnaise can be made and the eggs poached the night before and kept in a bowl of cold water and all you have to do is to put it all together. Simplicity itself.

6 eggs

lemon mayonnaise (see p134)

225 g/8 oz smoked salmon, roughly chopped

6 crispbakes

asparagus tips

Heat a large pan of water to a fast boil and add a splash of vinegar. Swirl it round with a whisk and break in an egg. Reduce the heat and leave until the yolk is covered with a white film. Remove with a slotted spoon and place in a bowl of cold water. Repeat with the rest of the eggs. Before using, place on 2 or 3 pieces of kitchen paper. If you can't face the poaching just use soft-boiled eggs. Bring a pan of water to the boil, put in the eggs which you have pierced with a pin at the blunt end and boil for 5 minutes then drain and cover in cold water. Place a crispbake on each plate and cover with smoked salmon. Just before serving spoon over the mayonnaise and garnish with lemon slices and 2 or 3 asparagus spears cooked for 2 minutes in boiling water and allowed to get cold. When you make the mayonnaise be sure that it is really thick and unctuous.

You can use 2 quail eggs per person instead, in which case place in boiling water and boil for 1 minute before removing into cold water and peeling.

Warm chargrilled vegetable salad with goats cheese and air–dried ham

SERVES 6–8

This is ideal as a communal first course for supper in the garden or you can serve it arranged on individual plates for a more formal dinner party. Goats cheese or fromage de chèvre is no longer the prerogative of France. There is a wonderful selection of British varieties to choose from in specialist shops or farmers' markets (see page 200).

1 red onion, peeled
3 courgettes
2 sweet peppers, 1 red and 1 yellow
1 bunch baby asparagus
1 aubergine
2 tablespoons cooked garden peas (optional)
225 g/8 oz air-dried Denhay or Parma ham
goat's cheese
best virgin olive oil
salt and pepper
parsley, chives, tarragon, marjoram, savory, mint

Cut the onion into rings and the courgettes and aubergine into thin strips lengthways. Remove the skin from the peppers either with a blow-torch or over a gas flame or failing this place in a hot oven for 10 minutes then place in sealed plastic bag for a further 10 minutes when you can rub off the skin. Remove cores and seeds and cut into strips. Grill on a very hot griddle, under a grill set at highest heat or in an oven set at 220°C/425°F/Gas Mark 7 until they are well browned but not dried out. Place on a large shallow serving dish, sprinkle with the garden peas, the rolled and chopped Parma ham and the diced goat's cheese and snip the herbs over top. Finally drizzle over a generous amount of olive oil and sprinkle with sea salt.

Tomato tart with crème fraîche & basil

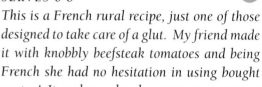

SERVES 6-8

This is a French rural recipe, just one of those designed to take care of a glut. My friend made it with knobbly beefsteak tomatoes and being French she had no hesitation in using bought pastry! It makes a lovely summer starter or it can be used as a side-dish with a terrine or cold ham. It is also excellent for a picnic.

1 packet shortcrust pastry
1 tablespoon mild Dijon mustard
crème fraîche
4–5 beefsteak tomatoes
stoned black olives
basil oil (see p146)
coarse salt and ground black pepper
tiny sprinkle sugar
1 garlic clove peeled and finely chopped
1 handful basil leaves

Roll the pastry out thinly and place in a well buttered 20 cm/10 inch flan tin, preferably with a loose base. It helps if you line the base with a circle of 'Bake-O-Glide' non-stick liner. Prick with a fork and bake blind in a pre-heated oven set at 180°C/350°F/Gas Mark 4 for 15 minutes. Remove and allow to cool. Spread thinly with the mustard and then with a thick layer of crème fraîche. Slice the tomatoes into fairly thick rings and lay on

STARTERS HOT

top in concentric circles. Sprinkle with salt, pepper and sugar and scatter with the garlic, torn basil leaves and olives then drizzle with the basil oil. Turn the heat up to 200°C/400°F/Gas Mark 6 and bake for 10 – 15 minutes or until the tomatoes are beginning to brown. Cool slightly and then transfer carefully to a serving platter. Decorate with sprigs of basil and serve warm.

Trick of the trade

Buy a ready-baked flan case and follow above procedure but use lesser quantities as these flan cases are smaller.

Goats Cheese and toasted walnut salad

SERVES 6   SUPER

This must be the quickest starter ever and is absolutely delicious. There are any number of producers of crottin goats cheese in this country so this is a good excuse to try them out.

3 Cotswold crottin goats cheese
1 small cos lettuce cut into ribbons
110 g/4 oz walnuts
teaspoon mild Dijon mustard
1/2 teaspoon sugar
salt and pepper
2 teaspoons white wine vinegar
50 ml/2 fl oz groundnut or sunflower oil
100 ml/4 fl oz walnut oil

Cut the goats cheese in half and place on a non-stick baking tray. Toast the walnuts in the oven until just coloured but watch them like a hawk as they burn easily. Grind half of them in a pestle and mortar until they start to look oily and mix together with the remaining ingredients. Place the goats cheese in the oven 10 minutes before you want to eat. Then take them out and arrange them on individual plates on the lettuce. Whisk the dressing and spoon over each one. Finally sprinkle over the remaining walnuts.

Warm smoked duck breast, with quince and red onion chutney

SERVES 4

If you have a trout-smoker, you can smoke the breasts yourself but there are several mail-order firms who supply these and they are even to be found in some butchers and delicatessens. Smoked chicken or venison can also be used but the combination of the rather rich duck and the slightly tart chutney is a good one, as the one offsets the other. If you have no quinces use the red onion, apple and sage relish (see page 181). Failing all else, unsmoked duck breasts can be used.

2 smoked duck breasts
1 head of radicchio or lollo rosso
4 tablespoons quince and red onion chutney (see page 182)

Heat the grill to high and cook the duck breasts (if smoked) for 2 minutes on each side. If using raw breasts, cook for 4 minutes on each side. Arrange the salad leaves on 4 plates. When the breasts have cooled but are still warm, cut each one horizontally into thin slices but do not sever completely. Divide into two portions each and arrange in fan shapes on each plate with 1 tablespoon of chutney.

STARTERS HOT

Kosher Jewish chopped chicken livers

SERVES 4–6

I ate this at a kosher lunch bar in London and thought it so good that I begged the recipe. It should be eaten warm or at room temperature and should be on the sloppy side, which is why chicken fat is best. Failing this, a mixture of olive oil and clarified butter will do the trick. It is emphatically not a pâté and the consistency is more like a 'dip'. For kitchen lunch or supper, serve in scooped-out baked potato halves.

350 g/12 oz chicken livers, trimmed
6 tablespoons chicken fat
2 hard-boiled eggs
75 g/3 oz onion, finely chopped
1 celery stalk, finely chopped, or 50 g/2 oz finely chopped fennel bulb
salt and freshly ground black pepper

Sauté the chicken livers in 2 tablespoons of the chicken fat, until they are cooked but still pink inside. Process, with the egg yolks, until finely chopped but not smooth. It is best done with a few short bursts. Tip into a bowl and mix in the rest of the chicken fat and the other ingredients, including the roughly chopped egg whites. Season and be very generous with the pepper.

This does not freeze well as you lose the crunchy texture of the chopped vegetables. You can, however, freeze the processed livers and add the other ingredients when they have thawed out. If you are not making it to eat on the same day, be sure and take it out of the fridge at least 3 hours before it is to be eaten.

Pumpernickel, rye bread or a mixed-grain loaf should accompany it.

Boned, stuffed duck, with truffles

SERVES 2–4

Boning is not nearly so difficult as it sounds and your guests will think you are a magician.

1 duck
1 shallot, peeled and finely chopped
110 g/4 oz minced pork
50 g/2 oz duck and chicken livers
25 g/1 oz fresh white breadcrumbs
salt and pepper
1 egg
1 small tin truffles
2 ham strips
10 g/½ oz shelled pistachio nuts
well flavoured stock
1 glass sherry
1 sachet gelatine
425 ml/¾ pint cooking liquor
5 small bay leaves

To bone the duck: place the duck breast down. With a pair of secateurs or scissors cut down each side of the backbone and remove it. Remove the wishbone. With a sharp, pointed knife cut away the flesh on each side of the duck working towards the breast-bone and keeping the knife edge towards the bone surface. Sever the thigh joints carefully. Insert the knife and work it round each bone until you reach the thighs and drumsticks, then sever and remove the thigh bones leaving the drumsticks in and the wings attached. Hold the carcass in one hand and very carefully cut away the flesh along the edge of the breastbone being careful not to pierce the skin or the stuffing will ooze out. Set the carcass aside and leave the flesh laid flat skin-side down, ready for stuffing. If you can't face the thought of all this, just remove the back-bone (as described) and the breast-bone.

Place the shallot, pork, livers, bread-crumbs, egg and seasoning in the food processor and whizz until smooth. Cut 6 thin slices from one of the truffles for decoration and chop the rest roughly. Mix this and the pistachio nuts into the pâté by hand. Smooth the pâté over the flattened duck and sew up. Wrap tightly in a tea cloth or piece of muslin, tying each end with string. Bring the stock made from the carcass and the sherry to the boil and lower the duck into it. Cover and simmer gently for 1½ hours.

Allow to cool in the liquid. Remove and take out the stitches. Refrigerate until quite cold.

Dissolve the gelatine in hot, not boiling, water and make up quantity with the cooking liquor, strain through a fine sieve and allow to cool until syrupy, then coat the duck with it. You will need to do this several times. Then place the truffle slices down the centre of the breast, dip the bay leaves in the jellied stock and decorate the bird with them. It will look so beautiful that you will have to photograph it for posterity!

Chicken-liver pâté, with paprika or with green peppercorns

SERVES 6–8

A rich, light chicken-liver pâté that is very quick to make and freezes well. You can alter the flavouring and, if you are lucky enough to have some truffles or truffle peelings, this is the ideal vehicle for them.

300 g/ 8 oz chicken livers
110 g/4 oz unsalted butter
1 shallot, peeled and chopped
75 ml/3 fl oz brandy
150 ml/¼ pint double cream
1 heaped teaspoon paprika or green peppercorns
pinch of dried basil or oregano
sliver of garlic, (optional)
salt and freshly ground black pepper

TO DECORATE

butter, melted
6–8 bay leaves
green or red peppercorns

Trim the livers and chop roughly. Melt the butter in a large frying-pan or wok, throw in the livers and cook until they are done but still faintly pink inside. Remove with a slotted spoon and transfer to the food processor. Cook the shallot in the pan juices for a few seconds and then add the brandy, cream and seasonings, including garlic, if using. Allow to bubble for a minute or so and then add to the livers and process until smooth and creamy. If using green peppercorns don't cook them as this makes them bitter. Spoon the pâté into dishes, pour over melted butter and decorate with bay leaves and whichever peppercorns you have used. Serve with thin slices of hot toast.

Easy grouse pâté

SERVES 2–4

The red grouse, Lagopus lagopus scoticus, is only native to this country and Archie considered it the most wonderful quarry. On one holiday in Scotland, when we had been after an elusive covey, he shot one which fell into the neighbouring loch. Being unable to bear the thought of losing it, Archie rushed down the hillside, leapt into the boat and was to be seen rowing furiously towards the farther shore, where he finally retrieved his hard-won prize. No bird has ever tasted so good. This recipe retains that special gamey grouse taste, redolent of the heather buds and juniper berries on which it feeds. It is also best made with old grouse, which are cheaper to buy, have more meat on them and, to my mind, more flavour. Before the traditionalists keel over in horror at the thought of using gin and not whisky, fear not, it really works, as, of course, juniper is one of its constituents.

| 1 old grouse |
| 50 g/2 oz butter |
| 50 g/2 oz bacon or pork dripping |
| 1 smoked bacon rasher |
| 1 teaspoon cranberry jelly or sauce |
| 75 ml/3 fl oz gin |
| 6 juniper berries, crushed |
| salt and pepper |

TO DECORATE

| juniper berries |
| butter, melted |

Cut the flesh off the grouse and dice it. Make stock with the carcass and reduce to 50 ml/2 fl oz. Sauté the grouse meat and rasher in the butter or dripping over a brisk heat, until still slightly pink inside. Transfer to the food processor and whizz until finely ground. Pour the gin into the pan and cook until well reduced then add the stock and other ingredients. Add to the ground-up grouse and process until really smooth. Spoon into an earthenware dish, cover with melted butter and decorate with juniper berries. Refrigerate for 2–3 days before using or freezing. Serve with crisp oatcakes.

Iris's spicy chicken-liver pâté

SERVES 8–10

My friend, Iris, always said that she hated cooking but I had my doubts after eating this at her house. It is a deliciously spicy recipe, which relies on the seasoning for its flavour.

| 450 g/1 lb chicken livers |
| 50 g/2 oz butter |

SEASONED BUTTER

| 175 g/6 oz butter softened |
| ½ teaspoon salt |
| ½ teaspoon freshly ground black pepper |
| ½ teaspoon grated nutmeg |
| pinch of ground cloves |
| 2 teaspoons finely chopped onion |

Beat all the flavourings into the softened butter. Sauté the trimmed and roughly chopped livers in the 50g/2oz butter and process until finely ground. Add the seasoned butter and the onion and blend until really smooth and creamy. Spoon into dishes, cover tightly with cling film and allow the flavours to develop for at least 24 hours in the fridge before using.

Game brown

SERVES 8–10

This wonderful, old-fashioned recipe deserves a revival. Many people nowadays have no idea what a brawn is, and would probably be put off by the idea of using a pig's head, but they are making a grave error. It was, of course, the thrifty countryman's way of using up everything when the family pig was killed and often also included a 'boiling fowl', again, an item non-existent nowadays. This gave me the idea for using up old pheasant. Any OAG (Old-Age Game) would do as the cooking is long and slow. If you can't get hold of half a pig's head, trotters will do but you must have something which has soaked in brine so try to include a piece of un-smoked bacon, preferably hock.

½ pig's head, brined

1 pig's trotter

1 old pheasant

stock or water to cover

1 onion, peeled

1 carrot, peeled

piece of celery

6 peppercorns

½ lemon

2 bay leaves

bouquet garni

300 ml/½ pint white wine

1 tablespoon vinegar

½ teaspoon quatre-épices or mace

1 tablespoon chopped fresh parsley

1 hard-boiled egg

Soak the pig's head overnight. Place in a preserving pan with water to cover and bring to the boil; then throw away the water.

Add stock or stock and water, the trotter, vegetables, peppercorns, lemon and herbs. Simmer really slowly for 5 hours, adding the pheasant 3 hours before the end of cooking time.

Remove the pig's head, trotter and pheasant and take off the flesh. Strain the liquor and reduce by fast boiling to half. Measure 750ml/1½ pints into a clean pan, add the wine, vinegar and spice and reduce to 570 ml/1 pint. Dice the meat – it is easier to do this when the meat has cooled and jellied. Add it to the reduced liquid and simmer for a further 20 minutes.

Adjust the seasoning. Remove from the heat and, when cool, stir in the parsley. Lay some slices of hard-boiled egg on the base of a 900 g/2 lb loaf tin and then spoon in the mixture. Cool and refrigerate.

Turn out, and serve with new or mashed potatoes (the classic accompaniment to *fromage de tête*, the equivalent French dish) or, better still, with Summer garden salad with herbs (see page 122) and sauce gribiche (see page 135). For sensitive guests, you could call it a mould or terrine!

STARTERS PATES, TERRINES & RAISED PIES

Pheasant terrine, with Calvados, apple and mushroom

SERVES 6–8

This is one of my favourite recipes. It is based on the classic French dish Faisan Normande, in which the bird is cooked with apples and Calvados. The same flavourings, with baby button mushrooms, make it quite mouth-watering. You can either serve it as a first course or as part of a summer buffet. Failing pheasant, try making it with guinea fowl or chicken. It is great for a buffet.

1 pheasant
225 g/8 oz minced, boned pork spare rib
8 streaky bacon rashers, de-rinded
110 g/4 oz pork fat
225 g/8 oz chicken livers, plus the pheasant liver
2 shallots, peeled and chopped
pinch of dried thyme
2 bay leaves
salt and freshly ground black pepper
55 ml/2 fl oz Calvados
1 thick slice of white bread, de-crusted
150 ml/1/4 pint stock
1 egg
50 g/2 oz apple, peeled and chopped
50 g/2 oz button mushrooms, sliced
25 g/1 oz butter

Remove the flesh from the pheasant and chop roughly. Place in a food processor and mince coarsely. Do the same with the pork and pork fat and 2 of the bacon rashers and cut up the livers. Put all this in a bowl, with the shallots, thyme, bay leaves, salt, pepper and Calvados. Mix well and leave to marinate for 2 hours. Pre-heat the oven to 180°C/350°F/gas mark 4.

Soak the bread in the stock, in which you have beaten up the egg. Sauté the apple and mushrooms in the butter for a few seconds. Flatten and stretch the remaining bacon rashers on a board with a knife. Line a terrine with all except 2 of the rashers. Add the soaked bread and sautéed apple and mushroom to the marinade mixture and spoon into the terrine. Lay the 2 bacon rashers on top and decorate with the bay leaves and a sprig of thyme. Cover with foil and a lid and sit in a pan, with boiling water to come half-way up the terrine; bake for 2 hours.

Test with a skewer at the end of this time and, if juices run clear, the terrine is cooked. Remove, allow to cool and then place a 900g/2 lb weight on top until cold. Refrigerate for at least 3 days, to let the flavours develop.

Either serve it in the terrine or turn it out and arrange in overlapping slices on a dish and garnish with watercress. Hand round hot french bread. If it is to be served in the terrine, either run a little melted pork fat over the top or decorate with thinly sliced, sautéed mushrooms and apple slices and cover with jelly made with gelatine and stock.

Rich raised game pie

SERVES 8–10

A really rich game pie is a celebration in itself and is ideal for a winter buffet. With about 900g/2 lb of mixed game of one sort or another you are home and dry. Don't despair if you haven't got quite enough, though, just make it up with chicken, turkey or pork. In fact, I rather overdid the quantity of meat in one of my pies so I made a terrine by lining a 450 g/1 lb loaf tin with bacon, filled it with the remaining mixture, covered it with foil and cooked it in the oven with the pie for 2 hours. I make no excuse for including this, as no country cookbook would be complete without a recipe for a raised pie. If you don't have access to any game just use pork or chicken and ham instead. It is wonderful picnic fare.

FILLING

900 g/2 lb mixed game meat, chopped

450 g/1 lb minced pork

225 g/8 oz pork fat, chopped

225 g/8 oz pork sausage-meat

110 g/4 oz bacon, diced

2 shallots, peeled and chopped

1 garlic clove, peeled and chopped

1 teaspoon dried mixed herbs

1 teaspoon juniper berries

2 tablespoons Madeira or port

salt and freshly ground black pepper

JELLY

600 ml/1 pint reduced, well seasoned stock

sachet of gelatine

HOT-WATER CRUST PASTRY

700g/1½ lb strong white flour

1 teaspoon salt

1 tablespoon icing sugar

225 g/8 oz lard

200 ml/½ pint water

Mix together all the pie ingredients, which is best done with clean hands. Put the carcasses on to make stock.

To make the pastry: pre-heat the oven to 150°C/300°F/gas mark 2. Sift the flour, salt and sugar into a bowl. Melt the lard in the water in a saucepan and then mix into the flour with a wooden spoon. Knead lightly and then cut off one-third and leave to cool. Line a 900 g/2 lb collapsible loaf tin with the pastry. Fill with meat. Paint the rim with egg. Roll the remaining pastry for a lid and lay on top; crimp the edges with a fork, make a steam hole and paint with egg. Bake for 2½ hours.

Remove the pie and leave to cool for 1 hour. Let down the sides of the tin, remove from the tin and place on a baking tray. Paint the sides with egg and put back in oven with heat turned up to 190°C/350°F/gas mark 5, until brown, about 30–40 minutes. Reduce the stock to 425 ml/¾ pint and dissolve the gelatine in it. When the pie is cool, pour stock in carefully through steam hole. When cold, serve and wait for plaudits.

STARTERS PATES, TERRINES & RAISED PIES

Smoked pigeon pâté

SERVES 6–8

An all-time favourite, and guests frequently ask for the recipe. It is a true example of 'sweet and sour'. The honey and lemon are just discernible through the rather strong, smoky flavour of the pigeon, and give it a certain lightness. Don't give up just because you haven't got a smoker for you can now buy 'SAVU' Food Smoker Bags from Lakeland which you fill with your chosen ingredients and pop into the oven. Failing this either borrow one from a fishing friend or fix up a make-shift affair with your barbecue or with a wok or stir-fry pan - see recipe for Spicy Hot Smoked Salmon Moulds, page xx.

8 pigeon breasts (4 pigeons)
5 streaky bacon rashers, de-rinded
110 g/4 oz unsalted butter
75 g/3 oz chopped shallot
75 ml/3 fl oz vermouth
1 teaspoon runny honey
2 teaspoons lemon juice
1 teaspoon stem ginger juice or dried ground ginger
1 tablespoon double cream
¼ teaspoon ground cloves
½ teaspoon mild Dijon mustard
pinch of dried dill weed
salt and freshly ground black pepper

Sprinkle 2 tablespoons of sawdust over the bottom of the smoker and put in the grid and drip tray. Remove the pigeon breasts from the carcasses with a sharp knife, place on the grid and then lay 3 of the bacon rashers on the top. Slide on the lid and put the smoke box over the methylated spirits container, which has been lit. Leave until it

has burned out. If using a smoker bag just follow the instructions.

Sauté the shallots and remaining bacon in the butter, until transparent. Transfer to a food processor or liquidiser. Cut the pigeon breasts into 2.5 cm/1 in dice and sauté for a few seconds, stirring constantly. Take out and put in the food processor. Pour the juices from the drip tray into the sauté pan, with the vermouth, honey, lemon juice, ginger juice, cream and the rest of the seasonings. Increase the heat and bubble furiously for a few seconds. Process the pigeon, bacon and shallots until really finely ground, then pour in the pan juices and blend until really smooth. Spoon into a pot or pots, smooth down and cover with melted butter. Refrigerate for 2 or 3 days, to allow the flavour to develop. Serve at room temperature and not straight out of the fridge. Freezes well.

To smoke over a barbecue: Light the barbecue and, when hot, sit an old roasting tin on top. Sprinkle the sawdust (obtainable from most fishing tackle shops), over the base of the tin. Lay the pigeon breasts on a grid on top with a plate to catch the juices underneath. Cover with foil (or close the lid if you have a covered barbecue) and proceed as for a trout smoker.

Salmon and caper terrine

SERVES 4–6

This recipe is very colourful and makes a stunning centre-piece for a summer buffet. It is not as difficult as you would imagine and I made no less than three for my granddaughter, Tabitha's, christening

225g/8 oz salmon

600 ml/1 pint water

110 g/4 oz smoked salmon pieces, diced

2 sachets gelatine

4 thin lemon slices

3 tablespoons crème frâiche or greek yoghurt

3 tablespoons Hellman's mayonnaise

2 teaspoons capers, drained

1 tablespoon chopped fresh dill

1 teaspoon lemon juice

pinch of cayenne pepper

salt and pepper

TO GARNISH

lemon wedges

fresh dill sprigs

Poach the salmon very gently in 600ml/1 pint water, lift out and remove the bones and skin. Dissolve the gelatine in 425 ml/¾ pint of the cooking liquor. Line the base of the tin with the lemon slices, spoon on the diced smoked salmon and pour on enough of the dissolved gelatine to cover and allow to set. Flake the cooked salmon into a bowl and mix with the crème frâiche or yoghurt, mayonnaise, capers, dill, seasoning and the remainder of the gelatine and spoon into the tin. Leave to set and then turn out and garnish with lemon wedges and sprigs of dill.

Smoked trout and fried almond pâté

SERVES 2–4

I think that this was one of my better midnight brainwaves and it has become my favourite fish pâté. Truite aux amandes is one of the classic French dishes so, I thought, why not combine smoked trout or salmon in a pâté with fried almonds, which give a nice crunchy texture?

225 g/8 oz smoked trout or salmon

25 g/1 oz flaked almonds

110 g/4 oz butter

2 tablespoons light crème frâiche

lemon juice, to taste

1 dessertspoon chopped fresh parsley

salt and pepper

pinch of cayenne pepper

TO DECORATE

fresh parsley sprigs

thin lemon slices

Fry the almonds in 25 g/1 oz of the butter until golden, but watch like a hawk because they burn very easily. Transfer to a dish and reserve some for decoration. Process the trout and 50 g/2 oz of the butter, until smooth; then add the crème frâiche, lemon juice, parsley and seasonings. Lastly add the almonds but only whizz them for a couple of seconds. Spoon into a dish and smooth the top. Cool and refrigerate.

Pour over the remaining butter, which you have melted, and decorate with the rest of the almonds, some sprigs of parsley and thin slices of lemon. Freezes well.

Serve with thin slices of white toast.

Watercress and pine nut vegetarian pâté

SERVES 4

This is actually so delicious that you could even serve it to non-vegetarians. It drove me nearly mad trying out various combinations before the fifth attempt finally passed muster with my 'tasting panel'.

75 g/ 3 oz watercress

75 g/3 oz Philadelphia cream cheese or similar

50 g/2 oz feta cheese

50 g/2 oz butter

75 g/3 oz pine nuts

lime juice

pinch cayenne pepper

salt and ground black pepper

Place the watercress, cheese and butter in a blender and whiz until creamy. Toast the pine nuts in the oven and add 50 g/ 2 oz to the mixture and process until smooth. Add lime juice to taste, the cayenne pepper, salt and black pepper. Be wary of the salt as the feta cheese is salty in itself. Finally stir in the remaining nuts and spoon into pots. Pour over some melted butter and decorate with watercress leaves. Serve with granary toast.

FISH

The smell of sea-fresh fish is evocative and conjures up visions of shoals of silvery creatures flashing through the ocean, or blue-black mussels be-jewelled with barnacles and trailing garlands of seaweed. If you go to France, almost any town on the Normandy coast will boast fish stalls on the sea-front with a gleaming array of *fruits de mer* and, if you suddenly decide to have a fish supper, at 7 o'clock in the evening, that is the time to go and choose your ingredients. Sadly there are not many fishmongers left, but don't despair as a great many have now taken to the road. I live in the heart of England and Keith, my travelling fishmonger, comes from Grimsby every week with wonderful fresh fish, probably from the morning's catch that he has bought straight from the fish market. He tells me that there are at least a dozen like him. Local markets and even Farmer's Markets are another source where you will often find an excellent fish stall selling a good selection of really fresh fish. Never buy anything which has the slightest smell of ammonia. It should have a whiff of seaweed and be firm to the touch, with bright-looking eyes.

Coquilles St Jacques mornay

SERVES 4

When served in half a scallop shell, this makes a really decorative and enticing dish. But do beware, however, and make sure that your guests are not allergic to shellfish. Soon after I was married, we were invited to a grand dinner party with Yugoslav friends. Coquilles St Jacques was the starter and you can imagine my horror when I saw Archie turn pale green and break out in a sweat. Our hostess took in the situation at a glance and arranged for the butler to pretend that there was an important telephone call, so that Archie could leave the table. It is always best to ask guests if they are allergic to, or particularly abhor, anything in particular. My downfall is green peppers, which is why you won't find any in my recipes!

8 scallops in their shells
50 g/2 oz butter
2 shallots, peeled and finely chopped
50 g/2 oz plain flour
300 ml/½ pint milk
25 g/1 oz cheese, grated
salt and pepper
dried wholemeal breadcrumbs
butter

Remove the scallops from their shells and separate the white from the coral. Melt the butter and cook the white bits of the scallops over a low heat for 2 - 3 minutes; then remove and keep warm. Cook the corals for 1 minute. Sprinkle in the flour, cook for a few seconds and then add the milk and seasoning and stir until thick. Add the cheese and then the scallops and heat through gently. Spoon into the shells, making sure that each contains 2 scallops. Cover with the breadcrumbs, dot with butter and place under a grill until lightly browned. Serve at once.

If you prefer, you can poach the scallops in white wine, add cream and sautéed mushrooms, place in the shells, surround with creamy puréed potato, sprinkle with breadcrumbs and brown under the grill.

Crevettes Theodor

SERVES 2 (OR 4 AS A STARTER)

A really 'show-off' dish, which, if you eat in the kitchen, will impress your guests with your expertise. You can even do it in the dining room with a camping gas heater and a wok. I had it on my first wedding anniversary at a little Greek restaurant and it has been a wonderful standby ever since. To be true to the original you should use potted shrimps but as these are now difficult to obtain and are prohibitively expensive just use shrimps, prawns or even tiger prawns. Provided you have the requisite sea-food, tomato purée and cheese, you can knock this up in a matter of moments. For young bachelors, it is a perfect dish with which to impress a would-be girlfriend.

225 g/8 oz prawns
50 g/2 oz butter
55 ml/2 fl oz sherry
3 tablespoons concentrated tomato purée
½ teaspoon dried mixed herbs
salt and pepper
2–3 tablespoons freshly grated parmesan or Cheddar cheese

Melt the butter in a wok and heat through the shrimps or prawns. Add the sherry,

FISH

tomato purée, herbs and seasoning and let it bubble for a second. Remove from the heat and stir in the cheese. Serve immediately. (If you do decide to go the whole hog and use potted shrimps you will need 4 pots and omit the butter}.

Don't feel too constrained by the amounts given, for it is the ideal dish to pour in a slosh of this or that in true television 'cheffy' style!

As a starter, you can spoon the mixture into ramekins or place a spoonful on to pieces of toast on individual plates. If using as a main course, serve with rice and a green salad.

Fish pie with crunchy topping

SERVES 6–8

Of all the 'comfort' foods, I think that fish pie heads the list. It can be a vehicle for leftover cooked fish, or be purpose-built, with an exotic selection to bring it up to dinner-party standard. For me, fish pie should always have a potato topping but, as I also like 'crunch', a sprinkling of breadcrumbs or crushed cornflakes does the trick. To vary the textures of the potato, I usually mix in blanched diced vegetables of one kind or another: celeriac, fennel, parsnip or carrot are some of the ones I use but it is not obligatory.

225 g/8 oz cod or halibut fillet, skinned
225 g/8 oz smoked haddock, skinned
225 g/8 oz rainbow trout
50 g/2 oz peeled cooked prawns
570 ml/1 pint milk
1 onion, peeled
1 bay leaf
6 peppercorns
50 g/2 oz butter
50 g/2 oz plain flour
squeeze of lemon juice
grated zest of ¹/₂ lemon
1 tablespoon chopped fresh chervil or flat-leaf parsley
1 kg/2 lb potatoes, peeled and cut up
milk
butter
1 tablespoon diced and blanched celeriac
wholemeal breadcrumbs
salt and pepper

Pre-heat the oven to 200°C/400°F/gas mark 6. Poach all the fish, except the prawns, in the milk, together with the onion, bay leaf and peppercorns. Remove the skin and bones, transfer the fish to an oven-proof dish and sprinkle over the prawns. Melt the butter, add the flour and pour in the strained milk to make a béchamel sauce. Stir in the lemon juice, zest and herbs and pour over the fish.

Cook the potatoes until soft in salted, boiling water. Mash well with milk and butter and then beat until creamy and stir in the celeriac. Spread over the fish, sprinkle with the breadcrumbs and bake for 20–30 minutes or until golden brown.

Serve with mange-tout peas.

FISH

Mackerel with green gooseberry sauce

SERVES 2

Going out in a boat to catch mackerel off the coast is a thrilling experience, with the sun shining on the choppy waves; and the excitement of pulling in your line with several fish dangling from it is hard to beat. Often, you never come across a shoal so, when you do strike gold, it is a real achievement. These freshly caught mackerel, smelling of the sea, are sublime but most of us have to make do with what we can buy from the supermarket or fishmonger. Mackerel is a very oily fish and benefits from the sharp contrast of a fruit sauce, such as green gooseberry, the French name for which is groseilles à macquereau (mackerel gooseberries), which are in season at the same time as the mackerel. They are best grilled.

| 2 mackerel, cleaned |
| plain flour |
| salt and pepper |
| green gooseberry sauce (see page 136), to serve |

Cut the heads off the mackerel and slash them diagonally 2 or 3 times on each side. Sprinkle lightly with flour and season with salt and pepper. Place on a grid and grill under a medium heat for 4–5 minutes on each side or until the skin is bubbling and brown.

Serve with the gooseberry sauce and riced potato. If you do not have a potato ricer, mash potatoes thoroughly but do not add butter or milk.

Flash-fried fillets of sea trout, with lemon butter sauce and braised lettuce

SERVES 6

Unlike salmon, whose whereabouts in the ocean were only discovered by chance by a submarine, the sea trout has kept its secret and no one knows where they go to when they migrate back to the sea. They congregate at certain times in river mouths and estuaries and, like salmon, enter the rivers to spawn. In the west country, they are known as 'peal', in Wales as 'sewin' and in Scotland as 'finnock'. Sea trout are notoriously difficult to catch and the best way to do it is at night. Unless there is a full moon, wading in a river can be quite scary, but all is forgotten when the magic moment arrives and you have hooked one of these silvery fish. Don't 'count your chickens', though, until you have actually got the sea trout on the bank, as they have notoriously soft mouths and the hooks slip out all too easily. To me it is king of the Salmonidae and its delicate flesh needs only a minute or two on a hot griddle or pan and a lemon butter sauce to complement it, with simple vegetables such as braised Little Gem lettuce and tiny new potatoes, to accompany.

You can use escalopes cut from the tail end of a salmon or fillets of rainbow or brown trout instead.

| 6 sea trout fillets, skinned |
| 75 g/3 oz butter |
| 6 Little Gem lettuces |
| salt and pepper |
| lemon butter sauce (see page 129), to serve |

FISH

Make the lemon butter sauce.

Heat 25 g/1 oz butter in a saucepan and sauté the lettuces until they start to brown. Cover tightly, shake and cook over a low heat for 5 minutes.

Melt the remaining 50 g/2 oz butter in a heavy frying-pan until foaming and then flash-fry the fillets; a bare 30 seconds on each side will be sufficient. Transfer to a warm serving dish. Pour the sauce over the fish or hand it round separately.

Serve with new potatoes and the braised lettuces.

Bank-side barbecued trout with 'freebies'

SERVES 4-6

This is a real example of making the best of what's around. The herbalist daughter of friends of mine had a family barbecue by her father's trout lake. The trout had been caught that evening. They were stuffed with various herbs, wrapped in leaves and barbecued on a boot scraper over a wood fire. They were moist, delicious and, unlike most lake trout, full of flavour.

4 trout weighing approximately 700g /
1½lbs each

meadowsweet

comfrey leaves for wrapping up the fish

salt and pepper

potatoes for baking

butter

water mint

Cook the potatoes in the embers of the fire for about 1 hour while you are having a pre-supper slurp of wine. Gut the fish, stuff the cavities with the herbs. Don't bother to chop them, just scrunch them up into bundles and push them in then wrap the fish in the comfrey leaves. Place on the grid over the fire when the embers are red-hot and cook until done, probably about 5 minutes on each side. Before serving, peel off the comfrey leaves and skin which will be charred. Split the potatoes and fill with knobs of butter and sprigs of water mint. Eat with chunks of fresh bread thickly spread with butter and quaff down plenty of white wine which has been cooling down in the water while you have been cooking. There is nothing so wonderful as sitting by a misty lake in the gloaming, trout dappling the water and the moon rising over willow trees.

FISH

Trout fillets with bacon and oatmeal

SERVES 2

Fishing in the Elan Valley meant a long hike as in those days there was no road. We walked from the dam all the way round with fishing tackle, saucepan, kettle and small calor gas stove. The fish did not take until suddenly in the evening I caught a monster. In order to get it into the pan I had to fillet it, but coated in oatmeal and cooked with the bacon and then washed down with strong sweet tea it was one of the best meals I have ever eaten.

To fillet a fish:

Step 1 *Cut off head.*

Step 2 *Place fish on board, flat stone or grassy bank, with the tail nearest your tummy and the dorsal (or back) fin to the right. Hold firm with left hand and run knife along backbone. (If left-handed, read left for right and vice-versa)*

Step 3 *Ease knife underneath, along rib-cage, pulling skin and flesh gently to the left with your left hand until you have uncovered it completely.*

Step 4 *Remove intestines*

Step 5 *Ease knife under tail end of backbone and lift. You should now be able to pull it off. The fish will now be lying skin down, opened out in two halves like a book.*

2 trout filleted
4–6 rashers bacon
butter for frying
fine oatmeal
salt and pepper

Fry bacon rashers in a little butter and when cooked remove to a plate. Heat plenty of butter until foaming and put in trout skin-side down. Sprinkle with oatmeal, salt and pepper and cook for a couple of minutes. Turn over and repeat procedure with any further trout. Sprinkle more oatmeal and cook for a few seconds until brown. Alternatively you can use a grill.

Serve with bacon, bread, lashings of butter and strong tea. Archie maintained that the best tea he ever drank was made in a billycan in the desert during the war. The leaves were never thrown away, the new ones simply being added to each brew-up and then ceremonially stewed over a five-gallon drum filled with sand and petrol. We did try it once, unsuccessfully. I think desert heat, dust, flies and thirst must have been what made it seem, in retrospect, so ambrosial!

By the way, all this can be done in the comfort of your kitchen with bought trout in which case, serve it with boiled potatoes.

Oriental fishcakes

SERVES 4–6

Fishcakes can vary from the stodgy, gluey commercial variety to a gourmet delight of contrasting tastes and textures. Even if used as a vehicle for leftovers, you can add capers or herbs to give them a 'lift'. To add a bit of crunch, this recipe includes fennel and an eastern flavour with Thai 7-spice seasoning and ginger.

350 g/12 oz cooked white fish, skinned and boned
225 g/8 oz potato, boiled and mashed

FISH

150 ml/¼ pint béchamel sauce (see p.126)

25 g/1 oz onion, finely chopped

1 dessertspoon finely chopped fennel

½ teaspoon minced fresh ginger

1 teaspoon lemon juice

1 teaspoon soy sauce

Schwartz Thai 7-spice seasoning , to taste

salt and pepper

plain flour, for dredging

1 egg, beaten with 1 tablespoon milk

dried whole-meal breadcrumbs

oil, for frying

Mix together the fish, potato, sauce, onion, fennel, ginger, lemon juice and soy sauce. Season to taste with salt, pepper and 7-spice seasoning. Divide into 12 cakes and dredge with flour. Now dip each separately in the egg and milk mixture and then coat with crumbs. Fry in oil or a mixture of oil and butter until golden on each side.

Serve with sauté potatoes and sugar-snap peas.

Mussels in white wine and cream

SERVES 2–4

One of my brothers-in-law lived on the Argyll coast. His land included a beautiful wild bay edged with rocks on which, at low tide, there were thousands of mussels. My daughter, Lucy, and I gathered some and announced our intention of making moules marinière. The family were horrified and thought we were mad. At supper time, they couldn't resist coming down to see if we were dead or not, and believed that each delicious mouthful would be our last! The most fantastic mussels I had recently were bought from a stall on the sea-front at Arromanches, within spitting distance of the Normandy landings. My host visited at least four stalls before settling on the one which had, according to him, the best, biggest and juiciest mussels, and he was right.

2 litres/4 pints mussels

300 ml/½ pint dry white wine

4 shallots, peeled and finely chopped

2 garlic cloves, peeled and finely chopped

pinch of dried thyme

150 ml/¼ pint double cream

1 tablespoon chopped fresh parsley

ground black pepper

Wash the mussels in several lots of water and scrub as clean as possible. Discard any that don't close when sharply tapped. Place in a large saucepan, with the wine, half the shallots and garlic, and the thyme and cook, covered, over a high heat, for about 5 minutes or until the shells have opened. Discard any that are still shut. Fish the rest out and place in a warm dish. Strain the cooking liquor through a clean tea-towel, to get rid of any sand or grit, and pour into a clean saucepan. Add the remaining shallots and garlic and reduce by fast boiling to half. Add the cream, divide the mussels between 4 bowls, pour over the sauce and sprinkle with parsley. Grind over some pepper.

Serve with hot french bread.

FISH

Salmon, poached or baked

SERVES 6–8

The saga of the salmon is a romance. It returns each year to its native spawning grounds, surmounting the hazards of man and Nature to deposit its eggs in the 'redds', or spawning grounds, or to fertilise them with its milt, before making the equally dangerous journey back to the ocean. Freshly caught salmon, still covered in sea lice, is hard to beat as a gourmet food and the same can be said for the wild brown trout. In case this puts you off, the presence of sea lice indicates that the fish were in the sea only a few days previously; they fall off after the fish has been in fresh water a week. Not everyone can get freshly caught wild salmon, however, and we must be thankful that farmed salmon and sea trout really do taste pretty good and the fish farmers who do this for a living can be said to have revolutionised the market, by bringing these delectable fish within everyone's reach instead of being a luxury for the few.

A whole salmon makes a wonderful centre-piece for any party and, if served cold, makes for trouble-free entertaining, as all the hard work has been done and you can sit back and relax. To poach a salmon is not difficult and you can nearly always borrow or hire a fish kettle, if you do not own one yourself. Failing this, baking in foil is the other option. Frozen salmon can be dry and tasteless, so try a Scottish friend's tip and cook it in milk, which will make it more succulent.

1 fresh or frozen salmon, weighing approximately 2.7 kg/ 6 lb

2.25 litres/4 pints milk

50 g/ 2 oz butter

1 onion, peeled and cut up

1 carrot, peeled and cut up

1 leek, cleaned and cut up

1 celery stalk, cut up

2 bay leaves

10 black peppercorns

grated zest of 1 lemon

1 teaspoon salt

To poach frozen salmon: Thaw the salmon completely. Then wipe dry and sprinkle salt and pepper on the inside. Pour the milk and all the other ingredients except the salmon itself into a fish kettle, bring to the boil and simmer very slowly for 5 minutes. Wrap the fish in a piece of muslin or a clean tea-towel and lower into the pan. Make up the liquid with boiling water if it does not cover the fish. Bring back to the boil very slowly and simmer very gently for 15 minutes.

Allow to get quite cold in the poaching liquor and then remove, skin and garnish.

Serve with mayonnaise, (see page 134) or Green sauce (see page 134). If it is to be eaten hot, remove from the pan, skin and place on a serving dish. Serve with Hollandaise sauce (see page 133).

To poach fresh salmon: Make a court bouillon (see page 16) and cook for 8 minutes per 450 g/1 lb; then follow the above procedure.

To bake in foil: Lay the fish on a piece of well buttered foil in a roasting pan. Fill the stomach cavity of the fish with sprigs of

FISH

fennel or dill, and slices of lemon and season with pepper and salt. Seal the foil and make into a loose parcel (if it is too tight, the steam won't be able to circulate). Pre-heat the oven to 190°C/375°F/gas mark 5 and cook for 8 minutes per 450 g/1 lb.

To barbecue a whole salmon: Wrap a fish of 5 kg/10 lb in a soaked and sodden copy of the *Telegraph* or *Times* or similar broadsheet (not a tabloid!) Place on the barbecue, cook until both sides are charred, and then peel off the paper and skin the fish carefully. Serve with baked potatoes and plenty of butter and a watercress salad.

Halibut with a dill sauce

SERVES 4

Halibut is widely available and has a lovely firm texture. The other plus is the fact that the bones are very easy to remove. The taste is so good that you don't want to overwhelm it with complicated spices or sauces, it speaks for itself. Butter, a 'spritz' of lemon juice, cream and snipped fresh dill are all you need to make a truly gourmet dish

2 halibut steaks roughly 2 cm/³/₄ inch thick
110 g/4 oz butter
lemon juice
crème fraîche
snipped fresh dill
salt and pepper

Heat the butter in a sauté pan until foaming then coat the steaks on each side and place in pan. Put on a lid and cook over a medium to low heat for 2 – 3 minutes then turn over and cook the other side for the same time. Remove the skin and carefully detach the 4 sections from the bones before placing on a serving dish. De-glaze the pan with a generous squeeze of lemon juice then add the crème fraîche and salt and pepper. Stir for a few seconds to amalgamate, taste and add more lemon juice if necessary then pour over the fish. Finally snip masses of dill over the top. If no fresh dill is available just use dried. Serve with baby new potatoes. It is so easy and simple and is one of my favourite fish 'quickies'.

FISH

GAME

When the market for pigeon collapsed, in 1960, to 6d (2½p) a bird, Archie and I decided to become game dealers. After a while, it became obvious that plucking the birds by hand was not viable, so we bought a Bingham plucking machine. Although it was pretty basic, it did a good job but it had an uncanny knack of going wrong just when we had guests. Archie's mechanical expertise only rose to changing light bulbs, so it fell to me to become the mechanic. As a result, there is nothing I don't know about fan belts, discs, cogs and oil nipples.

Game is one of the most underrated of foods and is for the most part low in fat. It is widely available during the shooting season. If you live in the country, it is worthwhile finding out the local shoots and buying direct from them, that is, if you don't mind doing the plucking and gutting yourself. Otherwise, find a butcher or game dealer or even a fishmonger and it can be found in most supermarkets in season. Once again Farmers' Markets are another source and there are some specialist firms which sell by mail-order. These are listed on page 200.

Contrary to received wisdom, game does not need to be 'hung' until it is 'high'. In Edwardian days, it was not considered fit for consumption until it had fallen off the peg and my father-in-law would not eat a woodcock or snipe unless this had happened!

My personal rule of thumb for hanging game is as follows. As grouse and partridge are often shot in near-summer conditions, they should only be hung for 2–3 days and the same applies to wild duck. Pigeon should not be hung at all, as they go bad very quickly, and, if their crops (throats) are filled with greenstuff (even in winter) this should be removed at once or the flesh will be tainted. In cold weather or winter you can hang any kind of game for a week to ten days.

I have often seen people pause in the supermarket when they see game on the shelf, look, wonder and then move on because they don't know how to cook it. There is nothing difficult about this and I hope the following recipes will lead some beginners at the 'game' to realise what they have been missing.

Many pheasant and partridges are reared but have plenty of time, once released into the wild, to mature and gain flavour. Some venison, too, is farmed but it is an excellent substitute for those who are unable to eat beef. Of the wild deer the most delicate is roe deer, which can be cooked like lamb, next on my list is fallow and then sika. Wild red deer, unlike the farmed deer, is strongly flavoured and benefits from immersion in a marinade. Rabbit is delicious and, for those who find it a bit strong, a soaking overnight in salt and water or milk is the answer. Hare can be overpowering but long, slow cooking is the answer. Pigeon is one of the best buys and can be gourmet stuff if cooked with flair and imagination. Wild duck, such as mallard, are another delight. The list of healthy and delicious ingredients which can be yours for the asking is long and these treats are there, ready and waiting.

GAME SEASONS

Grouse		August 12th – December 10th
Partridge		September 1st – February 1st
Wild duck (mallard)		September 1st – January 31st
Pheasant		October 1st – February 1st
Snipe		August 12th – January 31st
Woodpigeon		No close season
Woodcock	England and Wales	October 1st – January 31st
	Scotland	September 1st – January 31st
Rabbit		No close season
Hare	No close season, but may not be sold March to July inclusive	
Deer	Seasons for each species and sex vary in England and Scotland	

ROASTING TIMES

These times apply to young grouse, partridge and pheasant, and older birds will need longer.

Grouse	35–40 minutes at 200°C/400°F/gas mark 6
Partridge	30–35 minutes at 200°C/400°F/gas mark 6
Wild duck (mallard)	45 minutes at 200°C/400°F/gas mark 6
Pheasant	45 minutes-1 hour at 190°C/375°F/gas mark 5
Snipe	15 minutes at 230°C/450°F/gas mark 8
Woodpigeon	35-40 minutes at 200°C/400°F/gas mark 6
Woodcock	20-30 minutes at 220°C/425°F/gas mark 7
Hare	1½ hours at 190°C/375°F/gas mark 5
Venison	20 minutes at 230°C/450°F/gas mark 8, then reduce to 190°C/375°F/gas mark 5 and cook for 20 minutes per 450 g/1 lb.

ACCOMPANIMENTS FOR GAME

Grouse toast; fried crushed oatcakes; bread sauce; cranberry; bilberry or redcurrant jelly; game chips; mashed swede.

Partridge toast; fried breadcrumbs; bacon rolls; bread sauce; matchstick potatoes; cabbage.

Wild Duck orange and chicory salad; sauté potatoes, turnips.

Pheasant apple; onion; roast potatoes; fennel; calvados or cider sauce.

Snipe and Woodcock toast; lemon wedges; button mushrooms; watercress salad

Woodpigeon redcurrant jelly, mashed potato; cauliflower.

Rabbit onions; boiled potatoes.

Hare redcurrant jelly; port; soured cream; pasta.

Venison rowan jelly; wild mushrooms; new potatoes or pasta; red cabbage.

GAME

Old grouse braised in raspberry vinegar

SERVES 2–4

Archie and I always considered that old grouse had more flavour. If you cover them in softened butter and wrap them in bacon and then foil and cook them in a low oven for 3–4 hours, they will be very tender and you can then serve them with all the trimmings, such as fried breadcrumbs, bread sauce and a rich gravy. It is a crime to do anything other than roast young grouse for 35–40 minutes in a hot oven with butter and bacon. The following recipe is an excellent way of dealing with old grouse; the marinade of raspberry vinegar and oil makes them very tender and the addition of a few raspberries to the casserole gives a nice tang to the sauce and your dyed-in-the-wool traditional guest should be won over.

2 old grouse

4 tablespoons raspberry vinegar

2 tablespoons olive oil

1 onion, peeled and chopped

8 juniper berries, crushed

6 black peppercorns

1 bay leaf

50 g/2 oz butter

2 bacon rashers

1 tablespoon raspberries

150 ml/¼ pint stock

1 teaspoon plain flour

1 teaspoon redcurrant jelly (optional)

salt and pepper

Place the grouse in a china dish, with the vinegar, oil, onion, juniper berries, peppercorns and bay leaf, and leave for 2–3 hours or, if possible, overnight. Turn occasionally.

Pre-heat the oven to 200°C/400°F/gas mark 6. Heat 25 g/1 oz of the butter in a frying-pan until it is foaming and then brown the birds all over. Place, breast-side down, in a casserole, with the marinade, bacon, raspberries, stock and salt and pepper; cover tightly. Put some foil under the lid if it doesn't fit well. Place in the oven, leave for 10 minutes and then turn down to 150°C/300°F/gas mark 2 for a further 2 hours, or until really tender when pierced with a skewer. Half way through cooking, turn breast-side up.

When cooked, remove to a warmed dish and then press the cooking liquid through a sieve. Melt the rest of the butter in a pan, sprinkle in the flour, cook for a few seconds and then pour in the strained juices and stir until the sauce has thickened and the sauce looks glossy. Add the jelly if it seems too tart.

Serve with sauté potatoes and caramelized young turnips.

GAME FEATHERED

Poached partridge poulette

SERVES 4–6

Game gourmets are usually hard-pressed to say which they consider to be at the top of the epicurean tree – young English partridge or young grouse. Plainly roast young partridge get my vote but old ones can also be delicious and this is a good way for either. Served with a lemony sauce, which is normally associated with chicken or fish, this makes a lovely light lunch dish or would be equally good for a dinner party.

4 partridges
1 carrot, peeled
1 celery stalk
1 fennel bulb
6 fresh parsley sprigs
300 ml/½ pint white wine
salt and pepper

SAUCE POULETTE
25 g/1 oz butter
25 g/1 oz plain flour
600 ml/1 pint stock
juice of ½ lemon
2 egg yolks
2 tablespoons crème fraîche
1 tablespoon chopped fresh parsley
salt and pepper

Poach the partridges very gently, with the vegetables and herbs, in the wine and water to cover. For old birds, this will take anything from 1½–2 hours. If your partridges are young, they will only need ¾ hour or 1 hour at most.

Remove from the saucepan and carefully cut in half, unless you think your guests can manage a whole bird. Arrange on a serving dish and keep warm. Strain the stock and remove the fennel bulb. Cut into slivers and use it as a garnish.

To make the sauce: melt the butter, add the flour and cook for 2–3 minutes. Add the strained partridge stock (for chicken, use chicken stock) and stir over a low heat until the sauce thickens. Cook over a low heat for 5 minutes. Add the lemon juice and whisk in the egg yolks, crème fraîche and parsley. Do not re-heat or allow to boil or the sauce will curdle. Season to taste, pour over the partridges and tip the remainder into a sauce boat.

Serve with new potatoes or rice and fine green beans. If you want to do so, you can serve the birds cold, cut into slices, and pour over the well whisked, cooled sauce.

GAME FEATHERED

MMMM
or
Mighty muscovado marmalade mallard

SERVES 2

Flighting wild duck by river's edge or pond in the gloaming is a truly magical experience. The thrashing and creaking of bare branches in the wind against scudding clouds, and a barely glimpsed crescent moon, is the backdrop. Suddenly, they appear out of nowhere and plummet down. On these occasions, your meal will have been well earned, for they are difficult quarry. This recipe was the result of 'make do and mend' when last-minute guests turned up and I had not got certain ingredients. I had just made a batch of my dark Oxford marmalade so I decided to use it with a brace of mallard I had in the fridge. As so often happens it was the perfect choice of partners and on every occasion since it has elicited 'Ooh' and Aah's'. Ordinary marmalade would do just as well: just add a spoonful of black treacle or muscovado sugar if you have any in the cupboard.

2 mallard duck
1 onion, peeled
50 g/2 oz butter
2 tablespoons dark mighty muscovado marmalade (see page 179)
5 ml/2 fl oz rum
2–3 drops balsamic vinegar
55 ml/2 fl oz stock
salt and pepper

Cover the duck breast with salt and leave, uncovered, overnight in the fridge. Before cooking, brush off the salt and place the onion in the body cavity. Pre-heat the oven to 200°C/400°F/gas mark 6. Heat the butter in roasting pan, until foaming, put in the duck and baste well; then spread with the marmalade. Cook for 45 minutes, if you like duck pink, or 1 hour if well done. Remove to serving dish. Pour off excess fat and then add the rum, balsamic vinegar and stock and bubble until the sauce is dark and syrupy. Adjust the seasoning.

Serve with sauté potatoes and whole baby turnips or mange-tout peas. Plain orange or orange and chicory salad also goes well.

Pheasant 'Guidwife'

SERVES 2

The worst episode in my game-dealing career occurred one Christmas Eve, when a very important customer brought in 100 pheasants, which had to be made 'oven-ready'. No slouching around on Boxing Day for Lucy and me as we had to get cracking and do them all and, of course, we didn't get paid any overtime!

This is a wonderful recipe for the old stager with spurs a mile long and it freezes well. You can also adapt it for other game or poultry.

1 pheasant
2 large Spanish onions, sliced
oil for frying
4 heaped tablespoons fruit chutney
1 wine glass red wine
1 heaped teaspoon cornflour
salt and pepper

Brown the pheasant in the oil and set aside. Then fry the onions. Sit the pheasant on top and spread a thick layer of chutney over it.

Pre-heat the oven to 150°C/300F/Gas Mark 3 and cook for 1½ hours, or 2 hours for a very old bird. Thicken the juice with the cornflour. You can use the chutney and fried onion mixture for grilling pheasant, pigeon or chicken breasts.

If you have a claypot, just spread the onions over the bottom of the pot, coat the bird with oil, then sit it on top and cover with the chutney, put on the lid, place in a cold oven and set heat at maximum. Cook for 1½ hours.

Serve with creamy mashed potatoes and buttered parsnips.

GAME FEATHERED

Pheasant sausage with leek and lemon sauce

SERVES 4–6

This unusual pheasant recipe can be eaten either hot or cold and will earn you 'brownie points' from your guests, not least those who don't like to deal with bones. It is a good way of using up damaged birds.

1 pheasant

1 onion

1 carrot

1 celery stalk

2.25 litres/4 pints water

bouquet garni

salt and pepper

25 g/1 oz fresh white breadcrumbs

2 tablespoons milk (approximately)

1 shallot, peeled and finely chopped

10 g/½ oz butter

110 g/4 oz sausage-meat

1 egg, beaten

plain flour, for dredging

dried breadcrumbs, for coating

butter, for frying

salt and pepper

LEEK AND LEMON SAUCE

6 baby leeks or 3 large ones

1 tablespoon water

1 tablespoon lemon juice

2 egg yolks

50 g/2 oz unsalted butter, chilled and cubed

salt and pepper

Remove the flesh from the pheasant and weigh out 225 g/8 oz. Put the carcass in a saucepan, with the vegetables, water, herbs and salt and pepper and simmer for 1½ hours.

Soak the breadcrumbs in milk. Cook the shallot in the butter until transparent. Process the sausagemeat, pheasant and cooked shallot. Squeeze out the breadcrumbs and add to the pheasant mixture, with the egg, and whizz until really smooth. Transfer to a bowl and chill while the stock is cooking.

When the stock is ready, strain it into a shallow pan. Take tablespoonsful of the pheasant mixture and roll gently into sausage shapes, in the flour. Lift with a slotted spoon, lower into the gently boiling stock and poach for 20 minutes. Remove and cool slightly; then roll in the breadcrumbs and sauté in the butter until brown. Keep warm on a dish in a low oven.

To make the sauce: If small, cut the leeks into 10 cm/4 in lengths and cook, with the water, in a tightly covered pan over a low heat, for 8–10 minutes – they should be cooked but not sludgy. (If using large leeks, cut into rounds and cook for only 5 minutes.) Heat 1 tablespoon each of the leek and lemon juice in a pan, pull off the heat and whisk in the egg yolks. Season with salt and pepper. Whisk in the butter, a piece at a time, until it has melted.

Garnish the sausages with leek and serve with pasta shapes. Hand round the sauce separately.

To use as a first course: place 1 sausage on each individual small plate and garnish with leek and a spoonful of sauce.

To freeze the sausages: do so before rolling them in the breadcrumbs.

To eat cold, just remove from the poaching water and roll in finely chopped fresh parsley.

Serve with Lemon Mayonnaise (see page 134).

Snipe, 'Butcher's treat'

A friend was wildfowling one day and, at the pub afterwards, asked a local fowler how he would cook snipe. 'Oh!' he said, 'you want to do them Butcher's Treat.' Chris asked how this was done and was told it was dead simple. Just cut a large potato in half, hollow out each bit, stick the plucked snipe inside, wrap in foil and bake. He tried it and found it actually worked, so I thought I'd have a go. I've done it a bit differently but I highly recommend the end result, which is tender and juicy. The potato makes the snipe go further, so that it is possible to use 1 snipe per person, which would normally be downright mean as there is hardly enough on a snipe to feed a very hungry mouse. I suspect that, in times gone by, the snipe were put into the potato with a wodge of fat bacon and cooked in the hot ashes of the fire. The only explanation of the name I can come up with is that it was either invented by a Mr Butcher or that it was a speciality of the local butcher.

1 snipe per person

1 large baking potato per person

butter

salt and pepper

Pre-heat the oven to 240°C/475°F/gas mark 9. Cut off a small piece of the potato at the base, so that it sits level and doesn't fall over. Remove an oval or round disk from the top, to form a lid, and hollow out the potato to form a case (a melon baller is ideal for this). Place a piece of butter in the bottom, sit the snipe on top and season well with salt and pepper. Lay another piece of butter on top and replace the lid. Bake for 1 hour.

Wonderful juice will have collected at the bottom and you may need extra baked spuds or bread to soak it up. A green salad with vinaigrette dressing makes a good accompaniment, to 'cut across the fats'. Incidentally, neither this or the following recipe is for dieters!

Roast snipe on mushrooms

SERVES 4
Another way to make snipe go further.

4 snipe

4 squares of fried bread

4 large mushrooms

4 pieces butter

4 rashers bacon

salt and pepper

Pre-heat the oven to 230°C/450°F/gas mark 8. Cut a V at each end of the mushrooms and place one on each piece of fried bread, with a piece of butter and roast for 5–10 minutes. Then sit a snipe on top, cover with bacon and cook for 25–30 minutes. Extra mushrooms can be cooked at the same time, if liked.

Again, salad goes best with this.

GAME FEATHERED

Grilled pigeon breasts stuffed with garlic cheese

SERVES 4

When Archie threw in his lot as an office worker and decided to become a professional pigeon-shooter and offer a crops-protection service, we had serious amounts of pigeons to deal with and get to market.

My side of the business was to try to popularise them with a public who only ever connected them with pigeon pie. The No 1 rule with pigeon is 'short and sharp' or 'long and slow', anything else and the end product is dry and leathery. This was one of the first pigeon recipes that I created and it has become quite a classic. Guests always seem to enjoy it and ask for the recipe. It also freezes well. It certainly comes into the quickie bracket.

8 pigeon breasts (from 4 pigeons)
8 teaspoons cream cheese with garlic and herbs
plain flour, for dredging
1 egg, well beaten
dried breadcrumbs, for coating
butter and/or oil, for frying

Make a pocket in each breast with a sharp knife, by slitting lengthways, and fill with cream cheese. Dredge with flour and then dip in egg and coat liberally with breadcrumbs. If you have any egg left over, it pays to do an extra coating of crumbs over the slit, as the cheese tends to escape from this. (Freeze, if wished, at this point.) Deep-fry in hot oil for 3–4 minutes or shallow fry in a mixture of butter and oil for 3 minutes on each side.

Serve with a purée of potato, into which you have folded cooked, diced celeriac. If to be eaten cold, cut lengthways into thin slices. Arrange in a fan shape on plates, garnish with fennel and avocado and then drizzle with walnut oil and lemon juice and sprinkle with chopped walnuts.

Grilled pigeon breasts with redcurrant jelly and cream

SERVES 4

To be truthful I think that this was actually my first culinary pigeon invention and it really has stood the test of time, in this case half a century ! It is so simple and easy that it would be difficult to go wrong.

8 pigeon breasts
50 g/2 oz butter
1 tablespoon redcurrant jelly
cream
soy sauce
Salt and pepper

Cut the pigeon breasts into 2.5 cm/1 inch cubes. Turn the grill onto high, melt the butter in the pan from which you have removed the rack. When the butter is foaming and beginning to turn brown add the breasts, jelly and soy sauce tossing turning to coat well and cook for 3 – 4 minutes or until the pigeon cubes are still faintly pink inside then remove with a slotted spoon.

When the sauce begins to caramelize, add the cream and seasoning. Stir and scrape until it looks coffee-coloured. Serve with baked or boiled potatoes and peas. Lucy reminds me that we sometimes had it for supper served up on thick wodges of toast!

Pigeon and tangerine casserole

SERVES 2

The tangerines go exceptionally well with the pigeons and the long, slow cooking produces a very tender end result. I don't possess a slow cooker but I think it would be ideal for this recipe, and, of course, if you have an AGA, you could stick it in the simmering oven overnight. This freezes well.

4 oven-ready pigeons
4 tangerines or 2 oranges, peeled
butter, for frying
2 shallots, peeled and chopped
1 onion, peeled and cut up
4 bacon rashers, cut up
110 g/4 oz small button mushrooms
1 tablespoon plain flour
110 ml/4 fl oz sherry or Madeira
1/2 teaspoon dried mixed herbs
salt and freshly ground black pepper

Pre-heat the oven to 150°C/300°F/gas mark 2. Stuff the birds with a tangerine or half an orange. Brown in butter and remove to a casserole. Sauté the shallots, onion and bacon until pale gold, add the mushrooms and cook for a few minutes. Sprinkle in the flour and then add the sherry or Madeira and cook until it thickens. Pour over the pigeons and sprinkle on the salt, pepper and herbs. Cook for 2–3 hours, or until tender. You may have to thicken with a little cornflour as the juice from the tangerines and birds tends to thin the sauce.

Serve with new potatoes and green beans.

Pigeon bangers and mash

SERVES 2–4

Pigeon bangers are so good that my daughter's builder, a huge man, known in our family as the Big Friendly Giant, was so enamoured that he asked me to make him a few pounds for his freezer. You don't have to own a contraption for sausage making as they are fine without casing, and you can, if you wish, just make them into 'burger' shapes. You can use any kind of game. Try venison and porcini mushrooms but omit lemon and honey and substitute rowan jelly and add a few juniper berries, or grouse and cranberry jelly with thyme. The possibilities are endless.

6 pigeon breasts
100 g/4 oz belly pork
1 rasher de-rinded streaky bacon, chopped
2 tablespoons fresh breadcrumbs
1 teaspoon mixed herbs
½ teaspoon honey
½ teaspoon minced fresh ginger
1 teaspoon lemon juice
½ teaspoon green peppercorns , crushed
salt

Put the pigeon breasts, belly pork and bacon in a blender and process with short, sharp bursts until it looks like fine mince but is not puréed. Tip into a bowl, add the other ingredients and mix well by hand. Scoop out a tablespoon of mixture and roll into a ball, then dredge with flour and roll into sausage shapes.

Grill or fry and serve with plenty of mashed potato.

Woodcock with beurre noir and capers

SERVES 2

The classic way of cooking woodcock (and snipe) with the 'innards' does not appeal to many people, except perhaps the hard-core traditionalists. You can imitate tradition more palatably by mashing up some sautéed chicken livers and spreading them on the toast on which you have roasted the woodcock. Die-hards of the old school will have it that the birds should fly through a very hot oven for 8 minutes; I prefer the longer roasting time of 20 minutes. The combination, in the following recipe, of burnt butter and capers, really is delicious and I think even the most prejudiced anti-woodcock eater would be seduced by it into more positive thinking.

2 woodcock
25 g/1 oz butter

POTATO PURÉE

1 kg/2 lb potatoes
milk
butter
salt and pepper

BEURRE NOIR WITH CAPERS

75 g/3 oz butter
2–3 teaspoons capers

Pre-heat the oven to 220°C/425°F/gas mark 7. Boil the potatoes; then drain and mash well. Add butter and plenty of milk, beating vigorously until you have a purée the consistency of thick mayonnaise. Season well, place some kitchen paper under the lid of the saucepan and keep warm.

Melt the 25 g/1 oz butter in a small roasting pan and, when foaming, put in the woodcock. Season with salt and pepper and baste well, and then roast for 20 minutes.

Give the potato purée a final beating. Place a good dollop on each plate and sit a woodcock on top.

For the sauce, melt the butter in a pan and, when it begins to turn brown, remove from the stove and add the capers. Despite the name, don't on any account let the butter turn black. Spoon over the birds and serve immediately.

A watercress salad is all you need as an accompaniment.

Rabbit, fried with almonds and creamy sauce

SERVES 2

I never cook rabbit without thinking of a lovely story told by a friend about a Norfolk keeper. There was a conjuring show one Christmas in the village hall and the conjuror asked this old keeper to come up on stage. He said, 'Now, Sir, I am going to make this rabbit disappear', which he duly did. He then turned to the keeper and said, 'Now I am going to produce it from your coat pocket!' 'I shouldn't do that if I was you.' 'Why not?' asked the conjuror. 'I do keep my ould hob ferret in that there pocket and yew wouldn't have no rabbit left.'

This recipe elevates the humble rabbit to dinner-party level. The almonds go particularly well and I concocted a cream and anchovy sauce, with lemon juice to counteract any richness. It is a good idea to remove the bones from the rabbit joints, or get your butcher to do so.

| 1 young rabbit, jointed and boned |
| 1 egg, beaten |
| breadcrumbs, for coating |
| oil, for frying |
| 1 tablespoon flaked almonds |
| 25 g/1 oz butter |

CREAMY SAUCE

| 2 tablespoons water |
| 1 tablespoon lemon juice |
| 50 g/2 oz butter |
| ½ teaspoon cornflour |
| 150 ml/¼ pint single cream |
| 1 teaspoon anchovy essence |
| salt and pepper |
| chopped fresh coriander, to garnish |

Dip the rabbit joints in the egg and then coat with the breadcrumbs.

Fry the almonds in the butter until they are golden; watch them, as they burn very easily. Drain and put them on kitchen paper.

Heat the oil and fry the rabbit pieces for about 5 minutes on each side; then transfer to a warmed serving dish.

To make the sauce: Put the water, lemon juice and butter into a small pan and bring to the boil. Add the cornflour, mixed with a little water, and stir until it thickens; season with salt and pepper and, lastly, pour in the cream and anchovy essence. Scatter the almonds over the rabbit pieces and garnish with the chopped coriander.

Serve with new potatoes and spinach. Hand the sauce round separately.

GAME 'FURRED'

Rabbit risotto with ramsons pesto

SERVES 2   *F*

The Italians hold ramsons or wild garlic in high regard as I discovered when visiting Carluccio's delicatessen in Covent Garden where it was, to say the least, highly priced. Pairing wild rabbit and wild garlic together is a real marriage of 'freebies'. You should be able to find 'ramsons' any time from late January onwards but if you can't find any in your locality make the pesto with chives and garlic instead.

1 rabbit
2 tablespoons olive oil
2 shallots, peeled and finely chopped
350 g/12 oz Arborio or carnirolli rice
150 ml/¼ white wine
1 litre/1¼ pints stock
salt and pepper

THE PESTO SAUCE

20 g/1 oz ramsons
1 small garlic clove, peeled
2 tablespoons grated Parmesan cheese
1 tablespoon pine nuts
best virgin olive oil
salt and pepper

Remove the flesh from the rabbit and cut into cubes. Heat the oil in a large sauté pan and soften the shallots then add the rabbit and cook over a low heat for about 5 minutes, shaking the pan. Tip in the rice and stir until coated in oil then pour in the wine. Stirring continuously, keep adding a ladle full of stock each time it is absorbed. The rice should be cooked but still firm and unlike basmati rice, the end result gooey. Season to taste.

To make the pesto: Chop the ramsons roughly then blend with the other ingredients. Finally add enough oil for it to be thick but not runny.

Mix into the risotto but reserve a little to drizzle over the top. Finally sprinkle over some parmesan shavings.

Hare medallions, with cassis

SERVES 2

Hare is much appreciated as a gourmet food on the continent, where hare fetch far more money than a brace of pheasants. People in this country rarely ask for them but what a treat they miss. Hare should be hung, head-down, for up to a week, depending on the weather. In the old days, you would see them in butcher's shops with a little metal bucket attached to the head, to catch the blood, which would then be used to thicken the sauce. If, like me, you are squeamish, don't attempt this! The following recipe can be prepared ahead and then, if you don't want to use it immediately, put it in the freezer (they only take 1 hour to thaw). Roe fillet can be treated the same way but will feed twice the number.

2 fillets of hare
1 tablespoon best olive oil
1 garlic clove, peeled and finely chopped
butter, for frying
squeeze of lemon juice
1 teaspoon blackcurrant jelly
small pinch of cayenne pepper
75 ml/3 fl oz Cassis (see page 193)
1 tablespoon soured cream
salt and ground black pepper

GAME 'FURRED'

Remove the white skin and membrane from the hare and cut each fillet diagonally into four. Flatten with the heel of your hand, smear each side with the olive oil and sprinkle with garlic. Cover with cling film and leave for 30 minutes.

Heat the butter in a heavy pan, until foaming; blot the oil off the medallions with kitchen paper and sauté for 2 minutes on each side. They should still be pink inside. Transfer to a dish. Add the lemon juice, jelly, seasoning and cassis and bubble for a few seconds; then stir in the soured cream. Spoon a little over each of the medallions.

Garnish with triangles of fried bread and sautéed oyster mushrooms. Serve with matchstick potatoes and steamed, diced celeriac.

Hare and chestnut casserole

SERVES 6–8

If you are not a fan of strong-tasting furred game, try this recipe for a hare casserole. The meat is not marinated, so the gamey flavour is not accentuated. In fact, if you leave ordinary pork or a leg of lamb in a marinade for few days, the result will be very similar to wild boar or red deer. Conversely, I have fooled guests who swore they hated venison into thinking they were eating leg of lamb, by serving up a joint of un-marinated sika or roe deer with all the usual lamb trimmings, such as mint sauce or jelly!

A really good stock is essential. You can use a stock cube but it would be preferable to open a tin of beef consommé or buy a tub of fresh stock from the supermarket, some of whom also sell vacuum-packed chestnuts, though the tinned variety are perfectly all right. The glass of port is optional but I think it adds flavour and you could use Madeira, sherry or whatever is in the booze cupboard.

A young hare would only need 1½ hours; an old stager would take 2–3 hours or even overnight in the simmering oven of an AGA. As with all casseroles, it improves by being re-heated the day after you have cooked it.

1 hare, jointed
50 g/2 oz butter
2 shallots, peeled and chopped
2 tablespoons plain flour
1.2 litres/2 pints stock
1 glass of port (optional)
1 tablespoon red-wine vinegar
1 teaspoon Dijon mustard
½ teaspoon ground allspice
½ teaspoon ground dried thyme
2 dried bay leaves
1 tablespoon dark muscovado sugar
1 packet vacuum-packed chestnuts

Pre-heat the oven to 170°C/350°F/gas mark 3. Brown the shallots and hare joints in the butter in a frying-pan. Remove to a casserole. Sprinkle the flour into the frying pan, cook for a few seconds and then add the stock and stir until it thickens. Add all the other ingredients and pour the sauce into the casserole. Transfer to the oven and cook for 1½ hours, or until tender; reckon on 2–3 hours, or overnight in the simmering oven of an AGA for an old hare.

Serve with boiled potatoes and brussels sprouts.

GAME 'FURRED'

VENISON

After the war, Archie became a professional stalker for a friend who had a Scottish estate. After five years of laissez-faire, there had been a deer population explosion resulting in poor beasts, due to lack of food and in-breeding, so an intensive cull was necessary. One day, Archie shot three beasts in the snow, which had to be got down off the hill. He had the bright idea of roping them together, sitting on them and using them as a toboggan. Only when it was gathering speed did he realize that there was a rocky gorge and river below. He baled out just in time but the beasts were un-saleable. His friend was justifiably indignant as the price of venison was rocketing, due to meat rationing! Nowadays he wouldn't have worried as the price is abysmal.

Venison casserole with chipolatas

SERVES 4–6

Having been taken to task by one of my friends, who has traditional tastes, for making 'mucked-up' recipes, I thought I'd better redeem myself in his eyes. A good rib-sticking casserole seemed to be the answer. I did use red wine but you could equally well cut it out and use all stock, instead.

| 1 k g/2 lb venison |
| 2 tablespoons olive oil |
| 2 onions, peeled and chopped |
| 2 carrots, peeled and chopped |
| 2 celery stalks, chopped |
| 8 pork chipolatas |
| 2 tablespoons plain flour |
| ½ bottle red wine |
| 300 ml/½ pint stock |
| 110 g/4 oz bacon, diced |
| 1 teaspoon dried mixed herbs |
| 2 teaspoons redcurrant jelly |
| 1 teaspoon made mustard |
| 1 teaspoon Lea & Perrins Worcestershire Sauce |
| salt and pepper |

Pre-heat the oven to 150°C/350°F/gas mark 2. Carefully remove all the sinews and membrane from the meat and cut into 2.5 cm/1 in cubes. Heat the oil and brown the meat, vegetables and chipolatas. It is best to do this in small batches and I find a wok excellent, as it heats the oil to a high temperature and is roomy. Sprinkle in the flour and then the red wine and stock, stirring constantly until it thickens. Add the bacon, herbs, jelly and seasonings and transfer to a casserole. Cover and transfer to the oven; cook for 3–4 hours, or overnight in the simmering oven of an Aga.

Serve with mashed potato and swede and I think you will agree that you can't get more traditional than that!

GAME VENISON

Velvety venison casserole agro dulce

SERVES 8-10

The richness of this Italian peasant dish is offset by the agro dulce sauce and the crunch of the toasted pine nuts which are sprinkled on the top. It is splendid for a winter buffet or shoot lunch and can be made a day or two before as it improves with re-heating. It can be frozen. It is in fact the venison equivalent of an oxtail stew with the added bonus that you don't have to cope with the bones.

| 2 kg/4 lb venison, diced |
| 1 pig's trotter |
| seasoned flour for dredging |
| 4 tablespoons olive oil |
| 450 g/1 lb belly of pork |
| 1 pig's trotter |
| 2 small onions, stuck with cloves |
| 2 carrots, peeled and cut up |
| 6 small shallots |
| 225 g/8 oz swede, peeled and diced |
| 1 leek trimmed and sliced |
| 4 fat cloves garlic |
| 1 bottle Primitivo Italian red wine |
| 1 tablespoon concentrated tomato purée |
| 1 tablespoon redcurrant jelly |
| 25 g/1 oz dried porcini mushrooms |
| 1 teaspoon Italian dried herbs |
| 2 bay leaves |
| salt and ground black pepper |

AGRO DULCE SAUCE

| 1 tablespoon sugar |
| 300 ml/1/2 pint of the cooking liquor |
| 1 1/2 teaspoons balsamic vinegar |
| 4 tablespoons soaked raisins |
| 3 squares dark chocolate |
| salt and pepper |

TO GARNISH:-

| 50 g/4 oz toasted pine nuts |

Cut the meat into 5 cm/2 inch dice and roll in the flour. Heat the oil in a flame-proof casserole and brown the venison and pork. Add the remaining ingredients and place in a pre-heated oven set at 200°C/400°F/Gas Mark 6 for 15 minutes and then reduce the heat to 150°C/300°F/Gas Mark 2 and cook for 4 hours, or until tender. If you have an AGA, cook in the simmering oven.

To make the sauce; dissolve the sugar lumps in a small pan with a tablespoon of water. Boil without stirring until it caramelizes. Add the cooking liquor, balsamic vinegar, raisins and chocolate and season then stir into the casserole. Toast the pine-nuts and sprinkle over the top just before serving. It is so rich that you can either serve it with pasta such as tagliatelle or even omit this and just have hot ciabatta bread and a green salad. It may sound like a lot of trouble, but I can assure you it's worth it and it is one of those 'work of art' dishes that I mentioned in the introduction.

GAME VENISON

Roast roe haunch, stuffed with apricots and almonds

SERVES 8–10

This Moroccan stuffing of apricots and almonds complements the flavour of the venison and ensures that it isn't dry. As a general rule, roe haunches do not go much beyond the 2.3 kg/5 lb–2.7 kg/6 lb mark, so the stuffing also makes it go further. Leg of lamb is also excellent done this way.

1 roe haunch, weighing approximately 2.3 kg/5 lb
110 g/4 oz butter, softened
1 teaspoon mustard powder
1 teaspoon soft brown sugar
275 ml/¹⁄₂ pint stock
salt and pepper

STUFFING
25 g/1 oz butter
225 g/8 oz onion, peeled and chopped
2 pieces of celery, chopped
175 g/6 oz ready-to-use dried apricots
50 g/2 oz flaked almonds
2 cardamon seeds, crushed
50 g/2 oz fresh white breadcrumbs
1 egg, beaten
salt and pepper

Pre-heat the oven to 230°C/450°F/gas mark 8. Lay the haunch flat, with the thick bit facing you, and make a big pocket with a sharp, pointed knife; endeavour to keep the opening as small as possible.

For the stuffing: melt the butter and cook the onion until soft but not coloured. Add the remaining ingredients, mix well and allow to cool. Spoon into the pocket and fix with a skewer.

Mix the butter, mustard and sugar to a paste and spread over the haunch. Season well. Place in a roasting pan and roast for 20 minutes; then cover with foil and reduce the heat to 190°C/375°F/gas mark 5 for 2¼ hours, removing the foil for the last half hour.

Transfer to a carving dish. Pour some stock into the roasting pan and bubble on top of the stove; then strain and pour into a sauce boat.

Serve with roast potatoes, creamed celeriac and brussels sprouts.

Hot game pie

SERVES 4–6

Hot game pie is a wonderful excuse to use up all the odds and ends in your deep-freeze, which would not be enough on their own to feed a family. Anything can go into it, providing that you reckon on having approximately 700g/1½ lb of meat. I personally don't like to find bones in my pie, so I always remove the meat from whatever game I'm using and cut it into cubes. You can either cook it first and take the flesh off later, or remove it beforehand. A rough guide would be 1 rabbit, 1 pheasant and 1 pigeon. Of course, a whole hare would give you almost that amount on its own, so you might just roast the saddle and use the meat from the thighs and legs to mix in with your chosen game. It is also an ideal way to use up old birds. On the other hand, if you don't have much game, just use what you've got and make up the difference with chicken or turkey.

1 pheasant, 1 rabbit and 1 pigeon, jointed

50 g/2 oz butter or lard

plain flour, for dredging

1 onion, peeled and chopped

2 bacon rashers, de-rinded and cut up

110 g/4 oz button mushrooms

1 teaspoon redcurrant or rowan jelly

good pinch of dried mixed herbs

300ml/½ pint stock

1 tablespoon red wine (optional)

beurre manié (see page 15, optional)

SHORTCRUST PASTRY:

1 egg, well beaten

salt and pepper

You can use flaky pastry if preferred, in which case a 450 g/1 lb packet will be sufficient.

Melt the butter or lard in a large frying-pan and sauté the onion until just turning colour. Then dredge the joints in the flour and cook until golden. Transfer to a flameproof casserole. Add the bacon, mushrooms, jelly, herbs and seasoning. Pour in the stock and wine, if using, cover and cook for 1½–2 hours or until tender.

Pre-heat the oven to 200°C/400°F/gas mark 6. Fish out the joints, take the meat off the bones and lay in a 1.2-litre/2-pint pie dish. If the sauce looks too thin, bring to the boil and whisk in little pieces of beurre manié, until it is thick enough; then pour over the game meat and allow to cool. Roll out the pastry and cover the pie. Brush with the beaten egg and bake for 35–40 minutes.

GAME VENISON

MEAT

Modern marketing concepts must lead many people to believe that meat starts life in a plastic package. In the not-so-distant past, every butcher would have had charts of each type of beast hanging on his walls, showing the different cuts and joints. Now all packaged meat looks much the same and you could be forgiven for forgetting that beef comes from bullocks, lamb from sheep and pork from pigs. But, more importantly, you should remember that good meat comes from contented beasts, well nurtured. The end product must then be skilfully butchered and nicely presented. To be tender and succulent, a joint should be hung in a chiller for 3 weeks, but you will be lucky if you find a butcher who does this as they are few and far between. In these health-conscious days, it is almost impossible to get well marbled beef or lamb, yet it is these veins of fat which make the meat tender. In the same way, a nice thick layer of fat beneath the skin on a joint of pork will ensure crisp and crunchy crackling, so eschew any joints which have the skin tied round them. There are a growing number of organic meat shops which meet these needs, so my advice is to search one out or find a good butcher who knows his stuff and where his meat comes from. Farmer's markets are getting better and better and are another good source of both meat and poultry as are some of the mail-order outlets, some of which I have listed at the end of the book.

In this section, I have included a variety of recipes with cooking methods ranging from roasting to the long, slow cooking of the tougher cuts. Stews and casseroles improve by being heated up the following day, which allows the flavours and juices to impregnate the meat. These dishes are ideal for the working person, as they can be cooked the day before and re-heated or frozen for future use. They are also ideal for the single person to cook in a slow-cooker.

BEEF

A roast joint of beef, brown and crisp on the outside and progressing through the colour spectrum from palest pink to old rose in the centre, thus catering for those liking their meat well-done to those whose preference is 'rare', is the end-product of great expertise. The farmer starts this chain of events with his choice of breed and the way in which his animals are reared. Sadly, modern health faddishness dictates that he shall choose one of the modern breeds with lean meat and not much fat, but, fortunately, there are still herds of Aberdeen Angus whose meat is undoubtedly at the top of the gourmet tree. Beasts reared organically are undoubtedly the best. The next stage is to find a butcher who will take the trouble to hang the meat for up to 3 weeks, thus ensuring tenderness and flavour. Butchers with their own abattoir are to be preferred, as the animals then do not have to undergo long journeys and suffer the stress of overnight stays in waiting pens which results in the meat being tough.

Roast fore-rib of beef

SERVES 6–8

Having found your first-class butcher, ensure that he has hung your joint, which, for this recipe, is a fore-rib on the bone. This may be more of a bore to carve but gives incomparably more flavour.

2.7 kg/6 lb–3.6 kg/8 lb fore-rib of beef on the bone
110 g/4 oz butter, softened
1 tablespoon dry mustard powder
1 dessertspoon Lea & Perrins Worcestershire Sauce
salt and pepper
1 glass red wine
1 teaspoon brown sugar (optional)
1 dessertspoon plain flour (optional)
300 ml/½ pint stock

Pre-heat the oven to 200°C/400°F/gas mark 6. Make a paste of the softened butter, mustard, Worcestershire sauce, and salt and pepper and spread it on both sides of the joint. Put the joint on a rack in the roasting pan and place in the oven. Cook for 15 minutes per 450g/1lb (rare), 20 minutes (medium), or 25–30 minutes (well done), plus 15 minutes. Baste well every 20 minutes.

When cooked, transfer to a serving dish and allow to 'rest' for 30 minutes. This is most important, as the meat will then be juicier and it will be easier to carve. Incidentally, beef should always be carved in thin slices, unlike lamb.

Meanwhile, pour off the fat from the roasting tin and scrape up the brown bits. Swirl out with the wine and stock and pour into a small pan. Reduce by fast boiling, until syrupy, and adjust the seasoning. You may have to add a small teaspoon of brown sugar, to counteract the acidity of the wine. Some people like a thick gravy, in which case sprinkle a dessertspoonful of flour into the roasting pan before you add the liquid.

Serve with 'bag o' nails' potatoes (see page 106), Yorkshire pudding (see opposite), horseradish sauce and spring greens.

BEEF MEAT

Yorkshire pudding

SERVES 6–8

In addition to Yorkshire pudding, there are many other uses for batter, not least of which is to stretch leftovers. You can make it in individual 15 cm/6 in tins and, after cooking the batter, fill it with chicken in a sauce, mince or mushrooms. The possibilities are endless.

110 g/4 oz plain flour
pinch of salt
2 eggs
300 ml/½ pint milk and water (or use all semi-skimmed or skimmed milk)
50 g/2 oz dripping or lard or 2 tablespoons sunflower oil

Sift the flour and salt into a bowl and make a well in the centre. Break in the eggs and add half the liquid. Mix well and then beat in the rest of the liquid, until bubbles burst to the surface. The operation can be done in a food processor but a lighter batter will ensue if you do it by hand or with electric beaters. Leave to rest for 1 hour, to allow the starch grains in the flour time to swell and burst, thus producing a lighter pudding. This is not essential but advisable.

To cook, pre-heat the oven to 240°C/475°F/gas mark 9. Heat your chosen fat in a 20 cm/8 in × 25 cm/10 in roasting pan in the oven for 5 minutes. Pour in the batter and cook at this temperature for 5 minutes; then reduce the heat to 220°C/425°F/gas mark 7 for 30 minutes.

BEEF MEAT

Beef in beer, with crisp bread topping

SERVES 4

This recipe is suitable for any kind of stewing beef. The rich juices from the stewed meat and onions seep into the slices of bread, making the underside gooey and the top crisp. You can cook it the day before and it improves with re-heating; and it freezes well. Don't use a bitter beer; lager is best. You can cut out the stock and use all beer, but I think this tends to make it too bitter, not to mention the expense! Be sure to use an unsliced loaf, preferably one that has not been steam-baked, as the latter does not absorb the liquid nearly so well. Incidentally, the same applies if you are making a summer pudding. You can also use venison for this recipe.

700 g/1½ lb stewing beef
2 tablespoons plain flour
oil and/or butter, for frying
450 g/1 lb onions, peeled and chopped
900 ml/1½ pints boiling water
1½ beef stock cubes
300 ml/½ pint lager
2 teaspoons sugar
stale bread slices, with crusts cut off
salt and pepper

Pre-heat the oven to 170°C/325°F/gas mark 3. Cut the beef into 5 cm/2 in cubes and coat in the flour. Melt some oil and/or butter in a large frying-pan or wok and fry the onions until they are transparent and beginning to turn brown. Transfer to a square ovenproof dish. Melt some more butter and fry the meat until it is brown. Add to the onions and spoon into the dish. Dissolve the stock cubes in the boiling water. Tip any remaining flour into the frying-pan and add the stock and beer, stirring and scraping. Pour over the meat, until it is level. Reserve the extra liquid. Sprinkle over the sugar and season well. Lay the bread slices on top and trim to fit exactly. Spoon over a little of the reserved stock, place in the oven and cook for 3 hours. If the bread begins to look dry, dribble over more stock or beer.

Test the meat with a skewer at the end of the 3 hours and, if it seems tough, continue cooking until it is tender. For Aga owners, this is a perfect candidate for the simmering oven, where it could be safely left for 5–6 hours. Serve with mashed potato and lightly cooked sliced cabbage, plus the ale of your choice.

Steak and kidney pudding

SERVES 4

On a cold winter's day, nothing raises my spirits more than the thought of a rich steak and kidney pudding. It was a favourite in Dickens' day and has cockney connotations, being known in rhyming slang as 'Kate and Sid'. Fierce arguments rage as to whether you should cook the meat before you encase it in the suet crust but, for my money, you should put it in raw. The long, slow cooking makes it melt in the mouth and, as long as you keep the water topped up, it does not really matter how many hours steaming it undergoes. You can substitute venison and use pig's kidney if for any reason you do not wish to use beef.

SUET CRUST

225 g/8 oz plain flour

MEAT BEEF

1 teaspoon salt

1 teaspoon baking powder

110 g/4 oz suet

FILLING

450 g/1 lb stewing steak

225 g/8 oz ox kidney

1 large onion, peeled and sliced

50 g/2 oz mushrooms, sliced

2 tablespoons plain flour

1 teaspoon dried mixed herbs

pinch of ground mace

beef stock or water

dash of Lea & Perrins Worcestershire Sauce

salt and ground black pepper

To make the suet crust: sift the flour, salt and baking powder into a basin, mix in the suet and add enough water to make a stiff dough. Cut off a quarter for the lid and roll out the remainder into a circle 1 cm/½ in thick. Carefully lift into a 1-litre/1¾ -pint basin and press in, leaving some overhang. Roll the remaining pastry into a circle to fit over the top.

Cut the beef and kidney into 2.5 cm/1 in cubes. Mix together the flour, herbs and seasonings and coat the meat, onion and mushrooms well. Place in the basin, heaping up in the middle. Pour in the stock or water, to which you have added the Worcestershire sauce, so that it comes half-way up the basin. Wet the edges of the pastry, put on the lid and press well together to seal. Cover with greaseproof paper or foil, with a pleat in the middle, tie with string and steam for 3½ to 4 hours or longer.

Bring to the table in the basin, wrapped in a clean napkin, and serve with boiled potatoes and carrots.

Scotch minced-beef collops

SERVES 6

Collop comes from escalope, the French word for a thin slice of meat, no doubt a relic of the 'Auld Alliance' between Scotland and France. The following recipe was a favourite of my father-in-law and is a far cry from the grey, granite-like lumps served up at my school.

1 kg/2 lb best lean mince

1 dessertspoon sunflower oil

1 tablespoon pinhead or medium oatmeal

1 large onion, peeled and finely chopped

150 ml/¼ pint stock

1 good pinch of dried mixed herbs

2–3 drops of gravy browning

salt and plenty of ground black pepper

6 toast triangles, to serve

Pre-heat the oven to 150°C/300°F/gas mark 3. Heat the oil in a heavy frying pan until smoking or use a wok over a high heat. Add the mince and scrape and turn with a fork until it is sealed and there are no raw-looking lumps. Take off the heat and sprinkle in the oatmeal. Add the onion, stock, herbs, gravy browning and seasoning and transfer to a casserole. Place in the oven and cook for 2–3 hours, or overnight in the simmering oven of an AGA. Look at it occasionally and give it a stir. The end result should be a rich, savoury and shiny-looking mixture.

Garnish with toast triangles and serve with mashed potatoes and swede. You can, if you wish, use minced venison and, as a variation, instead of the toast triangles, serve it with dumplings flavoured with horseradish or herbs.

MEAT BEEF

Oxtail stew and dumplings

SERVES 6–8

This rich and succulent stew is one of the dishes I most look forward to in winter.

It was one of my husband, Archie's, favourites and Will Garfit, my dear friend, always sniffs hopefully when coming into the house, as he loves it. Constance, an old cousin of Archie's, was always held up as the queen of oxtail-stew-makers but she had the advantage of an AGA simmering oven, in which it could cook overnight. The highest accolade I could ever receive was 'almost as good as Auntie C's'. The perfect oxtail stew should be smooth, velvety and shiny and the colour of deep mahogany, and the meat should melt in the mouth. It is emphatically one of those dishes that are best when re-heated the next day and it freezes well.

2 small oxtails
plain flour, seasoned
4 tablespoons olive oil
2 large onions, peeled
2 carrots, peeled
1 leek, trimmed
3 fat garlic cloves, peeled
8 cloves
bottle of red wine
2 tablespoons concentrated tomato purée
1 tablespoon redcurrant jelly
dash of mushroom ketchup
25 g/1 oz dried porcini
1 teaspoon dried mixed herbs
4 bay leaves
salt and ground black pepper

Pre-heat the oven to 150°C/300°F/gas mark 2. Trim as much fat as possible from the oxtail and coat in the seasoned flour; then brown in half the heated oil. Transfer to a casserole with a slotted spoon. Wipe the pan if it looks burnt. Heat the remaining oil and brown the vegetables. Add the remaining ingredients, cover and place on the bottom shelf of the oven and cook for 5 hours, until the meat is falling off the bones; or cook overnight in the simmering oven of an AGA. Remove the vegetables, skim well and finish by blotting off the fat with kitchen paper.

Serve with dumplings, carrots and small glazed onions. Any stew left over can be made into oxtail soup (see page 4).

Tread's dumplings

This is my father's recipe for suet dumplings. I can't think why he gave it to me, as he didn't cook, but it is in his handwriting and it works. I give it verbatim, so no apologies for the cup measurements.

2 cups plain flour
2 tablespoons minced butcher's suet
3 teaspoons baking powder
1 teaspoon salt
1 cup milk

Minced butcher's suet may be a thing of the past so just use packet suet. Mix lightly but well. Drop dessertspoonsfuls into really fast-boiling, salted water and leave for 15 minutes without lifting the lid. Remember they swell, so use a really large saucepan.

MEAT BEEF

LAMB

There is nothing more delectable than a succulent leg of lamb or, better still, 'hill' lamb, which has a nuttier flavour. When choosing your joint, pick one with nice pearly-white fat; this denotes quality and youth. Sadly, nowadays, with the emphasis on low fat, the pre-packed objects that you buy bear little relation to this, as they have hardly any fat. Fat is essential if you want to produce a juicy joint, faintly pink on the inside, with a crisp, golden skin. If you have the freezer space, it pays to find a farmer or farm shop specialising in one of the lesser-known, old-fashioned breeds and purchase a whole or half beast. See directory on page xx. When in Scotland ask for a 'gigot' (pronounced Jiggut!) – the same word as in French and so, presumably, another relic of the 'Auld Alliance' between Scotland and France.

Roast leg of lamb

SERVES 6–8

For those of us who still cherish the tradition of sitting down to a family lunch on Sunday, a leg of lamb with roast potatoes and mint sauce is still defiantly British and precludes the worry of whether a roast of beef will be to everyone's taste.

1 leg of lamb, approximately
1.8 kg/4 lb – 2.3 kg/5 lb
1 tablespoon Provençal herb oil
(see page 147)
1 tablespoon redcurrant jelly
Schwartz lamb seasoning (available in supermarkets)
110 g/4 oz butter
1 onion, peeled and cut in thick rings
4–5 garlic cloves, unpeeled (optional)
2 fresh rosemary sprigs
1 dessertspoon plain flour (optional)
150 ml/¼ pint red wine
salt and freshly ground black pepper

Pre-heat the oven to 230°C/450°F/gas mark 8. Rub the joint with the oil, spread with the jelly and sprinkle generously with lamb seasoning and ground black pepper. Melt the butter in the roasting pan in the oven. Make a bed of the onion rings, garlic cloves and rosemary in the roasting tin and sit the joint on top. Roast for 30 minutes and then turn the oven down to 190°C/375°F/gas mark 5 for a further 1½ hours, basting frequently. Remove to a serving dish and allow to rest for 20 minutes.

Pour most of the fat out of the pan and bubble on top of the stove, with the stock and wine, scraping and stirring and squashing the garlic cloves. If you like a thick gravy, add the flour before pouring in the liquid. Strain into a gravy boat.

Serve with 'bag o' nails' potatoes (see page 106) and curly kale. For a change, you can omit the garlic and rosemary and substitute sprigs of mint, mint jelly to cover the joint and dried mint instead of lamb seasoning.

Shepherd's pie

SERVES 4–6

This can be 'progressive' i.e. a recipe to use up cold cooked lamb, as many people only like to eat lamb hot, or you can use fresh minced lamb, in which case, go for a pack of lean mince. The following recipe is for the latter. The only difference if you use cold cooked meat is that you don't have to fry it initially.

700 g/1½ lb lean minced lamb

1 tablespoon sunflower oil

1 onion, peeled and chopped

1 carrot, scraped and chopped

1 heaped tablespoon plain flour

1 teaspoon mixed herbs

300 ml/½ pint stock or water

1 tablespoon tomato ketchup

dash of Lea & Perrins Worcestershire Sauce

gravy browning (optional)

1 tablespoon frozen peas

1 tablespoon of chutney

TOPPING

mashed potato, to cover

butter

milk

salt and pepper

Heat the oil in a frying pan or wok and fry the onion and carrot for a few minutes. Then add the mince and fry until it has separated and looks crumbly – keep prodding with a wooden spoon. Sprinkle in the flour and herbs and stir well. Add the stock or water, ketchup, Worcestershire Sauce, salt, pepper and gravy browning (if using). Cook over a very low heat for 1-1½ hours. Blot off the fat with kitchen paper. Pre-heat the oven to 200°C/400°F/gas mark 4.

Adjust the seasoning and add the peas to the lamb. Transfer to a shallow dish and cover with the mashed potato, which should have had plenty of butter and milk beaten into it. Bake for 30 minutes or until well browned.

Serve with lightly cooked cabbage with caraway seeds.

Braised lamb shanks with white wine and rosemary

SERVES 4

I got the idea for this from Mauro Bregoli who, until he retired, owned the fabulous Manor House Restaurant, Romsey. He cooked knuckles of venison according to a recipe of his mother's which he remembered from his childhood in Italy. It was absolutely delicious, so I decided to have a go with lamb shanks, this being the nearest equivalent to knuckle of venison that I could think of. The end result was shiny and succulent and, I like to think, almost as good as Mauro's.

4 lamb shanks

olive oil

2–6 garlic cloves

2 fresh rosemary sprigs

300 ml/½ pint white wine

300 ml/½ pint water

1 lamb stock cube

2 teaspoons demerara sugar

10 g/½ oz beurre manié (see page 15)

salt and pepper

Pre-heat the oven to 200°C/400°F/gas mark 6. Brown the joint in the oil and lay in a large casserole, with the rosemary and garlic cloves. Pour over the wine and water and crumble in the stock cube. Season with salt and pepper and sprinkle in the sugar. Cover with a lid and place in the oven. After 20 minutes, turn down to 180°C/350°F/gas mark 4 and cook for a further hour.

Remove the lid of the casserole and continue cooking for a further 1½ hours or until tender when pierced with a skewer.

Remove the shanks to a dish and keep warm. Strain the liquid into a saucepan and reduce by fast boiling to 300 ml/½ pint. Drop small pieces of *beurre manié* into the boiling sauce, whisking constantly. On no account put in too much, as the sauce must not look too thick; it should be the consistency of single cream. Pour the sauce over the meat and serve with pasta and a green salad.

MEAT LAMB

PORK

People are always complaining to me that they can't seem to make their crackling crunchy nowadays. Once again, one of the problems is the lack of fat beneath the skin (crackling). If you buy pre-packed joints, try to make quite sure that the skin is an integral part of the meat and not just tied on after butchering. One of the best breeds for old-fashioned pork is Gloucester Old Spot. Several people are now rearing them, so it is worth searching for. Luckily, many farmers have got the message and are not rearing intensively, which you may notice if you see fields full of what look like miniature Nissen huts occupied by contented-looking pigs roaming about. The most delicious pork roast that I have ever eaten was from the privately owned pig of a Leicestershire farmer of my acquaintance, fed almost exclusively on household scraps. Before roasting, the depth of fat between the meat and skin must have been nearly 5 cm/2 in but, by the time the joint was cooked, most of the fat had melted away and was poured off to make delicious pork dripping. Potatoes roasted in either pork or beef dripping are a marriage made in heaven.

Roast pork, with crunchy crackling

SERVES 6–8

The best joint to go for when you want the 'crunch factor' is either loin or leg. Since a whole leg would be way over the top, weight-wise, for the modern nuclear family, a half-leg is usually sufficient; the same goes for loin. Unlike beef or lamb, pork should never be pink and underdone.

It should be cooked for 30 minutes per 450 g/1 lb and 30 minutes over, at 190°C/375°F/gas mark 5.

1 pork loin, weighing approximately 2.3 kg/5 lb

6 apples, cored but not peeled

1 teaspoon chopped fresh or dried sage

apple or redcurrant jelly

150 ml/¼ pint cider

salt and pepper

SAGE, APPLE AND CELERY STUFFING

25 g/1 oz butter

1 shallot, peeled and finely chopped

50 g/2 oz apple, peeled and finely chopped

1 celery stalk, finely chopped

50 g/2 oz fresh breadcrumbs

1 teaspoon chopped fresh sage

1 egg, well beaten

salt and pepper

Get the butcher to bone the joint but leave it untied. Have him score the skin or do it yourself, with a Stanley knife. Rub well with salt and leave, uncovered, overnight in the fridge. Pre-heat the oven to 190°C/375°F/gas mark 5.

To make the stuffing: cook the shallot, apple and celery, in the butter, until soft and transparent. Then mix in the breadcrumbs, sage, egg and salt and pepper. Spread a thin layer over the flesh side of the loin, roll it up and tie with string. Rub salt well into the skin and place the joint on a rack in the roasting

MEAT PORK

pan. Roast for 3 hours. Do not baste.

Mix the sage with the jelly and put 1 teaspoon into each apple. Then, 1 hour before the end of the cooking time, place the apples in the roasting pan.

When the joint is cooked, transfer to a heated serving dish and surround with the baked apples. Pour off the fat, add the cider and bubble the pan juices on top of the stove, scrapping any brown bits. When it is reduced and syrupy pour into a gravy boat.

Serve with Gudrun's honeyed potatoes (see page 107) and baby broad beans in cream sauce (see page 104).

Pork stir-fry, with lime and mushrooms

SERVES 2–4

This is one of those blissfully easy recipes which only take minutes to cook and, if you don't want the trouble of cutting up the meat, can be made with a packet of ready-sliced stir-fry pork, one of the few occasions when I bless pre-packed meat.

225 g/8 oz stir-fry pork
110 g/4 oz basmati
1 lime
2 tablespoons sunflower oil
50 g/2 oz shiitake mushrooms
bunch of spring onions, cut in rings
1 tablespoon Rose's lime marmalade
1 tablespoon soy sauce
1 teaspoon sesame seeds
salt and pepper

Cook the rice as per Prue's perfect rice (see page 98). Scrape off the lime zest and reserve; then squeeze the juice. Heat the rest of the oil in a wok or stir-fry pan, until it is smoking, and put in the pork. Shake and stir constantly for 1 minute. Then ease the pork up the sides of the pan and put in the mushrooms and spring onions. Cook for a further minute and then add the marmalade, soy sauce, 1 tablespoon of lime juice and the zest and mix well. Season with salt and pepper and transfer to a dish. Sprinkle with the sesame seeds.

Serve with the rice and a chicory salad.

MEAT PORK

HAM

It is a matter of preference as to whether you have smoked or un-smoked bacon or ham. Except in specialist shops, most of the smoked ham and bacon that you buy will have been given its smoky flavour by the application of 'smoke liquid', so it pays to seek out the 'real McCoy', if you can. There are dry cures and wet cures for ham. Some of the old recipes are hard to beat, especially the ones with molasses and beer. I do not have room here to enumerate them all but I highly recommend *Maynard, Adventures of a Bacon Curer,* published by Merlin Unwin Books. If you want to have a go at curing an un-smoked ham, follow one of his recipes. Don't attempt smoking, as it really is for the expert. I tried once, by hanging the ham from a hook on a tripod, covered with wire netting and old sacks to contain the smoke from the oak sawdust. The first two sessions were successful but, during the third and final one, I was called away to change a Land Rover tyre. A wind sprang up, the sacks caught fire and all I found on my return was a 'burnt offering'

Whole boiled ham

Cooking a whole ham seems to induce feelings of panic, but, in fact, it is quite easy and makes a wonderful addition to any buffet, or if you have a large quantity of people to feed. The best ham I ever remember used to come from our village shop long before the days of EU hygiene laws. The proprietor, Mr Pearson, used to cook his hams in the electric wash boiler. He brought it to the boil, turned it off and then left it overnight; next morning it would be cooked, succulent and tender. Whole hams weigh between 4.5 kg/10 lb and 7.2 kg/16 lb and should be soaked for at least 24 hours with a change of water once, if not twice (if it is very salty). For joints weighing up to 2.7 kg/6 lb, allow 25 minutes per 450 g/1 lb and reduce proportionately for larger joints, allowing 15 minutes per 450 g/1 lb for a ham weighing 6.8 kg/15 lb.

| 1 whole ham, weighing 6.8 kg/15 lb, soaked overnight |
| 1 onion, peeled and stuck with 4 cloves |
| 1 carrot |
| 2 bay leaves |
| 6 peppercorns |
| 2 tablespoons brown sugar |
| browned breadcrumbs, for covering |

Place the soaked ham in a preserving pan or ham kettle with water to cover and the remaining ingredients. Bring to the boil and skim well; then turn the heat down, so the water is barely simmering. Boil for 15 minutes to the 450 g/1 lb. Then take off the stove and leave in the cooking liquor for 2 hours.

Transfer the joint to a dish and carefully peel off the skin. (Save some of the stock and squares of skin. Freeze for pea soup or Duck and bean casserole, see page 88.) Sprinkle over the browned breadcrumbs and press well in. On no account use the packet kind!

If you wish to glaze the ham, remove from the liquid and place in a baking dish. Take off the skin, score the fat diagonally and press cloves into the intersections. Spread thickly with demerara sugar and bake for 1 hour in a pre-heated oven set at 200°C/400°F/gas mark 6. Serve with Cumberland sauce (see page 136).

OFFAL

Sadly, food scares and lack of information have almost made offal into a non-event. Admittedly, thrift and a desire not to be wasteful made these food items popular in the old days, because they were cheap and plentiful. However, even if we can't (or don't want to) cook sweetbreads, brains, hearts, tongue or the like, some still remain within our reach. Fresh lamb's kidneys, in their overcoats of pearly white fat, are top of the pops and pig's kidney and ox kidney are wonderful in stews, pies and suet puddings. Fresh calves' liver, thinly sliced and flash-fried, is without peer, and pig's liver and lamb's liver, provided they are fresh, come a close second. One very important point; if you are thinking of serving offal, do find out beforehand if your guests have an aversion to it.

'Shootable Stag' kidneys

SERVES 4 (OR 8 AS A STARTER)

My husband, Archie, came back from giving a lecture, singing the praises of a dish which had been cooked for him by his hostess who he described in those un-'PC' days as 'a very Shootable Stag' so obviously that is what the recipe was called by us! It is a very versatile recipe, because you can serve it as a starter or as a main course by increasing the quantities and serving it on a bed of rice or mashed potato. It is quick and easy and is another good recipe for the bachelor cook.

4 lamb's kidneys (8 for a main course)

plain flour, for dredging

50 g/2 oz butter

1 dessertspoon lemon juice

1 dessertspoon Lea & Perrins Worcestershire Sauce

1 tablespoon tomato ketchup

1 teaspoon made English mustard

1 teaspoon curry powder

pinch of cayenne pepper

salt

Trim the kidneys and cut in 4. Roll in the flour. Heat the butter over a low flame and add the remaining ingredients. Tip in the kidneys and cook over a low heat, until they are just done and still pink in the middle. Serve on squares of buttered toast.

This can be made the night before and heated up. The seasonings can be increased in quantity, if you like it hotter.

Sante's liver, with fried sage

SERVES 4

In the gourmet wasteland of Basingstoke, there used to be a jewel in the form of Franco's Ristorante, a lovely Italian family restaurant. Sante the owner/chef was an inspired cook and his Italian-based menu never failed to please. Like my other restaurateur friend, Mauro Bregoli, he never forgot his roots. In retirement he is still an assiduous gatherer of fungi and, like Mauro, a sportsman; sadly, he never found much local enthusiasm for the fruits of his forays. However, one of the staples on his menu was meltingly tender slices of calves' liver, accompanied by crisply fried sage leaves.

6 slices of fresh calves' liver
50 g/2 oz butter
1 tablespoon olive oil
4 shallots, peeled and chopped
12–18 fresh sage leaves
salt and freshly ground black pepper

For the best results, the liver should be fresh and not frozen. Get your butcher to cut paper-thin slices from the whole liver. Failing this, if you buy pre-packed sliced liver from the supermarket, you will probably have to slice them in half again, Heat the oil in a thick frying-pan and then add the butter. When it is foaming, put in the slices of liver and cook for 1–2 minutes on each side. Transfer to a warmed serving dish. Now throw in the chopped shallots and the sage leaves and cook until the latter are crisp and brown. Sprinkle over the liver and serve immediately. It must not be kept waiting.

Accompany by sautéed potatoes and spinach.

MEAT OFFAL

POULTRY

'Fings ain't what they used to be' on the poultry front but they are improving and even the supermarkets have got the message and have began to sell free-range and organic chickens. Nothing beats the flavour of a home- or farm-reared cockerel. I used to rear Marans, a breed of French origin, whose gentlemen wear grey and black striped suits and whose wives lay those unbelievable brown speckled eggs. As for boiling fowl, I don't think they exist any more. They were the 'tired ladies' whose usefulness as layers had come to an end, and who, at 3 or 4 years, were destined for the pot. Age and maturity gave them flavour, though long, slow cooking was the order of the day (see Chicken and barley broth page 2). I'm afraid, in today's world, you have to make do with chicken. France is still refreshingly free of politically correct 'noise police' and, in the Normandy village where I stayed recently, I was awoken by a wonderful cacophony of crowing cocks each morning. Happily, my next-door neighbour in the village I have moved to has a lovely vocal bird. I think he was nervous about my reactions until I put his mind at rest and I live in hopes of a boiling fowl one day!

Claypot roast chicken, with lemon and parsley stuffing

SERVES 6–8

I am a committed claypot cook and consider claypots to be an essential piece of culinary kit. Cooking in clay or earthenware vessels has been going on for thousands of years and was brought to a high state of perfection by the Romans, hence Romertoft or 'Roman pot', the name of one of the present-day makes in Germany. They are especially good for the busy hostess who doesn't want to keep rushing into the kitchen and basting her chicken or joint every 20 minutes. The result is moist and tender and, despite the chicken being covered, the skin will be crisp. All you have to do, in effect, is to soak your claypot in water for 10 minutes, put in your chicken or meat with seasonings and vegetables if wished, cover with the lid and place in a cold oven. You then switch on to highest heat, that is, 240˚C/475˚F/gas mark 9 and leave for 1/½ hours. A pheasant will only take 1 hour and a large chicken of say 2.3 kg/5 lb, 2 hours. The other advantage is that claypot cooking keeps the oven immaculately clean. You can buy claypots in several sizes and there is even a special shape for whole fish.

Haunch of venison or leg of lamb are brilliant cooked in a claypot. Except for pork, I use it for all my roasts.

You can even use them in a 2 or 4 oven AGA: give 30 minutes in the simmering oven and transfer to grid shelf on the floor of the roasting oven for 1–1½ hours (depending on the size of bird or joint).

Another advantage of claypot cookery is that, unlike traditional roasting, hardly any fat is used – just a suspicion of oil rubbed over the bird or joint. Wonderful juice exudes and can be made into gorgeous gravy, particularly if you scatter a few vegetables round the bird.

1 chicken, weighing 1.8 kg/4 lbs
1 dessertspoon sunflower oil
1 carrot, 1 peeled onion, 1 peeled celery stalk, all roughly chopped

STUFFING

10 g/½ oz butter
1 small onion, peeled and finely chopped
110 g/4 oz fresh breadcrumbs
grated zest and juice of 1 lemon
1 tablespoon chopped fresh parsley
1 egg, well beaten
salt and pepper

To make the stuffing: Melt the butter and cook the chopped onion in it, until soft. Add the breadcrumbs, lemon zest, half the lemon juice, parsley, egg and seasoning. Allow to cool. Spoon into the body cavity of the chicken.

Rub the bird with the remaining lemon juice and the oil and season well. Place, breast-down, in the claypot and surround with the vegetables. Cover and place in a cold oven. Switch on to 240°C/450°F/gas mark 9 and forget for 1 hour.

Turn the chicken breast-side up and continue cooking for 30 minutes. If the juices are still pink, cook for a further 15 minutes. When cooked, remove, transfer to a carving dish and allow to rest for 20–30 minutes.

Lucy makes a wonderful gravy by tipping the vetetables and the juices into a small saucepan and 'blitzing' them with her hand-held blender. Otherwise pour

POULTRY

the juices through a sieve into a saucepan, pressing the vegetables well, and reduce by fast boiling, until syrupy. Adjust the seasoning and pour into a sauce boat.

Serve the chicken with sauté potatoes and carrot with chopped spring onions.

To roast in the conventional way, prepare the chicken as above but spread with softened butter instead of oil. Place in a pre-heated oven set at 200°C/400°F/gas mark 6 and roast for 20 minutes per 450 g/1 lb, plus 15 minutes, basting once or twice during cooking.

Boiled chicken and parsley sauce

SERVES 6–8

This rather old-fashioned dish looks most appetising, with its covering of white sauce speckled with bright green parsley. You can vary it by using chopped hard-boiled egg instead of parsley, which is also delicious, and, if you want to turn it into a party dish, use the light lemony sauce poulette (see page 53), which, of course owes its name to the French word for pullet, or young pre-laying hen. If you don't want to boil a whole chicken, follow the same procedure but poach chicken breasts, and reduce the quantity of sauce.

1 chicken, weighing 1.8 kg/4 lb
1 onion, peeled
1 carrot, peeled
1 leek
1 celery stalk
bouquet garni
6 peppercorns
salt

TO SERVE

parsley sauce (see page 126)
fresh parsley sprigs
2 lemons, quartered

Choose a saucepan just large enough to take the chicken comfortably. Half-fill with water, bring to the boil and then put in the bird. Bring back to the boil and let it continue boiling for 5 minutes, skimming well. Add the vegetables and seasonings and simmer very gently for 45–50 minutes.

Test with a skewer. If the chicken is not cooked, simmer for a further 10–15 minutes. Remove to a serving dish and keep warm while you make the parsley sauce. Cover the chicken with sauce and garnish with sprigs of parsley and lemon quarters.

Serve with mashed potato and mange-tout peas.

POULTRY

Fricassée of chicken

SERVES 4–6

This is both 'progressive' cookery and comfort food. My daughter, Lucy, was furious when she found out that I had not included it in my first book and woe betide me if there is not enough turkey left over at Christmas to make fricassée. If you don't have any leftovers, 1 or 2 fresh chicken breasts can be stretched to feed a surprising number of people.

225 g/8 oz – 350 g/12 oz cold, cooked chicken

50 g/2 oz butter

1 onion, peeled and finely chopped

50 g/2 oz mushrooms (optional)

50 g/2 oz plain flour

600 ml/1 pint chicken stock

1 tablespoon double cream

salt and pepper

Cut the chicken in chunks and set aside. Melt the butter and cook the onion and mushrooms until soft. Sprinkle in the flour, stir well and then take off the heat. Pour in the stock, replace on the heat and continue stirring until the sauce thickens. Add the chicken chunks and cream, check the seasoning and heat through gently.

Serve with rice or riced potatoes and buttered carrots (see page 104).

Duck and bean casserole

SERVES 4–6

This hearty casserole, which is a kind of cassoulet, is another instance of 'comfort' food and is guaranteed to keep out the winter chills. Haricot beans or green or brown lentils are all perfectly good substitutes for the green flageolets. Before freezers, dried beans were very much a staple of the countryman's store-cupboard and the runner, haricot and the butter beans which had become old and stringy would have been dried both for food and for next year's seed. My French friend Rose Pénim always harvests her 'out of date' beans in this way.

This is very definitely one of those dishes that improves with re-heating; it also freezes well. Any beans left can be whizzed in the food processor with a little stock to make a lovely soup, especially if eaten with ciabatta bread split, cut in squares, drizzled with olive oil, covered with goat's cheese and browned in the oven.

1 small duck, quartered

570 ml/1 pint measure flageolet beans

1.2 litres/2 pints stock

1 large onion, peeled and chopped

4–6 garlic cloves, peeled and chopped

3 tablespoons olive oil

1 tablespoon concentrated tomato purée

1 smoked garlic sausage, cut in chunks

4 streaky bacon rashers, chopped

1 sprig each fresh rosemary, thyme and marjoram

2 bay leaves

salt and pepper

POULTRY

Wash the beans and soak them in cold water for 2 hours.

Drain and rinse the beans, place in a pan, with the stock, bring to the boil and then simmer for 1 hour.

Pre-heat the oven to 170°C/325°F/gas mark 3. Brown the onion and garlic in the oil, and then add the duck and brown it on all sides. Transfer the beans and stock to a casserole, mix in the onion, garlic and tomato purée and season well. Bury the duck quarters, breast-side down, and add the pieces of sausage and bacon. Strew the herbs on top, cover and place in the pre-heated oven for 3–4 hours, or overnight in the simmering oven of an AGA. Stir occasionally, so that the beans don't dry out, and add a little more stock, if necessary.

Serve with baked potatoes or hot french bread and a salad. For a change, instead of butter, try splitting the potatoes in half and drizzle over basil oil (see page 146) or pesto sauce. This is a real rustic French peasant dish and merits strongly flavoured accompaniments. Don't give it to your more lily-livered, anti-garlic friends!

Chicken with a creamy walnut sauce

This should really be made with 'wet' walnuts i.e. those newly harvested: but you have to spot them in the shops in early autumn. It is well worth the added chore of cracking the shells and extracting the nuts. However, those packets of walnuts lurking at the back of your cupboard will do just as well and the sauce is dreamy with either chicken or pheasant.

| 4 chicken thighs and drumsticks |
| 1 onion, peeled |
| 1 carrot |
| water |
| 75 g/3 oz stale white breadcrumbs |
| soaked in |
| 150 ml/4 oz milk |
| 75 g/3 oz walnuts |
| 1 clove garlic, peeled |
| 4 black peppercorns |
| salt and pepper |
| paprika |

Place the chicken in a pan with the onion, carrot and peppercorns. Cover with water, bring to the boil and allow to simmer for 1 hour or until really tender.

Remove chicken to a dish and discard the vegetables then reduce the stock by half. Process the walnuts and garlic and then add the soaked breadcrumbs and enough stock to make a creamy sauce.

Remove the meat from the bones and tear into strips, then mix with the sauce. Adjust seasoning, warm through and garnish with chopped parsley or chervil and drizzle over a little walnut or olive oil and sprinkle with paprika.

Can be eaten hot or cold, either way serve with rice and a salad of watercress or rocket and sorrel as it is very rich.

Trick of the trade

It is a good way of using up that left-over bread sauce and cold chicken which you can heat up in stock made from a stock cube.

Mick's hair drier duck, with damson sauce

SERVES 4

Mick is a dear friend, whose roast duck would pass muster with the hardest Chinese taskmaster. It is tender and juicy and above all has a crisp skin to die for. What, you may well ask, have hair driers got to do with cooking duck? The Chinese hang their ducks to dry in an airy place for 24 hours, so that the outside of the skin becomes crisp when roasted. This is not always practical and, anyway, many of us don't think that far ahead, so Mick's brilliant idea was to speed things up with his wife Jenny's hair drier. The last time I was privileged to eat duck at their house, I went into the kitchen and there spied the duck and the hair drier propped up on, of all things, half a crumpet! Why a crumpet? I asked myself, and Mick assured me that this set it at just the right angle. More mundanely, I use the cold setting of a fan heater.

1 duck, weighing 1.3 kg/3 lb–1.8 kg/4 lb
1 onion, peeled and chopped
300 ml/¹⁄₂ pint stock
salt

DAMSON SAUCE

450 g/1 lb damsons or plums
4 cloves
1–2 tablespoons muscovado sugar
1 tablespoon balsamic or wine vinegar
1 teaspoon soy sauce

Remove the duck from its plastic wrapping and dry well with kitchen paper. Leave, uncovered, in the fridge, for 24 hours.

Take out 1 hour before you intend to cook it, hang it up or place on a wire grid and dry with a hair drier, propped up at the appropriate angle, until the skin is papery. Pre-heat the oven to 200°C/400°F/gas mark 6. Prick the duck all over, rub well with salt and sit on a grid over a pan containing the onion. Place at the top of the oven and roast for 20 minutes. Then turn the heat down to 180°C/350°F/gas mark 4 for a further 2 hours. *Do not baste.*

Remove to a serving dish. Make a gravy by pouring off the fat (keep this and freeze it; it is wonderful for roasting vegetables), leaving the meat juices, add the stock and bubble until well reduced. Strain and season.

To make the damson sauce: Cook the damsons and cloves over a very low heat, until soft and mushy. Remove the stones and cloves. Add the sugar, vinegar and soy sauce and liquidise.

Cut the duck into 4, tuck napkins into collars and attack! Eat the bones in your fingers. Serve with a crunchy vegetable, such as mange-tout peas, and new potatoes, if you think roast potatoes will be too rich.

Trick of the trade

If you can't get damsons or plums, use 2 tablespoons damson jam, omit the sugar and add more vinegar.

POULTRY

Christmas turkey, with three stuffings

SERVES: A FAMILY PARTY

In the early days of our marriage we decided to rear 100 turkeys in our barn to supplement our income. When the time came to pluck them we had to hang them on the 'tie rods' which kept the walls of our old house together. Luckily they didn't collapse with the weight of the turkeys! It was a pretty gruelling business and led to stiff hands. We were very popular with our friends and neighbours as 'oven-ready' was a newly coined phrase and birds in a plastic bag were a rarity and supermarkets were only just in the offing.

Why is it that the mention of turkey at Christmas time seems to strike fear into the hearts of even the most experienced cooks (though they would never admit it)? No one thinks twice about roasting a chicken or turkey at any other time of the year but Christmas seems to be different and we worry whether our turkey is going to be dry, or under or over cooked.

The great secret is to get your act together well beforehand, with as many things as possible in the deep freeze. Unfortunately, the turkey cannot be stuffed until Christmas Eve at the earliest or, better still, Christmas morning. Always let your stuffing get completely cold before letting it anywhere near the bird as, if it is warm, it can provide a breeding ground for salmonella and other bacteria. You can make the stuffing ahead of time and freeze it, but be sure to thaw it properly. There are now wonderful vacuum-packed chestnuts on sale at some of the supermarkets, which obviates the time-consuming chore of peeling fresh ones.

Try to choose a fresh turkey, if possible, even if you freeze it yourself. Fortunately, many breeders have gone back to basics and are now producing the Norfolk Black and Broad-Breasted Bronze turkey which have more flavour. Once again there is nothing better than your local Farmer's Market for good organic or free-range turkeys. Hens are generally more tender than cocks, though, if you want a monster, you'll need a cock, as the biggest hen won't weigh much more than 7.2 kg/16 lb. The following stuffing is colourful and Christmassy but you could vary it by using diced walnut, apple and celery, wild mushrooms and all kinds of other wonderful combinations

| 1 turkey weighing 6.8 kg/15 lbs |
| 225 g/8 oz butter, softened |
| olive oil |
| salt and pepper |

SWEETCORN AND CRANBERRY STUFFING

| 50 g/2 oz butter |
| 1 onion, peeled and finely chopped |
| 1 celery stalk, finely diced |
| 2 tablespoons fresh or frozen cranberries |
| 2 bacon rashers, finely chopped |
| 1 small tin sweetcorn kernels, drained |
| 175 g/6 oz fresh breadcrumbs |
| 2 eggs, well beaten |
| salt and pepper |

SAUSAGEMEAT STUFFING

| 450 g/1 lb pork sausagemeat |

CHESTNUT STUFFING

| 450 g/1 lb chestnuts, peeled and chopped |
| stock, to moisten |

POULTRY

GRAVY

150 ml/¼ pint port

1 dessertspoon cranberry jelly

600 ml/1 pint stock

salt and pepper

Make the giblets into stock (see page 15) as soon as you get the turkey home and either freeze or refrigerate it. Remove the liver first, and freeze for future use.

Trick of the trade

With a small, sharp, pointed knife cut out the turkey's wishbone. This will make carving much easier. You can roast it separately, for those who want to pull it for luck.

Loosen the turkey skin and spread the softened butter underneath; you can even do this before freezing and it is one more chore done.

For the sweetcorn and cranberry stuffing: sauté the onion and celery in the butter, until soft; then add the cranberries and cook for a few minutes. Mix in the remaining ingredients and season well. When cold, spoon into the body cavity of the turkey, leaving enough room at the rear end for the sausagemeat, which acts as a stopper and prevents the cranberry stuffing from escaping.

For the chestnut stuffing: heat together with a little stock until soft, then when it is cold, insert in the neck cavity and fold over the flap of skin.

Sit the bird in a roasting pan, smear all over with olive oil, season well, cover with foil and place in a pre-heated oven set at 175°C/350°F/gas mark 4 for 20 minutes to the 450 g/1lb, plus 20 minutes; baste every 30 minutes. Three-quarters of an hour before cooking is complete, add the chipolatas and the bacon rolls and, for the last half hour, remove the foil and turn the heat up to 200°C/400°F/gas mark 6. When done, remove to a warmed serving dish and allow to 'rest' for at least 30 minutes.

To make the gravy: pour most of the fat out of the roasting pan and then add the stock, port and jelly and allow to bubble, scraping and stirring. Then strain into a saucepan and reduce by half.

Serve the turkey with bread sauce (see page 130), cranberry sauce (see page 136), 'bag o' nails' potatoes (see page 106), a purée of swede and brussels sprouts or whichever vegetable you prefer.

POULTRY

Turkey and ham croquettes

SERVES 24

Post-Christmas, for my family, is incomplete without turkey croquettes. As each successive meal of cold turkey and ham appears the vibes concentrate and there is suddenly a concerted cry of 'when are you going to make croquettes?' Properly made, these are good enough for a dinner party, so increase the quantity and put some in the freezer. You can also use cooked chicken or pheasant.

225 g/8 oz cooked turkey
110 g/4 oz cooked ham
50 g/2 oz butter
1 shallot, peeled and chopped
50 g/2 oz plain flour
300 ml/½ pint concentrated turkey stock
1 teaspoon mushroom ketchup
1 tablespoon chopped fresh parsley
plain flour, for dredging
2 eggs, well beaten
dried Granary breadcrumbs, for coating
oil, for frying
salt and pepper

Cut up the turkey and ham and mince finely in the food processor – the texture of the croquettes should be smooth. Melt the butter and soften the chopped shallot in it; then sprinkle in the flour, cook for a few minutes and pour in the stock. Cook, whilst stirring, until thick; then add the turkey, ham, ketchup and parsley and mix well. Season to taste and then spread on an oiled plate to cool, with some cling film over the top to prevent a skin from forming.

When cold, scoop up dessertspoonfuls, coat with flour and roll into neat cork shapes. Dip into the egg and then coat with the breadcrumbs. Pour the oil into a frying-pan – to a depth of 2.5 cm/1 in and fry the croquettes until golden all over, shaking to turn them; or fry in a deep-fryer. Drain on kitchen paper.

Serve with curly kale puréed with crème fraîche (see page 105) and sautéd potatoes.

It's also nice with Cumberland sauce (see page 136).

Pot-roast guinea fowl, with spiced crab apples

SERVES 2–4

This is my version of pintade Normande. Many of these classic foreign dishes are the result of local goodies, of which this is a classic example, as of course, Normandy is where most of the apples grow which are made into cider and that fiery drink, Calvados. It's a shame that so many of our own wonderful apple orchards have disappeared and, with them, the mistletoe to which they are host.

Guinea fowl can be dry, so it is best pot-roasted in a high-sided casserole, with fruit. If you don't have access to wild crab apples, the ornamental variety will do admirably or, as a last resort, cooking apples.

1 guinea fowl
1 tablespoon olive oil
25 g/1 oz butter
1 shallot, peeled and chopped
4 tablespoons spiced crab apples (see page 184)

2 tablespoons crème fraîche

300 ml/½ pint cider

Pre-heat the oven to 180°C/350°F/gas mark 4. Heat the oil and butter and sauté the shallot; then brown the bird all over. Put breast-side down, in a high-sided casserole with 3 tablespoons of the spiced crab apples, cover and place in the oven for 1 hour. After 15 minutes, turn on to its side. Then, after another 15 minutes, on to the other side.

Cook for 15 minutes and then, for the final 15 minutes, cook breast-upwards. Transfer to a heated serving dish and garnish with the spiced crab apples. Add the cider to the cooking juices and reduce until you have a good gravy consistency then blend, press through a strainer, add the crème fraîche and hand round separately.

Serve with sauté potatoes and creamed celeriac.

FAMILY FARE

These recipes are nearly all old favourites, with no pretensions to grandeur, and are what you would give family or close friends to eat informally, in the kitchen or in front of the telly. A telephone call from a chum is the kind of scenario I often encounter, 'Just calling on my mobile. I'm within 5 miles of you, can I call in? Love to see you!' Of course you say yes and tell them they'll have to take pot luck. Often, these impromptu visitations are the best form of entertaining. Friendly gossip or chat and a convivial glass of wine or mug of ale are the best accompaniment, ending up with a tot of home-made liqueur, perhaps.

Archie's curry

SERVES 2

When Archie was in The Hague, before the war, he and his father used to go to the Hotel des Indes where the speciality was Rystavel, quite literally a 'rice table' or Indonesian curry smorgasbord. A Dutch friend of mine says the usual number of dishes is twelve, though in Java it can rise to one hundred and twenty. To be authentic, each course is meant to be borne in by a beautiful maiden, though history does not relate whether this was so in Archie's case! This particular curry, hailing as it does from the Far East, is rather sweet, and is particularly good made with pigeon, though chicken or beef are equally good. Long, slow cooking is the answer and, as with casseroles, it is even better when re-heated.

225 g/8 oz pigeon breast, cut in 1 cm/¹/₂ in cubes

1 tablespoon sunflower oil

110 g/4 oz apple, peeled and diced

110 g/4 oz onion, peeled and diced

2 garlic cloves, peeled and chopped

50 g/2 oz any kind of dried fruit

1 dessertspoon bramble or other jelly

1 dessertspoon mango chutney

1 teaspoon black treacle

25 g/1 oz creamed coconut

1 teaspoon dried mixed herbs

2 teaspoons hot curry paste

2 teaspoons mild curry powder

salt

Heat the oil in a heavy-based frying-pan or, better still, use the oil from the curry-paste pot. Fry the apple, onion and garlic for a few minutes. Add the cubed pigeon breasts and the remaining ingredients. Cook on the lowest possible heat for 1 hour, stirring occasionally to prevent it from sticking. Cover and cook for a further hour. At the end of this time, the curry should look nearly black and be very thick.

Serve with Prue's perfect rice (see below), poppadums, sliced bananas, sliced tomato and onion and yoghurt with chopped cucumber.

Prue's perfect rice

This is my fail-safe method of cooking basmati rice so that the grains remain separate and don't end up as a glutinous mass Wild or brown rice can be cooked the same way but it needs to be cooked for 30 – 40 minutes.

225 g/8 oz basmati rice

1 dessertspoon sunflower oil

salt

Heat the oil in a saucepan and tip in the rice. Shake well, until each grain is coated. Pour in enough boiling water to come 2.5 cm/1 in above the level of the rice. Add salt. Cover and cook over a low heat for 15 minutes. Turn off the heat, place a double thickness of kitchen paper beneath the lid and leave for 15–20 minutes.

FAMILY FARE

Bubble and squeak, with bacon

SERVES 2

I have always longed to know why this is called 'bubble and squeak' but I have never discovered the origins of the name. In Ireland it is called 'colcannon' or 'champ' which is made with spring onions, and in Scotland 'kailkenny' or 'rumbledethumps' which has cheese added. To be really authentic, the mixture of cabbage and potato should be cooked in beef or pork dripping. It was, of course, staple food for cottage-dwellers before the advent of fridges, as it was one way of not wasting cold cooked cabbage and potato. To make this rather more substantial, I have included bacon, though the great nineteenth-century chef, Francatelli, advocated using slices of cold cooked beef, fried as an accompaniment. Alternatively you could add diced corned beef and make a kind of 'corned beef hash'.

1 savoy cabbage, cooked

450 g/1 lb potatoes, cooked

dripping or bacon fat, for frying

4 bacon rashers, cut in pieces

salt and pepper

Chop the cabbage roughly. Heat the fat in a large heavy-based frying-pan and fry the bacon. Remove and mix with the potatoes and cabbage. Spoon into the pan and flatten. Cook over a low heat and, every so often, stir and scrape with a spatula so that there are nice brown bits distributed throughout. Finally, allow to cook until a crisp brown layer has formed on the bottom. Place under the grill, to brown the top. Spoon on to plates and enjoy.

Toad in the hole

SERVES 4–6

I make no apology for including this delicious old-fashioned recipe. It swam back into my consciousness when a friend asked me to stay to supper on the spur of the moment, only to discover that all she had in the fridge was a packet of sausages and some eggs. We looked at each other and with one voice said 'toad-in-the-hole'! Her husband was very approving and said it revived happy childhood memories. My version uses sausagemeat balls, as I personally don't like overcooked sausage skin, and the batter is flavoured with chopped parsley, but the method is the same as for the traditional one.

450 g/1 lb sausagemeat

50 g/2 oz dripping or lard

1 quantity of Yorkshire pudding batter (see page 71)

1 tablespoon finely chopped fresh parsley

Pre-heat the oven to 220°C/425°F/gas mark 7. Make the batter and stir in the chopped parsley. Roll the sausagemeat into 16 balls. Heat the dripping or lard in a 20 cm/8 in x 25 cm/10 in roasting tin and cook the balls for 5 minutes in the pre-heated oven. Pour in the batter and cook at this temperature for a further 5 minutes. Then reduce the heat to 220°C/425°F/gas mark 7 for 30 minutes.

Serve with lightly cooked cabbage and onion gravy (see page 127).

Spanish omelette

SERVES 4

My daughter, Lucy, was taught how to make this by her godfather's Spanish cook, Alfonso. It is staple food in Spain and is equally good eaten hot or cold, as picnic fare; you will find it amongst the tapas at the humblest bar or as an hors d'oeuvre in the grandest restaurant.

1 large onion peeled and roughly chopped
2 large potatoes, peeled and diced
8 eggs, roughly beaten
olive oil, for frying
salt and pepper

Put 1 tablespoon of olive oil in a heavy-based frying-pan and heat. Tip in the onion and potato and cook over a low heat until soft. Add to the bowl of beaten eggs and season well. Wipe the pan clean with kitchen paper, pour in a little more oil and let it get really hot before pouring in the egg mixture. Stir with a fork for the first couple of minutes and then turn down the heat and let the omelette cook slowly. When the bottom half looks firm, put a spatula or egg lifter underneath and slide on to a plate. Now invert the frying-pan over the plate and turn over so that the top of the omelette cooks. Replace on the heat and cook until set. If you don't want to do this, just put the pan under the grill for a minute or two, to set; it should be quite firm but not dry. Eat hot or cold, cut in wedges.

Serve with french bread and tomatoes.

Pasta with Mauro's marvellous mixture

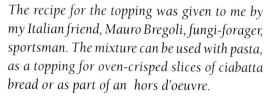

SERVES 4–6

The recipe for the topping was given to me by my Italian friend, Mauro Bregoli, fungi-forager, sportsman. The mixture can be used with pasta, as a topping for oven-crisped slices of ciabatta bread or as part of an hors d'oeuvre.

450 g/1 lb tagliatelle
1 tablespoon olive oil
1 quantity of Mauro's marvellous mixture (see page 186)
110 g/4 oz parmesan cheese, shaved in flakes with a peeler
fresh basil leaves, torn, to garnish

Bring water to the boil in a large saucepan, add salt and the olive oil and then throw in the pasta and cook for 12 minutes or until *al dente*. Drain and mix in the MMM. Sprinkle over the parmesan shavings and garnish with torn basil leaves.

Butternut squash risotto

SERVES 4

Some years ago this would have been considered exotic as squash were then thought of as American. Nowadays they can be easily grown in your garden or you can buy them almost anywhere and they have the added advantage of being very good keepers. Teamed with risotto rice and parmesan it is a marriage made in heaven and can be a marvellous last minute choice for supper when you have unexpected guests.

FAMILY FARE

1 butternut squash, peeled

2 shallots, peeled and finely chopped

2 cloves garlic, peeled and chopped

4 tablespoons olive oil

350 g/12 oz Arborio rice

600 ml/1 pint vegetable stock

salt and pepper

parmesan cheese

basil

Cut the squash into 2.5 cm/ 1 inch cubes and rub with olive oil and spread over an oven proof dish. Place in a pre-heated oven set at 200°C/400°F/Gas Mark 6 for about half an hour or until brown and caramelized. Meanwhile soften the shallots and garlic in 2 tablespoons of oil in a large, deep frying pan or sauté dish. Tip in the rice and coat well with the oil then pour in a ladle of stock at a time, stirring constantly. When the rice is soft but still 'al dente' turn off the heat. Stir in the squash cubes and sprinkle with parmesan and torn basil leaves. For non-vegetarians you can use chicken stock and some diced cooked chicken as well as the squash and crumble some crisply fried pancetta over the top.

Creamy smoked haddock kedgeree

SERVES 2–4

This must be one of my all-time favourites and dates back to my childhood, when I used to stay with my godmother. Breakfast was a veritable feast, with bacon and eggs, sausages, kedgeree, all served in silver dishes and kept hot on a copper hotplate, fuelled with methylated spirits. A whole cold ham and cold game in season completed the picture. Every time I eat kedgeree it brings back these memories. This version happened as a result of my looking in the fridge and expecting to find cream; there was none, so I substituted Hellman's mayonnaise, which was quite delicious. Of course, undyed, fresh smoked haddock is best but, for speed, a packet of boil-in-the-bag is fine.

450 g/ 1 lb undyed smoked haddock fillet, skinned and boned

225 g/8 oz cooked basmati rice (see page 98)

2 hard-boiled eggs, chopped

2 spring onions, cut in rings

50 g/2 oz butter

1–2 tablespoons Hellman's mayonnaise or soured cream

$1/2$ teasspoon curry powder

1 dessertspoon mango chutney juice

squeeze of lemon juice

pinch of grated nutmeg

salt and plenty of freshly ground black pepper

chopped fresh chives, and parsley to garnish

Simmer the haddock over a low heat with 2 tablespoons of water until just done - about 8 minutes. Then take out and save the juice. Remove any remaining skin and bones, flake the fish and thenfork into the rice, with the juice. Mix in all the other ingredients, heat through and garnish with the chopped herbs.

VEGETABLES

Compared to only a few years ago, we are spoilt for choice when we shop for vegetables. There is, of course, nothing like growing your own and there is nothing like the miracle you feel when you pull your first carrot of the year or dig a new potato. Not everyone is so lucky however, but take heart and wend your way to the nearest 'pick-your-own' or farm shop. These are worth their weight in gold and have opened up a whole new world to those who thought they were forever bound for supermarkets. The fact that there is a little bit of earth to wash off should alert you to the fact that your chosen purchase has actually been grown naturally in the ground and has not evolved by some sinister scientific means in a laboratory, scrubbed, measured to the exact millimetre, chilled and flown to your supermarket. Oddly shaped vegetables are part of the fun of growing them yourself and some can elicit quite Rabelaisian comments! Home-grown or locally-grown vegetables, too, unlike supermarket produce which may be flown in from the other side of the world, will only be available in season, and all the better for it. This removal of the seasonal barrier has taken away the delight of eating the first pea, bean or early carrot – a source of regret, to my mind.

It is not practical to list all the recommended varieties of vegetable as they change all the time; do go for some of the salad potatoes, however. They are wonderful for salads and for sautéing. Another good recent introduction is 'cultivated' fungi, euphemistically styled 'wild mushrooms'. If you decide to become a 'fungi' fanatic you will also be joining the 'freebie' club, about which more anon. These are amongst my all-time favourites and even if you are unable to experience the pleasure of gathering your own wild mushrooms, you can equally well make do with the bought variety; they are delicious.

Baby broad beans in cream sauce

SERVES 2–4

When it comes to broad beans, the only way to harvest them is to commit infanticide. Eating them when tiny carries them straight into the gourmet bracket. Marjoram makes a perfect marriage with the delicate young beans and brings out their slightly nutty flavour. A very light, creamy sauce completes the picture and makes them one of my favourite vegetables. They go well with pork, ham or poultry. 'OABs' (old-age beans) with leathery 'overcoats' can be made into a delectable soup (see page 5).

450 g/1 lb podded baby broad beans
25 g/1 oz butter
2 teaspoons cornflour
about 150 ml/¼ pint milk
1 tablespoon single cream
1 tablespoon chopped fresh marjoram
salt and pepper

Cook the beans in boiling, salted, water for about 4 minutes; then drain. Toss them in the butter and then add the cornflour, mixed with a little of the milk and stir until it thickens, thin with the remaining milk and use more, if necessary. Add the cream and marjoram and season lightly.

Braised florence fennel

SERVES 2–4

Florence fennel is the fat, white bulb with ferny fronds which is the vegetable variety of the herb. Like the herb, it goes well with fish and can also, with the addition of ham, cream and parmesan, make an excellent supper dish.

Blanched and braised, it goes particularly well with fish, chicken or pheasant.

2 fennel bulbs
25 g/1 oz butter
salt and pepper

Pre-heat the oven to 200°C/400°F/gas mark 6. Trim off any brown bits and coarse-looking outer leaves, though these do actually soften with cooking. Cut in 4 lengthways and blanch for 2 minutes in salted, boiling water. Melt the butter in a flameproof casserole and add the fennel quarters. Season well, cover and bake for 30 minutes, or until golden brown.

Buttered carrots

SERVES 4–6

The first carrots of the year pulled from your garden are ambrosial. They hardly need cooking and emerge from the pan sticky, sweet and juicy. No need to scrape them: just wash, cut off the tops and show them some boiling water for 2–3 minutes; then toss in a little butter. Their older relations can be cut up, cooked for a bit longer and then mashed and flavoured with coriander or similar. Try cubing them, blanching in boiling water until just al dente and then folding them into mashed potato or other root vegetables. The following recipe was evolved by my daughter, Lucy, during her university days.

1 kg g/2 lb old carrots
50 g/2 oz butter
1 tablespoon sugar
1 tablespoon finely chopped fresh parsley
salt and pepper

VEGETABLES

Peel the carrots and cut into very thin slices or put them through the alumette or fine-slicing disk of your food processor. Put them in a saucepan, with the butter, sugar and salt or pepper, and cook over a very low heat. Shake occasionally and give the odd stir. When just cooked – still firm or al dente, stir in the parsley and serve immediately.

Celeriac mashed with coriander

SERVES 2–4

Celeriac is a most versatile vegetable. There are so many things you can do with it, from celeriac salad with rémoulade (see page 118), to a variety of soups; and it is a good texture-enhancer for puréed potato. Like fennel, it goes well with fish. Don't be put off by its rather unappealing, knobbly appearance, though, nowadays they have bred a smoother variety. With the old-fashioned kind, you have to cut off all the contorted roots, wash and scrub well and then peel and cut up. It is also a boon to those who are on a low carbohydrate diet as it can stand in for potato.

1 celeriac root

lemon juice or vinegar (optional)

butter

1 teaspoon coriander seeds, crushed

salt and freshly ground black pepper

Wash, peel and cut up the celeriac. If doing so in advance, acidulate the water with lemon juice or vinegar. Cook in salted, boiling water for 15 – 20 minutes or until soft. Drain (save the water for stock and freeze it). Mash well and beat in the butter. Season well with salt and plenty of ground black pepper and sprinkle with the coriander seeds.

Curly kale, puréed with crème fraîche

SERVES 6–8

Curly kale makes a wonderful substitute for fresh spinach and brightens the kitchen garden at a time where there is not much else around. It is a hardy brassica that goes on producing its permanently waved green leaves over a long season. The ultimate epicurean delight, if you grow it yourself, is to have a final meal of the tender centre shoots, steamed and served with melted butter, before you pull it up to make way for summer vegetables. The following recipe takes care of the coarser leaves, which are what you usually find when you buy it loose from a greengrocer or pre-packed from a supermarket.

bag of curly kale

25 g/1 oz butter

1 teaspoon cornflour

2 tablespoons crème fraîche

1 teaspoon sugar

salt and pepper

Like spinach, kale cooks down to half its volume. Wash well and strip the green from the stalks. Put the leaves in the food processor and chop finely in short bursts (pulses). Cook in salted, boiling water for 5 minutes. Drain well, press out as much liquid as possible and return to the pan, with the butter. Add the cornflour, mixed with a little water. When it has thickened slightly, add the crème fraîche, and season with sugar, salt and pepper.

French beans, with bacon and cheese

SERVES 2–4

Young french beans are so meaty that you don't need many as a vegetable accompaniment. They make a marvellous salad (see page 124) and have great affinity with lamb stew, to which they can be added at the last minute so that they don't become sludgy and khaki coloured. The following recipe could be bulked up with the addition of hard-boiled egg, and pasta instead of bacon, to make a vegetarian main course.

| 450 g/1 lb french beans |
| 25 g/1 oz butter |
| 1 streaky bacon rasher, de-rinded |
| 25 g/1 oz mature cheddar cheese, shaved into flakes with a peeler |
| salt and pepper |

Trim the beans and cook in salted, boiling water for 3 minutes. Drain well, toss in the butter and season with salt and pepper. Grill the bacon rasher until crisp. Crumble it over the beans and sprinkle with Cheddar cheese shavings.

Serve with grilled lamb chops, pork or veal escalopes.

'Bag o' nails' potatoes

SERVES 4–6

Humanity owes a huge debt to Sir John Hawkins, who is said to have brought back the potato from the New World in 1563. Never has there been such a versatile ingredient. It can be a main course, or part of a soup or a salad and there are varieties to cater for every eventuality. The variety I favour for the following recipe is either Desirée or Maris Piper; it must be a 'floury' potato for the best results. During World War Two and after, there was a rather notorious nightclub called The Bag 'o Nails, but roast potatoes were the last thing on those patrons' minds. The recipe's name comes from a pub of the same name, just opposite the Royal Mews, where my husband Archie and I met clandestinely before we married. We considered the menu ambrosial; don't laugh when I tell you that it was generally spam fritters (there was still rationing) and these gorgeous roast potatoes, meltingly crisp on the outside and floury within. They are still mandatory with any roast joint and the Christmas turkey.

| 1.2 kg/2 lb large, floury potatoes |
| oil or dripping |
| salt |

Pre-heat the oven to 180°C/350°F/gas mark 4. Peel the potatoes and cut in half lengthways, to produce a shallow, oval disk. Bring to the boil in plenty of salted water and cook for just long enough to be soft on the outside but not cooked right through. Drain, lay a double thickness of kitchen paper over the saucepan and replace the lid for 5 minutes. Score the potatoes lightly with a fork and place, cut-side down, on a large, shallow roasting tin. Sprinkle with salt and spoon over oil or melted dripping (you can do this ahead of time and even, if pressed, the night before). Place on the bottom shelf of the oven and roast for 1½ hours. Drain off any excess fat and transfer to the top shelf for a further hour. If the meat or poultry has to be roasted at a lower temperature than this, put the potatoes on the top shelf and, when you have taken the meat out to rest, turn the oven up to 200°C/400°F/gas mark 6 for 15–20 minutes.

Parsnip patties

Parsnip engenders either hate or love on the culinary front. For those who love it, there are endless possibilities; these patties might even change the mind of the antis. The great bonus is that they can be made and cooked ahead of time and then re-heated at the last minute; they can also be frozen. The slight tartness of the apples complements the parsnip and counteracts any sweetness. Parsnip can be made into a delicate soup and I always put a few chunks into the pan when I am roasting potatoes. Like celeriac, parsnips cook very quickly and so are a boon for the last-minute cook.

450 g/1 lb parsnips, peeled and chopped
50 g/2 oz apple, peeled and chopped
pinch of grated nutmeg
plain flour, for coating
1 egg, well beaten
oil, for shallow-frying
salt and pepper

Steam the parsnips and apples. Mash them well and season with salt, pepper and nutmeg to taste. Take a dessertspoon at a time, coat in flour and roll into a ball. Dip in the egg and coat again in flour; then shape into cakes or rolls. Fry in hot oil until golden on the outside.

Gudrun's honeyed potatoes

SERVES 4–6

My Swedish sister-in-law gave me this potato dish, which was her speciality. She was a very good cook but had no sense of time, so you never knew when you were going to eat. My brother-in-law was a very distinguished naval officer and, soon after they were married, an invitation came asking them to dine with his admiral. They were 2 hours late so, unsurprisingly, a promising naval career came to an end! These potatoes are particularly good with duck or pork.

1 kg/2 lb potatoes, peeled
50 g/2 oz butter
oatmeal
1 tablespoon runny honey or golden syrup
salt and pepper

Cook the potatoes whole in salted, boiling water until just tender. Cut carefully in 4 lengthways and then into thick chunks. Heat the butter in a frying-pan and sauté the potatoes briefly on all sides. Sprinkle with a little oatmeal and then drizzle the honey over them. Continue cooking, turning them repeatedly until they become golden. Season with salt and pepper and serve immediately.

VEGETABLES

Potato purée, with diced root vegetables

SERVES 4–6

This delicate purée is a far cry from mundane mashed potato. It can be served on its own with a sprinkling of chopped herbs or you can fold in a spoonful or two of lightly cooked diced root vegetable and a chopped green herb for colour. If you don't want to use diced vegetables, try mixing in chopped cress or watercress, carrot, celeriac or swede, whichever takes your fancy. For the purposes of this recipe I have suggested carrot. It is a good way of using up that carrot or quarter of swede that you find lurking in the bottom of your fridge and which is not enough to serve on its own.

1 kg/2 lb potatoes, peeled and cut up

butter

milk

2 tablespoons carrot, lightly cooked and diced

1 tablespoon chopped fresh parsley

salt and pepper

Cook the potatoes until quite tender, in plenty of salted, boiling water. Drain the potatoes and cover the pan with a folded tea-towel or double thickness of kitchen paper. Replace the lid. Leave for 5 minutes. Mash with a potato masher until all lumps have gone. Now add plenty of butter and milk and beat until you have a purée the consistency of thick mayonnaise. An electric whisk or a hand-blender is best for this. Season really well and fold in the diced carrot, which should still be slightly crunchy.

Sprinkle with chopped parsley.

Lucy's red cabbage, fennel and apple

SERVES 2–4

This evolved as a result of my daughter, Lucy, finding she did not have enough red cabbage to serve on its own. A trawl through the fridge revealed a fennel bulb and some leftover apple sauce, so she decided to combine these unlikely ingredients. It was a resounding success and has now become a family favourite.

½ red cabbage

1 fennel bulb

1 apple

10 g/½ oz butter

1 tablespoon wine vinegar

1 teaspoon brown sugar

salt and pepper

Slice the cabbage and fennel thinly and chop the apple (unless you have some leftover apple sauce!) Melt the butter in a fairly large, heavy-based saucepan and tip in the cabbage, fennel and apple. Shake well to coat and then add the rest of the ingredients. Cover tightly and cook over a low heat for 1 hour, stirring occasionally.

Serve with pork chops.

VEGETABLES

FUNGI
'FREEBIES'

These are one of Nature's most bountiful gifts which, until recently have not been appreciated in Britain. Italy and France have been fungi-fanatics for centuries, which is why, when you go abroad, they feature so much on menus. In Russia and Eastern Europe, country-dwellers have relied on dried and pickled fungi to add flavour and nourishment to their food through the winter months. Gathering wild mushrooms is a magical experience (and I don't mean the hallucinogenic kind). To see a giant puffball gleaming in the grass or the luminous pearly grey of an oyster mushroom clinging to a tree is quite a revelation. Do not, however, take any risks and under no circumstances eat any of your gatherings without first being absolutely sure that they are not poisonous. Always take a field guide with you and, when you get home, double-check with a comprehensive book such as *Mushrooms and Other Fungi of Great Britain and Europe* by Roger Phillips, published by Pan Books. I have a great friend who is as mad about wild mushrooms as I am and, when we discover what we think is a gastronomic treasure and decide to eat it, his wife always looks on anxiously, in case we have made a mistake! Luckily, most of the supermarkets now sell some commercially-grown varieties of 'wild' mushrooms, such as yellow and grey oyster mushrooms and shiitake mushrooms. Some even have packs of some of the wild ones, and dried varieties are now widely available.

Always carry your harvest in a basket so that any spores can alight on the ground: a plastic bag tends to make them go slimy anyway. Most mushrooms can be dried, preserved in oil, and some can be frozen. The latter should be cooked straight from the freezer and must not be allowed to thaw, or they become unpleasantly flabby.

Chanterelle tart, with hazelnut pastry

SERVES 4–6

Next to ceps, chanterelles are my favourite fungi. They like to grow where there are birch trees and so are often plentiful in the highlands of Scotland. When Archie and I were on a self-catering fishing holiday with Will Garfit, I noticed a profusion of chanterelles along the banks of the River Dee, so I decided to pick some. My chanterelle soup received plaudits but had to be described as 'mushroom' or they wouldn't have eaten it. When finally told the truth, they pulled faces but had to agree they'd eat it again. This delicate tart makes a good contrast with the slight crunch of the hazelnuts and the flavours complement each other well.

225 g/8 oz chanterelles

50 g/2 oz butter

2 onions, peeled and finely chopped

1 litre/1¾ pints double cream

3 eggs, well beaten

salt and pepper

HAZELNUT PASTRY

225 g/8 oz plain flour

1 teaspoon icing sugar

½ teaspoon salt

175 g/6 oz cold butter, cut in pieces

25 g /1 oz chopped hazelnuts, roasted

1–2 tablespoons cold water

Melt the butter and cook the onions until soft; then add the chanterelles and cook for a few minutes. Set aside.

To make the pastry: sift together the flour, sugar and salt and tip into a food processor, with the butter. Switch on and process until the mixture is like fine breadcrumbs. Transfer to a bowl and gently mix in the hazelnuts; then add enough water to bind together. Press into a ball and refrigerate for 30 minutes.

Pre-heat the oven to 190°C/375°F/gas mark 5. Roll out the pastry and line a greased 23 cm/9 in loose-based flan tin with it. Spread with the onion/chanterelle mixture. Beat together the cream and eggs, season well and pour over. Bake for 45 minutes.

Eat hot or warm, with a spinach or rocket salad sprinkled with garlic croûtons.

Hedgehog mushrooms, sautéed with garlic

SERVES 1–2 DEPENDING ON YOUR HARVEST

Instead of gills, these forest mushrooms have little spikes on the underside of the cap. They are very good but take quite a bit of spotting. However, when you see one, there are usually several more in the vicinity. They grow amongst conifers and broad-leaved trees. Quantities can't be specified as it all depends on how many mushrooms you've got.

hedgehog mushrooms

oil, for frying

plenty of garlic, peeled and chopped

salt and pepper

cooked pasta

chopped fresh parsley

Parmesan cheese, shaved into flakes with a peeler

Trim any dirty bits off the stalks and wipe the caps. Fry in smoking-hot oil for a few seconds and, when the juice has exuded (there will be a lot) throw it away, otherwise the mushrooms will taste bitter. Heat some more oil, and throw in the garlic and the mushrooms. Fry for 2–3 minutes, season well, then tip over the cooked pasta and sprinkle with parsley and parmesan shavings.

Lawyer's wig, with cream and mace

SERVES 1–2 DEPENDING ON YOUR HARVEST

This delightful-sounding name is another alias for the shaggy inkcap, a mushroom that you may easily find growing on the edge of your lawn or by the compost heap. Pick them young, before the gills turn black. Its domed appearance is quite easy to identify, with its fringed and shaggy appearance. The flesh should be white and gills white or pink and have a sweetish smell. They have passed their 'sell-by date' when the gills have turned black and the dome looks dingy. You will not find this in the shops or supermarkets so quantities cannot be specified.

They can also be fried in butter with fresh-chopped parsley or tarragon.

lawyer's wig mushrooms
butter
cream
1 teaspoon cornflour
good pinch of ground mace
salt and pepper
thick slices of bread, toasted, to serve

Fry the mushrooms in butter until they begin to exude juice, about 2–3 minutes. Add the cream and seasonings and the cornflour, mixed with a little water. When it thickens, spoon on to thick slices of toast.

FUNGI

Puffball slices, fried in egg and breadcrumbs

SERVES 2–4

There are several varieties of puffball but by far the best is Lagermannia Gigantea, the giant puffball. They generally grow in grass or on pasture and it is quite an experience to see a collection of these shining globes, ranging in size from a golf to a football. My most unlikely sighting was in the grass area of Parson's Green, in London. The local inhabitants were astonished, to say the least, when they saw me garner the monster and secrete it in a plastic bag. Gather them only when they are firm and shiny. They are past it if, when you touch them, they collapse like a pricked balloon. Cut into thick slices, they can be frozen successfully but are then best cooked straight from the freezer.

1 giant puffball mushroom
plain flour, for dredging
1 egg, well beaten
wholemeal breadcrumbs, for coating
1 tablespoon sunflower oil
25 g/1 oz butter
streaky bacon rashers
salt and pepper
chopped fresh parsley, to garnish

Cut the puffball into slices 2.5 cm/1 in thick. Dredge well with flour, dip in the beaten egg and then in the breadcrumbs. Heat the oil and butter and cook the bacon rashers until crisp; then remove. Fry the puffball slices on each side, until golden. Season well, serve with the bacon rashers, and garnish with the chopped parsley.

Serve with wholemeal baps.

Mixed wild mushroom and lentil stew

SERVES 4–6

V

I believe that this herby and comforting stew would convert even the most convinced carnivore that there are acceptable alternatives to meat. One of the essential ingredients is the Provençal herb oil (see page 146). But, if you haven't made any, either go out and buy some or use double the quantity of dried herbs. Long and slow cooking is the answer and, as with all stews and casseroles, it is even better re-heated the next day.

450 g/1 lb Puy lentils
225 g/8 oz fresh wild mushrooms or
110 g/4 oz dried mixed wild mushrooms
2 tablespoons Provençal herb oil
1 onion, finely chopped
1 carrot, chopped
2–3 garlic cloves, peeled and chopped
2 bay leaves
1 teaspoon concentrated tomato purée
1.2 litres/2 pints vegetable stock
salt and freshly ground black pepper

Soak the lentils in water for 1 hour or longer. Heat the herb oil in a saucepan and fry the onion, carrot and garlic until soft. Add the fresh mushrooms and cook for a few seconds. If using dried mushrooms, soak in a little warm water for 20 minutes and then drain (add the water to the stock) and add to the vegetables. Strain and rinse the lentils and tip into the casserole, with the remaining ingredients. Cover tightly and simmer gently for 2–3 hours or overnight in the simmering oven of an AGA. Serve with a green salad and hot french bread.

SALADS

Things have come a long way from the days of the 'limp lettuce leaf and, sliced tomato' salad. There is a fantastic variety of salad leaves available, so there is no excuse not to eat healthily. Pink radicchio and Florence fennel, to name but two, are to be found at the smallest greengrocer and, of course, in supermarkets. I first ate them on a trip to Italy and smuggled back some seeds, which I managed to grow successfully.

Salad can be an accompaniment such as summer garden salad, with snipped herbs (see page 122), or a dish in its own right, such as Tarragon and Star Anise Chicken (see page 119) which makes a good main course for a summer buffet. Freshly picked lettuce straight from the garden, dressed with a vinaigrette sauce, takes only a matter of moments to make and should please the most demanding gourmet; leftovers in your fridge can often be turned into an unrepeatable culinary triumph.

Celeriac salad, with rémoulade sauce

SERVES 4–6

This French dish forms part of hors d'oeuvre from the grandest restaurant to the smallest auberge deep in the country, but you can use it as an accompaniment. Contrary to expectations, the sauce is not really a mayonnaise as it is made with mild Dijon mustard, oil and vinegar. A friend of mine complained that it was bitter but, when 'grilled' by me, it transpired that she had used ordinary French mustard not mild Dijon – fatal! You have to be very careful, when adding the oil, not to pour it in too fast, or the sauce will curdle, in which case you may have to cheat by adding an egg yolk and whizz it up in the food processor. Some recipes use chopped anchovies but I just add a few drops of anchovy essence.

Celeriac rémoulade is best made the day you want to eat it.

1 large or 2 small celeriac
4 tablespoons Dijon mustard
3 tablespoons boiling water
150 ml/¼ pint – 275 ml/½ pint sunflower oil
1 tablespoon white-wine vinegar
1 tablespoon single cream
2–3 drops anchovy essence
salt and pepper

Peel the celeriac. I find it easiest to cut the celeriac into 1 cm/½ in slices and then peel and cut into julienne strips. Plunge into salted, boiling water and, when the water has come to the boil again, strain it in a colander and run under the cold tap. Drain well and pat dry with kitchen paper.

Place the mustard in the food processor, switch on and add the boiling water, drop by drop, and then enough oil, to give a thick, mayonnaise-like sauce. Finally, add the rest of the ingredients and mix into the celeriac.

American chicken salad

SERVES 10–12

This recipe was given to me by a dear American friend; it was her standby whenever she had to do the catering for a family celebration. It entered my repertoire and has never failed to elicit complimentary comments. The dressing may sound complicated but it can be made up to 2 days in advance and refrigerated. You can also use turkey or pheasant.

450 g/1 lb cooked chicken, diced
450 g/1 lb cooked ham, diced
1 kg/2 lb salad potatoes, cooked and sliced
1 celery stalk or fennel bulb, chopped
spring onions and paprika, to garnish

COOKED SALAD DRESSING

150 ml/¼ pint concentrated chicken stock or consommé
150 ml/¼ pint wine vinegar
5 egg yolks, lightly beaten
2 tablespoons made English mustard
1 teaspoon salt
¼ teaspoon pepper
pinch of cayenne pepper
150 ml/½ pint double cream
75 ml/3 fl oz butter, melted

To make the cooked salad dressing: put everything except the cream and butter into a bowl over a pan of hot water. Stir constantly, until it begins to thicken. Add the cream and butter, and allow the sauce to cool.

Put the chicken, ham, potatoes and celery or fennel in a large salad bowl, add the dressing and mix well. Garnish at the last minute with the spring onions and a sprinkle of paprika.

Tarragon and star anise chicken breasts

SERVES 2-4

This is a quick and easy version of chaud-froid of chicken. It very nearly comes into the 'quickie' category and can be adapted to 'jazz up' left-over cold roast chicken if you suddenly want a summer dish. You can use it for pheasant breasts or even for whole poached salmon or trout and Lucy's addition of star anise is inspirational.

6 chicken breasts
600 ml/1 pint chicken stock
1 teaspoon tarragon vinegar
1 star anise
1 sachet gelatine
2 tablespoons Hellman's mayonnaise
2 tablespoons crème frâiche or greek yoghurt
1 tablespoon chopped fresh or dried tarragon
salt and pepper to taste

Bring the stock, tarragon vinegar, star anise and tarragon to a gentle boil and poach the chicken breasts in it for 20 minutes then leave to cool in the liquid. Take them out, arrange on a dish and refrigerate. Strain the stock and reduce by half then add

the gelatine which you have previously dissolved in a little of the liquid. Add the remaining ingredients and when cold but not set, spoon over the breasts which can be left whole or sliced diagonally. Decorate with sprigs of tarragon.

Triple tricolor salad

SERVES 6–8

On a hot sultry summer night, when appetites are flagging, there is nothing quite so tempting as a beautifully arranged tricolor salad. This one is not only three coloured but also has three different smoked meats to tempt the palate. It can be made simply with the sliced avocados, tomatoes and mozarella cheese, representing the colours from which it takes it name, but air-dried ham is usually included. The most famous is Parma ham, from the Italian town of that name. In Spain, it is called serrano ham. Twenty years ago, when in the mountains of the Sierra Morena, I often saw hams hanging beneath farm entrance-arches, drying in the air. In those days, it was one of the tapas served at every bar, cut into rather chewy chunks. Denhay Farms in Dorset produce a delicious air-dried ham from whey-fed pigs which is cured in a mixture of apple juice, honey curing salts and herbs. There are now any number of smokeries and you can buy their products by mail-order and/or on the internet or from supermarkets.

110 g/4 oz Denhay air-dried ham or similar

110 g/4 oz smoked venison

110 g/4 oz smoked duck or chicken

2 large beefsteak or slicing tomatoes

2 ripe avocados

2 buffalo-milk mozzarella cheeses

basil oil (see page 146)

red-wine vinegar

salt and pepper

fresh basil leaves, to garnish

Slice the tomatoes, avocados and cheese and arrange, with the meats, in concentric circles on a large platter. Drizzle with plenty of oil, sprinkle a few drops of vinegar, season with salt and pepper and garnish with basil leaves.

Serve with hot ciabatta bread and a bowl of olives.

French bean and tomato salad

SERVES 2–4

Staying with a friend in France recently was, as always a wonderful gastronomic experience. Her bean and tomato salad was perfection and it is so simple to make. It is best to use slightly more mature french beans than the tiny ones in packs. Choose those that look as if the beans are half-formed in the pod. It is worth the extra trouble of stringing them.

450 g/1 lb french beans

450 g/1 lb tomatoes, peeled and de-seeded

1 tablespoon best-quality olive oil

1 teaspooon balsamic vinegar

salt and ground black pepper

fresh thyme and marjoram leaves, to garnish

Top and tail and string the beans; then cut them in half. Cook in salted, boiling water until tender, about 8 minutes. To peel the tomatoes, cut a cross at the stem end and pour boiling water over them. Leave for 1 minute and then peel. Cut in half and scoop out the seeds with a spoon or melon baller and discard. Chop the flesh into chunks. Mix together with the beans, oil, vinegar and seasonings, put in a pretty bowl and snip the herbs over the salad just before serving.

Greek mushroom salad

SERVES 2–4

This is another standard component of the French hors d'oeuvre tray. It is very easy and quick and benefits from being made the day before you are going to eat it. Some recipes include tomato but I prefer this very simple one, with just mushrooms, lemon juice, olive oil and garlic. Don't be alarmed by the quantity of mushrooms; they will shrink in volume by half. Small button mushrooms are best but, failing these, bigger ones can be thickly sliced. Closed-cap mushrooms are, however, essential.

450 g/1 lb extra-small button mushrooms

2 tablespoons good olive oil

2 garlic cloves, peeled and finely chopped

1 tablespoon lemon juice

salt and pepper

1 tablespoon chopped fresh parsley, to garnish

Cook the garlic in the oil for 5 minutes. Add the mushrooms, lemon juice, salt and pepper and simmer, covered, for another 5 minutes. Remove the mushrooms with a slotted spoon to a dish. Reduce the cooking liquid by fast boiling, until it looks thick and syrupy. Pour over the mushrooms, sprinkle on the parsley and leave to cool.

SALADS

Salmon and quails' eggs in poppadums, with potato salad

SERVES 2–4

Quail's eggs are widely available now, although there was a time when they were thin on the ground. Acquaintances of ours who had a quail farm once invited us to dinner. They lived in the rural wilds of Dorset. Having been shown round the farm, we repaired to the house. Our jaws dropped a mile when we beheld the butler, who was a Pathan complete with turban. It transpired that our host had been in the Indian army and the same family of Pathans had been in his family's service for several generations. The trouble was that, every three years or so, the incumbent had to return to Afghanistan and settle any outstanding blood feuds, which meant that, if the outcome was fatal, there was a gap on the domestic front. Ironically it seems that even after many years nothing has changed!

Combining these delicately flavoured eggs with salmon adds a gourmet touch to your meal.

225 g/ 8 oz cold, cooked salmon

8 quail's eggs, hard-boiled

POTATO SALAD

450 g/1 lb cold, cooked potato cut into 2.5 cm/1 in dice

425 ml/³⁄₄ pint lemon mayonnaise (see page 138)

4 poppadums

oil, for frying

lemon slices and fresh fennel or, dill fronds, to garnish

Mix the vegetables with 275 ml/½ pint of the mayonnaise and divide amongst 4 plates. Fry the poppadums in a little oil. It is easiest to have 2 forks, so that you can flatten them as necessary. They don't take long and you can cook them a day or two in advance and keep them in an airtight tin.

At the very last minute, place one poppadum on each plate and on top a portion of salmon and 2 quail's eggs. Spoon over the remaining mayonnaise and garnish with lemon slices and fresh dill or fennel fronds.

Summer garden salad, with snipped herbs

SERVES 6–8

To be eaten at its best, this quintessentially summery salad should be made from the first fruits of your labours in the kitchen garden but, if you live in a town, don't despair: there may be a local Farmers' Market. If not, the salad can be made from pre-packed young vegetables. Even supermarkets now sell one or other of the varieties of salad potato mentioned.

The important thing is to pour on the basil or herb oil while the vegetables are hot and to snip over the herbs at the last minute. Use whatever is available and experiment with your 'mix and match' selection. Not out of the garden, I know, but I do add a can of green flageolet beans, which seem to complement the rest of the ingredients.

450 g/1 lb Charlotte, Ratte or Pink Fir
Apple salad potatoes, cooked

225 g/8 oz French or golden beans, cooked

225 g/8 oz garden, sugar-snap or mange-tout peas

225 g/8 oz carrot, cooked and diced

225 g/8 oz celeriac, cooked and diced

1 baby leek, blanched and cut into
2.5 cm/1 in lengths

1 tin green flageolet beans, drained

1–2 garlic cloves, peeled and finely chopped

3–4 tablespoons basil or Provençal herb oil (see page 146)

1 tablespoon sage and shallot vinegar (see page 144)

coarse sea salt and ground black pepper

2 bunches of spring onions

fresh parsley, thyme, marjoram, rosemary, basil, Good King Henry and salad burnet leaves

Cook all the vegetables lightly, so that they are still crunchy. If you have really tiny new carrots, just cook them whole. Keep all the cooking liquids as you will then have a fantastic vegetable stock to freeze. Put all the cooked vegetables, flageolet beans and garlic into a large bowl but keep the spring onions for decoration. Pour on the oil, vinegar and seasoning and mix well. Stick the spring onions round the edge, like a fringe, and, at the last minute snip over a generous amount of herbs.

Serve with Game Brawn (see page 31) or as a vegetarian dish in its own right.

Peta's tuna fish salad

SERVES 4–6

This dish always formed part of our alfresco lunch when we were partridge shooting in Spain. As we had eaten breakfast at 6.30 am, the sight of the long table with check cloth, bottles of red and white wine and a wonderful assortment of salads and starters was always welcome, and we fell on Peta's salad like ravening wolves. There were no side plates, just baguettes which we cut in half and used to mop up the sauce. The fantastic backdrop of the Sierra Morena mountains added to the euphoria, not to mention all the smells from the wild thyme and rosemary released by the hot sun. The following recipe is both quick and versatile and can either be a starter or main course. As a main course, serve with hot french bread and a green salad. As a starter, omit the potato and sweetcorn and serve in ramekins. If in a hurry, you can use Hellman's mayonnaise or similar. It is always popular with children.

2 × 200 g/7 oz tins tuna

6 hard-boiled eggs, roughly chopped

450 g/1 lb cooked potato, cut into chunks

1 large Spanish onion, peeled and chopped

350 g/12 oz tin sweetcorn kernels

425 ml/3/4 pint mayonnaise (see page 134)

pinch of curry powder

salt and freshly ground black pepper

Mix all the ingredients together. The mixture should be rather sloppy, so add more mayonnaise if necessary. Add cooked peas, chopped tomatoes or anything else which takes your fancy.

SALADS

SAUCES

Sauces can be sublime, if used with discretion to bring out the best in the principal ingredient. The test of time is that we unconsciously associate certain pairings of sauces with foods as marriages made in heaven, and feel cheated if they do not materialise. Roast chicken and bread sauce, or boiled mutton and caper sauce are as 'trad' as you can get, although, sadly, we now have to make do with boiled lamb, as mutton is rarely available. Mustard sauce is associated with such fish as herring and mackerel, and parsley sauce with boiled chicken or steamed haddock, to name but a few partners. Those who cook the best of country food should be familiar with many of these sauces, as they will set off the food you cook to perfection. The following are the principal basic sauces, with variations.

ROUX-BASED SAUCES
and Variations

Roux-based sauces should never taste of flour. If they do, you have not cooked the roux for long enough. Roux consists of equal quantities of butter and flour cooked together over a low heat for 2–3 minutes. The saucepan is then drawn off the heat and the liquid is poured in, whilst the mixture is being stirred. This is the basic method of making béchamel sauce and from it spring any number of variations.

Béchamel sauce

SERVES 6–8

40 g/1½ oz butter
40 g/1½ oz plain flour
600 ml/1 pint liquid, either milk or stock
salt and pepper

Melt the butter in a saucepan, tip in the flour and let it cook for 2–3 minutes. Pull off the heat and pour in the liquid, stirring constantly. Return to a low heat and continue stirring until it thickens; then cook for a further 5 minutes. It is now ready for any flavouring.

For a coating sauce, increase the quantities of butter and flour to 50 g/2 oz. If you use milk as the liquid, bring it to the boil with a bay leaf, a slice of onion and 3 peppercorns and then let it infuse for 15 minutes before straining it and pouring it on to the roux.

Caper sauce: Make with the cooking liquor from boiled lamb; add 1 tablespoon of capers and, just before serving, 2 egg yolks, beaten in 1 tablespoon of cream. Do not allow to boil after this addition or it will curdle.

Cheese sauce: Add 110 g/4 oz grated cheese and ½ teaspoon mustard to the basic béchamel and cook until the cheese has melted and blended in with the sauce.

Egg sauce: Add 2 chopped hard-boiled eggs to the basic béchamel.

Parsley sauce: Add 2–3 tablespoons of chopped fresh parsley to the basic béchamel.

Tarragon sauce: Use reduced stock for the liquid to add to the roux and add 1–2 tablespoons of chopped fresh tarragon. Just before serving, stir in 2 egg yolks, beaten in a little cream. Serve with poultry or game.

Velouté sauce. The butter and flour should be reduced to 25 g/1 oz and the liquid should be composed of stock or *fumet* (see page 15/16) of the main ingredient, plus wine. When you have made the sauce it should then cook over a very low heat or in a double saucepan for 1½ hours. This is what gives it the *velouté*, or velvety, texture.

SAUCES

Rich onion sauce

A wonderful accompaniment to roast lamb; or serve this with poached eggs, when it becomes oeufs soubise.
This, again, is based on a béchamel sauce.

110 g/4 oz onion, peeled and chopped
25 g/1 oz butter
25 g/1 oz plain flour
300 ml/½ pint milk
1 tablespoon double cream (optional)
salt and pepper

Melt the butter in a saucepan, add the onion and cook over a very low heat, until soft. Do not allow it to colour. Sprinkle in the flour and then proceed as for Béchamel Sauce (see page 126). Just before serving, add the cream.

Onion gravy

This is an essential accompaniment to bangers and mash or toad-in-the hole. It can also be an alternative to rich onion sauce (see opposite), to go with roast lamb; all you need to do is surround your joint with sliced onions and they will cook to a deep brown. You can then make your gravy in the roasting pan as usual.

225 g/8 oz onion, peeled and chopped
50 g/2 oz butter
1 teaspoon demerara sugar
25 g/1 oz plain flour
425 ml/¾ pint stock
dash of Lea & Perrins Worcestershire
Sauce
salt and pepper

Fry the onions and sugar in the butter, over a moderate heat, until they turn a deep brown. Sprinkle in the flour, stir constantly and pour in the stock. When it is bubbling, add the Worcestershire sauce and season to taste.

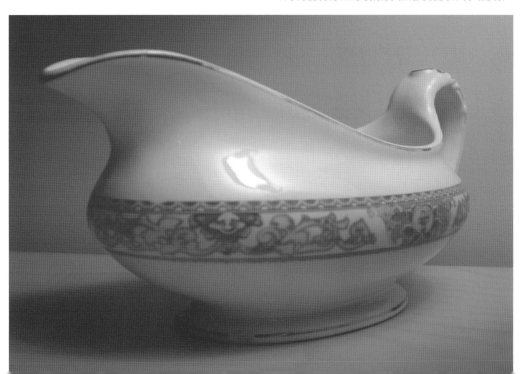

SHORT SAUCES

These are sauces made from the pan juices which have exuded from the meat or fish that you have cooked, usually after grilling, pan-frying or roasting. Wine, vegetable water or brown sauce is added to what the French call the jus, or juice, so it is really a grand name for a 'tarted up' kind of gravy. Sometimes, brandy is poured in and set alight or flambéed and, when the flames have died down, cream is added. Redcurrant jelly can be added to the roasting pan of lamb or game. The possibilities are endless, so do experiment.

Basic brown sauce

25 g/1 oz butter
1 carrot, peeled and chopped
1 onion, peeled and chopped
1 leek, trimmed and chopped
600 ml/1 pint brown stock (see page 15)
bouquet garni
salt and pepper

Brown the vegetables in the butter; then add the stock and *bouquet garni* and simmer for 1 hour.

Strain, pressing well to extract the juice from the vegetables. Skim off any fat with kitchen paper and then reduce by fast boiling to 275 ml/½ pint. You can freeze it for later use. Season before use rather than before freezing.

Lady Durham's sauce

This recipe is dated 1904 and comes from the book of recipes Lady Durham kept for her cook. It is the perfect partner for roast game, duck, goose or guinea-fowl.

pan juices from a roast bird
1 lemon, squeezed
2 tablespoons Lea & Perrins Worcestershire Sauce
2 tablespoons Harvey's Sauce
3 tablespoons (45 ml) port wine
1 good dash of cayenne pepper
salt
1–2 tablespoons (15–30 ml) stock
or water and a stock cube

Put all the ingredients in the pan with the juices and bubble for a few seconds, scraping in the brown bits. Add stock, then pour into a sauceboat.

BUTTER SAUCES

These are usually used as a light sauce for asparagus, fish or poultry. It is important not to let the butter overheat or it will separate.

Sauce bercy

50 g/2 oz shallots, peeled and chopped

300 ml/½ pint white wine

50 g/2 oz tomato, peeled, de-seeded and chopped

1 tablespoon capers, rinsed and drained

juice of ½ lemon

salt and pepper

110 g/4 oz unsalted butter, chilled and cubed

Simmer the shallots in the wine, until it has reduced to about a quarter of the original quantity. Then add the tomato and cook for a few minutes. Add the capers and lemon juice and season well. Heat through and then draw off the heat and whisk in the butter, a piece at a time. Serve immediately.

Lemon Butter Sauce Heat the juice of a lemon and whisk in 110 g/4 oz of butter as above. Season to taste.

OTHER HOT SAUCES

Bread sauce

This comes under no special heading except a 'must have' with roast chicken, turkey, pheasant, partridge and grouse. There would have been a revolt in this family, with banners and placards 'We want bread sauce' if I had ever failed to produce it with any of the above. As a family we prefer a robust version, with plenty of onion chunks, and not the version where you infuse the sauce with an onion stuck with cloves and then remove it before serving; but this is purely a matter of personal taste. Stale bread is preferable and, if possible, from a traditional and not a steam-baked loaf.

6–8 slices of bread, crusts cut off
1 onion, peeled and roughly chopped
600 ml/1 pint milk
25 g/1 oz butter
salt and plenty of freshly ground black pepper

Heat the onion in the milk, until it comes to the boil. Make breadcrumbs in the food processor and tip into the milk. This is not absolutely necessary, as you can just put in the bread slices, let them steep in the milk and then beat with a fork. Season generously, beat in the butter, cover and place over a very low heat for 5 minutes. Then pull off heat, until needed. If too thin, add more crumbs; if too thick, add a drop of milk. You can add cream for a luxurious version.

Tomato sauce

This is excellent with pasta or as an accompaniment to a turkey meat loaf and, for those who like Mexican food, it can be jazzed up with chillies and peppers.

If you have a glut of summer tomatoes, you can make large quantities of the sauce and freeze it. You will remember the taste of summer garden produce when you bring it out.

1 kg/2 lb tomatoes, peeled and de-seeded
1 tablespoon olive oil
225 g/ 8 oz onion, peeled and chopped
2 garlic cloves, peeled and chopped
1 dessertspoon sugar
1/2 teaspoon mustard powder
1 teaspoon vinegar
salt and pepper
1 tablespoon snipped fresh basil, to serve

Heat the oil and cook the onion and garlic for 2 minutes; then tip in the tomatoes and cook for 15 minutes.

Squash well with a potato masher and add the sugar, mustard, vinegar and seasoning. Cook for a further 5 minutes and snip in the basil, just before serving.

Trick of the trade

Use 2 x 400 g tins of chopped tomatoes if you are short of time and have no fresh tomatoes in the house or garden.

SAUCES

Lucy's asparagus sauce

3 shallots, peeled and finely chopped

1 dessertspoon lemon juice

3 hard-boiled egg yolks, crushed

225 g/8 oz butter, chilled and cubed

1½ hard-boiled egg whites, finely chopped

salt and pepper

Simmer the shallots in the lemon juice. Remove from the heat and then add the egg yolks and stir until amalgamated; season and whisk in the butter, a piece at a time. Then stir in the chopped egg whites.

Serve with asparagus, broccoli or fish.

WARM SAUCES

The classic way of making a 'warm' sauce is with egg yolks, lemon juice or reduced wine and vinegar and butter in a bain-marie or a heatproof basin over hot water. It is, in effect, a warm version of mayonnaise, using slowly melting butter instead of olive oil. Even self-possessed cooks sometimes go to pieces, when cooking these sauces, but, once you have mastered the process, you will wonder what all the fuss was about. For nervous cooks, there is another way; make it in the food processor. I have given both versions.

Trick of the trade

Do not use very newly laid eggs, nor should they come straight out of the fridge. Do have all your ingredients to hand and your time planned, so that the sauce does not sit too long after you have made it – you may have to hustle the serial drinkers into the dining room still clutching their pre-prandial 'snifters'!

Classic béarnaise sauce

SERVES 6–8

This is a 'must' with any kind of steak and can be good with stronger-tasting fish, such as tuna or swordfish.

2 shallots, peeled
55 ml/2 fl oz white wine
2 tablespoons tarragon vinegar
3 peppercorns
3–4 egg yolks
110 g/4 oz–175 g /6 oz unsalted butter, chilled and cubed
lemon juice
salt and pepper
1 tablespoon chopped fresh tarragon

Heat the shallots, wine, vinegar and pepper corns into a small saucepan and reduce, by fast boiling, to 2 tablespoons. Strain the liquid into a bowl, with the egg yolks, and whisk together. (You can do this ahead of time; then cover with cling film and refrigerate until you want to make the sauce.)

Place the bowl with the egg mixture over a pan of simmering water on a low heat. Whisking constantly, add 1 or 2 bits of butter at a time and keep on adding more as they melt. When the sauce is the consistency of double cream, pull off the heat, add a few drops of lemon juice and, if you want to join your guests for a drink, add a couple of bits of butter and cover. Just before serving, whisk in the chopped tarragon.

Trick of the trade

If the sauce starts to curdle, add an ice cube and a few drops of lemon juice and when it has cooled the sauce slightly, fish the ice cube out. Whisk in another egg yolk and serve immediately.

Blender béarnaise: Tip the reduced liquid and egg yolks into a blender or food processor. Melt the butter until hot but not foaming. Switch on the machine and pour in hot butter in a thin stream, until the mixture has thickened. Keep warm in a bowl over hot water and whisk just before serving.

SAUCES

Hollandaise sauce

The classic sauce to go with fish. The greatest dedication to epicurean cuisine was shown by my daughter Lucy when she was at university. Two of her friends were acting as a ghillies on a river in the Hebrides. Part of the wages was permission to keep one salmon. Cooking conditions were primitive: only one calor-gas ring and no saucepans. With the salmon steaks fried in butter, Lucy then made the hollandaise in a breakfast cup over hot water in the kettle. She said it was indeed a meal fit for the gods, as the salmon was so fresh it still had the milky curd which disappears after a very few hours.

3–4 egg yolks
1 tablespoon white wine
1 dessertspoon lemon juice
110 g/4 oz unsalted butter, or as needed, chilled and cut in small pieces
salt and pepper

Proceed as for béarnaise sauce (see page 132) but do not reduce the liquid. Whisk well whilst you are adding the butter, so that the sauce is light and frothy.

Blender hollandaise: Follow the same procedure as for blender béarnaise (see opposite).

COLD SAUCES

Classic mayonnaise

One of the secrets of successful mayonnaise is to have eggs which are a few days old and not straight out of the fridge. All the other ingredients should be at room temperature. It really isn't difficult and takes only minutes to make. If you wish, you can use electric hand-beaters but it really isn't necessary, a fork or wire whisk will do the job equally well and not make so much washing up!

2 egg yolks
1 level teaspoon mild Dijon mustard
300 ml/½ pint sunflower or olive oil
1 dessertspoon white-wine vinegar or lemon juice (for lemon mayonnaise)
salt and pepper

Place the yolks in a bowl with the mustard and beat with a whisk. Start pouring in the oil, drop by drop, until the sauce begins to thicken. you can then start pouring in a steady stream. Beat in the vinegar, or if making lemon mayonnaise, the lemon, and season.

Trick of the trade

In hot weather, and sometimes for no discernible reason, mayonnaise can separate. To re-constitute it, break 1–2 more yolks into a clean bowl and pour in the separated mixture very slowly and carefully, whisking all the time; it should thicken.
Whole-egg blender mayonnaise: Break 1 whole egg into the liquidiser or food processor with the mustard. Switch on and proceed as above. This is less rich and excellent for potato salad.

Trick of the trade

This is a last resort in a crisis. Add some top-quality olive oil or herb oil to Hellman's or other proprietary mayonnaise, with a dash of wine vinegar.

Green sauce

This pungent and herby sauce goes well with cold pork and with smoked eel. You can vary the herbs to your taste.

1 small onion, peeled and chopped
1 teaspoon capers, chopped
1 hard-boiled egg, chopped
2 anchovies, chopped
2 tablespoons each chopped fresh parsley and chives
1 tablespoon watercress or spinach blanched, drained and wrung out in a cloth and then finely chopped
1 tablespoon wine vinegar
4 tablespoons olive oil
salt and pepper

Combine all the ingredients, except the vinegar and oil. Add these last, and whisk well with a fork.

Tartare sauce

To be served with fried fish.

1 shallot or small onion, peeled and finely chopped
2 gherkins, finely chopped
1 teaspoon capers, chopped
1 dessertspoon chopped fresh parsley, dill, fennel or tarragon

SAUCES

1 quantity of classic mayonnaise or blender mayonnaise (see page 134)

Add all the other ingredients to the mayonnaise and mix well.

Sauce gribiche

A delicious sauce to serve with avocado pears, fish, raised game pie and terrines.

3 hard-boiled eggs
1 level teaspoon mild Dijon mustard
1 tablespoon each chopped fresh
parsley, chives and chervil
150 ml/ ¼ pint olive oil
1 dessertspoon wine vinegar
salt and freshly ground black pepper

Separate the yolks and whites. Chop the whites and reserve. Mash the yolks with the mustard and herbs. Pour in the oil, a drop at a time, and then in a steady stream; then add the vinegar. Season to taste and, finally, stir in the egg whites. Don't worry if it separates – it doesn't matter!

Horseradish sauce

Serve with roast beef and any cold smoked fish. It is best made at the last minute, as the pungency tends to dissipate. If possible, grate the horseradish in a food processor, to avoid running eyes, and don't rub your eyes!

2 tablespoons grated horseradish root
300 ml/½ pint cream, lightly whipped
1 teaspoon vinegar
salt, to taste

Mix all together and serve immediately.

Vinaigrette sauce

A classic French salad dressing, for anything rather rich which needs a tart sauce.

4 tablespoons olive or Provençal herb oil
(see page 146)
1 dessertspoon vinegar or herb vinegar
(see page 144)
½ teaspoon mustard
½ teaspoon sugar
salt and pepper

Best made and served in a screw-topped jar, as it needs to be shaken whilst being poured.

Coats' salad dressing

This used to be one of Archie's specialities. Friends watching always commented on the amount of sugar, but the end result is well worth it. French friends with very orthodox tastes have been completely converted and it is now their standard dressing.

1 dessertspoon mild Dijon mustard
1 tablespoon sugar
1 dessertspoon red-wine vinegar
5 tablespoons sunflower or olive oil
salt and pepper

Mix together the mustard, sugar and vinegar. Then whisk in the oil or shake in a screw-topped jar and season. This keeps in the fridge for up to a week.

FRUIT-BASED SAUCES

Cranberry sauce

Good with turkey and any game, and with roast lamb for a change.

225 g/8 oz cranberries

1 tablespoon water

runny honey

Place the cranberries in a pan with the water. Cook with lid on pan for a few minutes, until berries have burst and are mushy. Then stir in honey to taste and beat with a fork. Do not overcook or it will taste bitter. Cool and refrigerate.

Green gooseberry sauce

In France, gooseberries are called groseilles à macquereau or 'mackerel gooseberries'. They are always served with mackerel or herring as they are both in season at the same time. A similar sauce made with rhubarb can also be served with these fish. Both are good served with teal or mallard.

To make the sauce, top and tail some green gooseberries and stew in 1 tablespoon of water until mushy. Add just enough sugar to sweeten but the sauce should be really tart. Whizz in the food processor and allow to get cold.

Cumberland sauce

This is the classic sauce to go with cold ham or bacon. It also goes well with venison and wild duck.

1 orange

225 g/8 oz redcurrant jelly

1 glass port

juice of 1 lemon

dash of Lea & Perrins Worcestershire Sauce

2 drops of Tabasco sauce

½ teaspoon ground ginger

1 teaspoon dry mustard powder

Peel the orange zest carefully with no pith, cut into julienne strips and blanch in boiling water for 5 minutes. Strain and reserve. Squeeze the juice. Simmer the juice and the rest of the ingredients for 15 minutes. Add the orange zest strips. Cool and refrigerate.

SAUCES

BASIC KITCHEN EQUIPMENT

This list just covers what I consider to be the essentials. There are so many gadgets that you can buy which after the first excitement lie un-loved and unwanted in a drawer until they are given to a bric – brac stall at the fête.

1 set really good saucepans, stainless steel

1 non-stick heavy sauté pan with lid (Don't spare the pennies, you get what you pay for.)

1 non-stick pan for milk and sauces

1 cast iron enamelled casserole with lid

1 'Mermaid' omelette/pancake pan

1 Wok or stir-fry pan. Optional but they are very useful, not least for browning large quantities of meat or mince

1 heavy duty chopping board

1 Chef's chopping knife. Always try out to see if they feel comfortable, they should almost seem to chop by themselves. Again don't spare expense.

1 medium knife

1 boning/filleting knife

1 serrated Victorinox tomato knife. They're cheap, sharp and useful for paring and all sorts of jobs

1 Magimix food processor, 5100

1 500 watt Braun hand-held blender with small bowl for chopping herbs

1 good quality electric whisk

1 medium balloon whisk

Wooden spoons, including one with a slanted edge to the bowl for sauces.

1 pair kitchen scissors

1 'Add and weigh' kitchen scales. Salter Aquatronic are excellent. Pricey but worth it

1 Romertoft Claypot or Chicken Brick. To my mind one of the most important items in any kitchen

Bake O'Glide non-stick re-usable sheets

These are what I could not do without. Bowls, terrines, cake tines and other gadgets are all personal choice.

EQUIPMENT

STORE CUPBOARD FLAVOURINGS

The list of flavourings could be endless but these are what I would say were staples.

Green and black peppercorns
Coarse and fine sea salt (which are free from artificial additives)
Whole nutmegs
Cloves
Ground cloves
Mace
Ground allspice
Coriander seeds
Thai 7 spice seasoning
Dry and fresh ginger
Ground ginger
Cinnamon sticks
Ground cinnamon
Vanilla pods
Vanilla sugar, (a vanilla pod stuck in a jar of sugar, you can also put one in a jar of pudding rice)
Cardamon seeds, (black)
Mixed or Italian herbs
Dried dill
Tarragon
Thyme
Dijon mustard
Concentrated tomato purée
Soy sauce
Mrs Ball's chutney sauce
Mango chutney
Curry powder
Curry paste
Runny honey
Sunflower oil for frying
Best quality virgin olive oil
Red and white wine vinegar
Balsamic vinegar

FLAVOURINGS

HERBS

Herbs have finally come into their own as an important, complementary flavouring ingredient in cooking. Only a few years ago, all you could obtain, apart from the dried variety, were the obvious herbs such as parsley, thyme and sage. Now, almost every garden centre has a wide selection and many nurseries have sprung up which specialise in herbs. Supermarkets and some green-grocers sell them in pots or fresh in packets and, just off Berkeley Square, at the very heart of Mayfair, you will find pots of herbs on the pavement outside the famous herbal shop Culpeper House, named after that doyen of herbalists, Nicholas Culpeper, who wrote the definitive herbal. Of course all the commonly used herbs originated in the wild but if you are on the look-out, many of them can be garnered when you are walking in the country. To use something that you have picked yourself to flavour a dish somehow gives you a kind of atavistic pleasure and you feel you are really going back to basics. I think the ultimate example of this is my recipe for the 'Bankside trout'. I have included many 'freebies' in the following list of herbs, their habit and season. The 'fruit freebies' can be found in the section for puddings and preserves.

A herb garden on a sunny summer's day is absolute bliss; the scents and aromas are quite intoxicating. They are very decorative and can happily be grown amongst other plants in flower beds. Freshly picked herbs are best and, even if you only have a windowsill or box, don't despair, as herbs like poor soil conditions and a sunny position.

The best methods of preserving are:

Drying Hang up in a airy, warmish place or spread loosely on a baking tray and place in a very low oven or in an airing cupboard.

Freezing Place loose on a tray and, then put into bags or chop and freeze with a little water in ice-cube trays.

In oil or vinegar (see page 144).

GARDEN HERBS

Basil Annual. Likes lots of sun and plenty of water. Oval, pointed leaves. Essential ingredient in pasta sauces, pesto sauce, tomato salad or soup, lasagne and many other dishes. Never chop leaves; always tear. Use fresh or freeze.

Bay Perennial shrub. Can be grown in a pot and much favoured by topiarists. As a shrub, will reach 6 metres in height. One of the main ingredients of bouquet garni and added to many stews and casseroles. Whole or ground, dried leaves used to flavour pâtés and terrines. Dry.

Chervil Annual. Parsley-like leaves, with a slightly aniseed flavour. Good for flavouring soup. Use also with fish or eggs as a change from fennel. Freeze.

Chillies Perennial, not strictly a herb but easily grown in a pot in greenhouse or on a sunny windowsill. Very attractive and decorative and could be used as a pot plant. Very satisfying to pick those brilliant red pods off the bush, instead of shovelling them into a plastic bag. Use fresh or dry and thread them in decorative strings in your kitchen.
Warning: Wash your hands well after handling chillies and on no account touch your eyes.

Chives Perennial of the onion family. Easily grown in a pot where, if cherished and fertilised, will become luxuriant. All kinds of uses, especially in salads, soups, mayonnaise and as a garnish. Best fresh, but will freeze. Garlic chives are a stronger-tasting variety.

Coriander Annual. Parsley-like plant. Can be grown in a pot. Leaves for use in salads and soups. The ripe seeds, when crushed, are used in Greek, Turkish and Thai dishes. Ground coriander seeds, dhania, are a principal ingredient in curry. Frying in oil releases the typical aroma.

Dill Annual, with feathery leaves. An essential ingredient of gravadlax and many Scandinavian recipes. Enhances fish dishes and patés and cucumber and courgette soup. Dry or freeze.

Fennel Annual. Tall with feathery spikes. Use in fish dishes. Stronger than dill. The dried seeds can be used in oriental dishes. Ground fennel seed, saunf, is a principal constituent of Indian garam masala powder. Dry or freeze. Do not confuse with bulb fennel, which is a delicious vegetable.

Good King Henry or Poor Man's Asparagus Perennial. Grow in flower border. Use leaves in salads. Cook immature flower spikes like asparagus. Very delicate. Use fresh.

Horeseradish Vigorous perennial. Very strong, hot root, especially in winter. Grate and make sauce for beef, smoked salmon and trout. Use fresh, as it loses its potency when dried or bottled.

Marjoram Perennial Pretty, round-leaved plant with attractive purple flowers. Goes well with broad beans and in pâtés, casseroles and Italian dishes. Use fresh or dry.

Mint Invasive perennial. Best grown in a pot or container as it spreads like mad. Several varieties, including apple mint, which has a very delicate flavour. Use as a flavouring in savoury and sweet dishes. Dries and freezes well or can be preserved in golden syrup, (see page 147).

Parsley, Curley-leaved Biennial. Takes well to pot life, provided that you don't neglect it. Universal flavouring. Best used fresh but can be frozen.

Hamburg Parsley Flat-leaved biennial. Has a stronger flavour and is preferred by many top chefs. Use leaves for flavouring or garnish and roots as a vegetable (they are wonderful). Leaves, as above.

Rosemary Perennial. Decorative and aromatic shrub. Pointed, spiky leaves with blue, pink or white flowers. Very aromatic. Use fresh or dried with lamb, poultry, game and many pasta dishes.

Sage Perennial shrub. Both grey- and purple-leaved varieties suitable for flavouring and look decorative in borders. Very strong, so use sparingly with duck, goose, and in stuffings. Use fresh or dried.

Salad Burnet Perennial that seeds itself freely. Pretty, ferny leaves with a cucumber flavour. Use fresh, torn or snipped in salads.

Savory, Summer Annual. Use in Mediterranean dishes and with all varieties of dried and fresh beans and, especially, broad beans. Plant amongst rows of vegetables prone to blackfly, to which it is a deterrent. Use fresh or dried.

Savory, Winter Perennial. Will grow in a pot. Decorative in borders. Use as a flavouring as above.

Sorrel Perennial. Same family as the dock. Delicate, lemony flavour. Will grow in a biggish pot but best in a border. Delicious as a soup and in sauce (see p9). Use fresh.

Tarragon Invasive perennial. Tall spires of lance-shaped leaves. Essential in sauce béarnaise, poulet à l'estragon, in salads, mayonnaise or with mushrooms. Use fresh or freeze.

Thyme Perennial. Takes well to pot life. Very strong and aromatic. Use in bouquets garnis, stews, pâtés and Mediterranean dishes. Use fresh or dried.

This is not a comprehensive list of herbs, just my particular culinary favourites. They can also be used to make exquisite flavoured oils and vinegars, which make wonderful Christmas presents or donations to fêtes or charity fairs, where they will sell like hot cakes if you put them in pretty bottles.

Note: When making a batch of these herb oils and vinegars I try to use some very small bottles so that I can put a selection into a basket or box for presents.

GARDEN HERBS

SEASONAL WILD HERBS AND FRUIT 'FREEBIES'

FEBRUARY–MARCH

Wild Garlic or 'Ramsons', a member of the *allium* or onion family. Grows on woodland or roadside verges with a strong garlicky smell. White starry flowers like 'Star of Jerusalem' and leaves like lily of the valley. Much prized in Italy and Switzerland. Use in pesto sauce and with rabbit or pheasant.

APRIL

Dandelion, dent de lion (lion's teeth) or piss-en-lit (pee-in-your bed) as it is known in France for it's diuretic properties. Few people would fail to recognize its serrated leaves and yellow flowers. Delicious if used sparingly in salads. Can be blanched under a flower pot which makes it less bitter.

Elderflower The flowers have a delicate fragrance which is indescribable, especially on a warm, sunny day. Grows in hedgerows and in towns where, during the war, it was to be found on any bomb site. With gooseberries it is a 'marriage made in heaven (see page 175), made into a cordial or elderflower wine it is fantastic (see pages 191 and 194)

Wild Strawberry Grows in woods on chalky downland. Has a long season and can sometimes be found as late as November. Not prolific so has to be used sparingly, more as a flavouring.

MAY – JUNE

Bilberries and Cranberries To be found on moorland. Not prolific so use as part of a stuffing for game or as a sauce (see p136) Both have commercial counterparts which can be bought in most supermarkets, the latter coming from America.

Good King Henry Waste places and roadside verges in the South of England. Triangular, spear-shaped leaves which are very good in salad. Immature flower spikes known as 'Poor Man's Asparagus'.

Sorrel Grows on downland or poor mountainous pasture. The small spear-shaped leaves are very delicate and a special culinary asset if obtainable, in fact the gourmet version of the garden variety.

Herbs See previous page for garden varities. Mint, to be found by rivers. Marjoram and thyme grow on hillsides and can sometimes be found on roadside verges, especially on chalky land.

Nettles Stinging nettles. Grow anywhere. Supposed to have been introduced by the Romans as a means of increasing blood circulation in the cold weather by flagellation with bunches of nettles. Delicious as a soup (see page 9) or in a sauce with fish. Pick young tips early in growing season. DO WEAR GLOVES !

Comfrey Grows by the edge of rivers and lakes, particularly chalk streams. Use to wrap fish on barbecues.

SEASONAL WILD HERBS

Water Mint Grows by the edge of rivers or lakes. Use like garden mint.

Rowanberries Universal. The trees grow in gardens, hedgerows and towns. Excellent as a jelly but best teamed with crab-apple, as rather bitter on its own. (See page 176) Good with game and cold meat.

Samphire Coastal plant which grows from west coast of Scotland to Cornwall and down the east coast where it is most prolific. he ultimate in 'freebie' gourmet plants. (See page 24).

Wild Cherry Quite rare but can be found in hedgerows. Harvest before the birds get to them. Best pickled in sweet spiced vinegar (see page 183)

Wild Raspberry Grows on the edge of woods and sometimes just outside. Very 'more-ish' but not very prolific. Use more as a flavouring rather than the main ingredient as not very prolific. Glorious flavour.

JULY
Meadowsweet Grows in ditches and by water's edge. Good with fish.

AUTUMN
Hazelnuts and Spanish Chestnuts Hazelnuts are pretty universal. Good with rabbit and fish. Spanish chestnuts grow in the south. You will be lucky if you beat the grey squirrels to either of these goodies but if you do, chestnuts are a great addition, particularly to game. (See p52) Otherwise take off the prickly outer husk and roast over a log fire in winter.

Crabapples Late autumn, good for jellies and pickles

Rosehips Found in hedgerows. Use for jellies and cordial.

Sloes, Bullace, Mirabelle Plums All found in autumnal hedgerows. Good for jams, jellies and alcolholic beverages.

This is not a definite list, as to include everything would fill a book on its own. I have just listed those most commonly available.

HERB VINEGARS, OILS AND CONDIMENTS

These are really as easy to make as falling off the proverbial log and will save you money; the price of the commercially produced ones is exorbitant. All you need to do is to hoard any attractive bottles, or beg them from your improvident friends, in return for a bottle of the finished product. Wash them really well, preferably in a dishwasher, and then get going. Do not wash the herbs. Try to pick them on a dry, sunny day, or trust to luck if you buy them in a packet.

Raspberry vinegar

500 ml bottle white wine vinegar
raspberries

Pour a third of the vinegar out to compensate for the law of Archimedes and fill with raspberries until the vinegar comes to the top of the bottle. That is all you have to do. Leave for a few days before using.

Tarragon vinegar

500 ml bottle of white-wine vinegar
6 or more fresh tarragon sprigs, the length of the bottle

Pour a little of the vinegar out and stuff in as many of the sprigs as possible, making sure that they are completely immersed. Screw on the top and place on a sunny windowsill for 2 or 3 days. Store in a cool, dark cupboard. Your home-made variety will be as different from the commercial ones as chalk from cheese.

Sage and shallot vinegar

500 ml bottle of cider vinegar
1 shallot, peeled
fresh sage sprigs, as above

Follow the tarragon vinegar instructions.

Garlic vinegar

500 ml bottle of red-wine vinegar
10 garlic cloves, peeled and crushed

Bring the vinegar to the boil and pour over the garlic. Leave for 1 month. Strain and bottle.

Mint and apple vinegar

500 ml bottle of cider vinegar
$\frac{1}{2}$ apple, cut in slivers
fresh mint leaves

Stuff the apple slivers into the bottle and then as much mint as you possibly can. Fill up with vinegar. It is absolutely delicious.

HERB VINEGARS

Provençal herb oil

This strongly aromatic oil is fantastic with a bean salad or sprinkled on ciabatta bread crisped in the oven, and can be used to liven up a stew or casserole if it seems boring. It must be made with hard-stemmed herbs.

500 ml bottle of good olive oil

sprig each fresh thyme, marjoram, winter savory and rosemary

2–3 bay leaves

1 teaspoon mixed peppercorns

1 garlic clove, peeled

1 dried chilli

The sprigs should be really generous so that the bottle is stuffed with greenery. You can increase the number of chillies if you want the oil to be hotter; also the garlic. Make sure the sprigs are totally immersed and top up with more oil to cover, when you have used some.

Chilli vinegar

500 ml bottle red-wine vinegar

25 g/1 oz dried red chillies

Bring the vinegar to the boil. Cut the chillies up with a pair of scissors and pour over the vinegar. Bottle when cold. Strain as you use.

Chilli sherry

This, according to a naval friend who was once Flag Lieutenant to an Admiral, was mandatory in the wardroom. He was not alone, as other naval friends attested to this predilection, which, presumably, enlivened boring ship's consommé.

½ bottle of dry sherry

6 dried red chillies

Insert the chillies in the sherry bottle. The longer they are left the hotter it will become.

Don't drink it neat, but it's good in a Bloody Mary.

Basil oil

This is absolutely beyond compare if you get it right and is heavenly with a tricolour salad. Great care must be taken not to leave the basil in the oil for too long or you will get a rotten sludge.

500 ml bottle of good olive oil

3–4 generous branches of fresh basil

Stick the basil into the bottle of oil, screw on the top and stand on a sunny windowsill for no more than 2–3 days, 4 at the most. Have ready a clean bottle. Strain the oil into it and store in a cool, dark place. Don't worry if the oil looks cloudy: it will become crystal clear in a month or so. This applies to any of the herb oils.

HERB OILS

Archie's mustard

At the time when my late husband, Archie, dreamed this up, you could only buy dry mustard powder, Dijon and whole-grain mustard, so his really was a forerunner of the many commercial varieties of flavoured mustard on sale today. However, friends and aficionados, having once tasted it, say it has no equal.

8 tablespoons dry mustard powder

1 small pot dark French mustard

1 small pot mild Dijon mustard

4 tablespoons whole-grain mustard

2 teaspoons dried minced or powdered garlic

2 teaspoons dried mixed herbs

2 tablespoons sugar

Place all the dry ingredients in a bowl and mix together; then add the mustards and beat well with an electric hand-beater. Spoon into a screw-topped jar and close tightly. Leave for 24 hours.

Taste and, if too vinegary, add some more sugar. It improves with keeping.

Heather's preserved mint

My daughter, Lucy's, mother-in-law gave me this amazing recipe for preserving mint. It is so easy to do and takes care of the mass of mint that appears in mid summer. As a basis for mint sauce, it is unparalleled and cuts out all the tiresome chore of chopping.

masses of fresh mint

golden syrup

Dry the mint in a low oven or airing cupboard. You don't have to take off the leaves, just pick it on long stems. When it is absolutely crinkly and crunchy dry, rub the leaves off the stalks, crush them between the palms of your hands and pack into sterilised, warmed jars. Heat the syrup so that it is runny and pour over the pulverized mint, until it is completely covered. Screw on the tops and Bob's your uncle, as they say!

To make mint sauce, just spoon as much as you want into a sauce boat and thin with vinegar. Spread a little over a joint of lamb before roasting or over chops or cutlets before grilling.

HERB CONDIMENTS

PUDDINGS

The choice of pudding is important when planning a meal. A sturdy main course should have something light to follow so that your digestion does not have to work overtime, but circumstances may overrule this culinarily correct concept. My husband Archie, when asked what pudding he wanted, always used to think for a few minutes and then say 'Choccy Pots', no matter what the previous courses were. Similarly, my son-in-law, whose nickname is 'Piggy', is seriously addicted to bread and butter pudding and the like. He is not alone, and there is a rebirth of these old favourites, some of which, like castle puddings, you will find in this chapter. Sorbets and ice creams are a godsend, and you make them when fruit is at its best. This is where 'pick your own' or the hedgerow come into their own, or, if you are lucky enough, your garden.

No matter what you choose, a pudding should be a celebration of the end of the meal, which is indeed how the French view it, as they serve the cheese before the pudding, which I thoroughly endorse.

HOT PUDDINGS

Rice pudding

SERVES 4–6

No apologies for starting the pudding section with rice pudding. Except for those who hated it as children, most men drool when they see it, and this version is about as far from school dinners as you can get. The secret is the infusion of cardamon seeds, a tip I was given by my friend Shamim.

600 ml/1 pint milk
2 - 3 cardamon seeds
110 g/4 oz sugar
50 g/2 oz pudding rice
25 g/ 1 oz butter

Crack the cardamoms, remove the husks and put the seeds in the milk together with the sugar and the rice and bring to the boil. Simmer for 10 minutes, stirring constantly. Pour into a buttered 1.2 litre/2 pint pie dish and place in a pre-heated oven set at 130°C/275°F/Gas Mark 1 for 3 hours. Stir every 30 minutes or so until it is thick and creamy, you may need to add a little more milk occasionally to prevent it drying out. Turn heat up slightly for the last half hour to brown the skin. You can use a vanilla pod instead of the cardamon seeds or even a stick of cinnamon.

Apricot bread and butter pudding

SERVES 4–6

Bread and butter pudding came into being as a means of using up stale bread. It has been going for over 200 years and was sometimes known as Nursery or Newmarket Pudding. This is a tarted-up version of the old favourite, and makes a change from the more conventional recipe.

1 small sliced milk loaf
butter, softened
apricot jam
3 large eggs
110 g/4 oz sugar
300 ml/½ pint milk
300 ml/½ pint crème fraîche
1 packet dried apricots
sultanas
1 tablespoon brandy
icing sugar, sifted, to decorate

Remove the crusts from the slices, butter them, spread with a thin layer of jam and cut in half. Beat the eggs and sugar, until pale and fluffy. Bring the milk and crème fraîche to the boil and pour on to the egg mixture. Butter an 845 ml/1½-pint enamel or pyrex dish and line the sides and bottom with the slices, buttered-side down. Sprinkle with the dried apricots and sultanas and continue with layers of bread slices, butter-side up and apricots and sultanas. Pour over the liquid and leave to stand for 15 minutes.

Pre-heat the oven to 170°C/325°F/gas

HOT PUDDINGS

mark 3. Sprinkle over the brandy and stand the dish in a pan of boiling water, to come halfway up the dish. Bake for 45 minutes. Glaze with some of the apricot jam, flash under a hot grill for a few seconds, sprinkle with icing sugar and serve.

Castle puddings with treacle

SERVES 6

These are a real old favourite and can be served plain, with an accompanying sauce, or be made with jam, treacle or with dried fruit incorporated in the main mixture.

110 g/4 oz butter
110 g/4 oz caster sugar
3 eggs
110 g/4 oz self-raising flour
8 teaspoons treacle

TREACLE SAUCE

4 tablespoons treacle
2 tablespoons water
1 squeeze lemon juice

Pre-heat the oven to 190°C/375°F/gas mark 5. Beat together the butter and sugar, until light and fluffy. Add the eggs, one by one, sprinkling in a tablespoon of flour after each addition to prevent the butter from curdling. Butter 12 dariole moulds or similar and put a teaspoon of treacle in each one. Half-fill each mould with the batter and bake for 20 minutes. Unmould and serve with the treacle sauce, made by dissolving the treacle in the water and lemon juice.

'Freebie' elderflower fritters

SERVES 6–8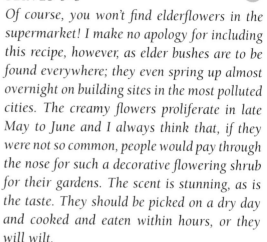

Of course, you won't find elderflowers in the supermarket! I make no apology for including this recipe, however, as elder bushes are to be found everywhere; they even spring up almost overnight on building sites in the most polluted cities. The creamy flowers proliferate in late May to June and I always think that, if they were not so common, people would pay through the nose for such a decorative flowering shrub for their gardens. The scent is stunning, as is the taste. They should be picked on a dry day and cooked and eaten within hours, or they will wilt.

8–12 elderflower heads
110 g/4 oz plain flour
pinch of salt
2 tablespoons sunflower oil
150 ml/¼ pint lager or water
1 egg white
oil, for frying
icing sugar, sifted, to decorate
lemon wedges, to serve

Sift the flour and salt together and mix to a batter with the sunflower oil and liquid. Allow to stand in a cool place for 1 hour. Beat the egg white until it holds stiff peaks.

Fold in the egg just before using the batter. Heat some oil in a deep pan or deep-fryer. Dip the flower heads in the batter and then drop into the smoking-hot oil and fry until golden brown. Drain on kitchen paper. Pile on to a dish, sprinkle with icing sugar and serve with lemon wedges.

Fruit and nut crumble

SERVES 4–6

In a competition I judged in The Field, this recipe, by Elizabeth Edwards, was the winner, and the unusual combination of rolled oats and nuts makes the fruit crumble a real winner. Blackcurrant, quince and apple, plum or damson make a perfect basis; just use whatever is handy. You can cook the fruit in the dish and freeze it but it is best to make the topping and freeze it separately. Then all you have to do is to sprinkle it on top and put it in the oven for the requisite time.

900 g/2 lb fruit

sugar

CRUMBLE TOPPING

175 g/6 oz plain flour

110 g/4 oz unsalted butter

110 g/4 oz demerara sugar

75 g/3 oz rolled oats

75 g/3 oz flaked almonds

75 g/3 oz ground almonds

Pre-heat the oven to 200°C/400°F/gas mark 6. Cook the fruit lightly, spoon into a dish and allow to cool. Sweeten to taste before using.

For the topping, rub the butter into the flour until it resembles fine breadcrumbs; or process for 15 seconds in a food processor. Tip into a bowl and mix in the rest of the ingredients. Spread over the fruit and bake for 30–40 minutes.

Serve with crème fraîche or, for traditionalists, custard.

Guards pudding

SERVES 4–6

Definitely a 'Piggy pudding' and always popular with male guests, but the ladies have been known to have a surreptitious second helping or a scrape of the dish in the kitchen. You should use raspberry jam but strawberry will do, or, at a pinch, apricot. If you have no cake to make into crumbs, use 4 trifle sponges, whizzed in the food processor.

75 g/3 oz unsalted butter

75 g/3 oz caster or granulated sugar

2 eggs

75 g/3 oz cake crumbs

3 tablespoons raspberry or other jam

1/2 teaspoon bicarbonate of soda, dissolved in a little hot water

Process or beat the butter and sugar, until light and fluffy, and then break in the eggs, one by one, and process again. Add the cake crumbs and give the mixture few short bursts (pulses), until mixed. Lastly, stir in the jam and the bicarbonate solution. Spoon into a well greased 845 ml/1½ pint pudding basin, cover with greased foil, pleated to allow room for expansion, and tie with strings. Put on a plate or trivet in a saucepan, pour in boiling water and steam for 2 hours. Check the water level from time to time and top it up, as necessary. Invert the pudding on to a dish and serve with cream or custard.

HOT PUDDINGS

Honey and walnut pancakes

SERVES 8

Golden honey is one of nature's marvels. The intricacies of the social structure of a beehive puts human society into perspective. There is a queen-bee, who is cosseted and nurtured by her workers with one aim, the continuation of the hive. The chosen spouse dies after consummating the marriage and the queen lays eggs, which hatch and are fed on the honey gathered by the workers, who can fly up to two miles to find nectar from flowers. The flavours of different honeys are as distinctive as the vintages of a wine. There is cinnamon-coloured, strong-tasting heather honey, lime honey, acacia honey, Greek honey from Mount Hymettus – beloved of the Gods of ancient Greece and redolent of sun-baked rosemary, thyme and lavender – and many more.

My first introduction to bee-keeping was through our jobbing gardener, who rejoiced in the name of Mr Funge. He was a misogynist who lived in a thatched cottage with a garden full of flowers and vegetables, at the end of which stood a row of thatched bee skeps (hives). His only trip to London was to acquire an Italian queen-bee. My father, travelling in the same railway carriage, was somewhat alarmed when Mr Funge produced a matchbox from his waistcoat pocket to show him his new acquisition, as Italian queens had a reputation for being very fierce.

Honey is a wonderful cookery ingredient and can be used both in puddings and for cooking meat and vegetables and sauces. The following recipe combines honey and walnuts, the sweetness being offset by the apple.

1 quantity of Yorkshire pudding batter (see page 71)

butter, for frying

50 g/2 oz walnut pieces

2 tablespoons honey, plus extra for brushing

450 g/1 lb apple, peeled and chopped

juice and shredded zest of 1 orange

lemon juice, for brushing

icing sugar, sifted, to decorate

Pre-heat the oven to 200°C/400°F/gas mark 6. Heat the knob of butter in a 15 cm/6 in frying-pan and pour in a little batter, tilting and turning the pan to coat the base evenly. Cook over a medium heat, until brown, and then turn over and cook the other side. Repeat until all the batter has been used. Pile on to a plate and set aside.

Whizz up the nuts and honey to a spreading consistency in the food processor. Cook the apple in a little orange juice, until soft but not soggy. Spread each pancake with the honey mixture and then place a spoonful of apple on one half; fold over and lay in a buttered, shallow, ovenproof dish. (You can prepare them ahead of time to this point.) Brush with a mixture of honey and lemon juice and bake for 15 minutes. Sprinkle with icing sugar and decorate with strips of orange zest.

HOT PUDDINGS

Queen of puddings

SERVES 4–6

This goes down well with grown-ups and children alike and the main part can be made in the morning or the previous day, so it makes for an easy pudding after a Sunday roast.

PUDDING

110 g/4 oz fresh breadcrumbs

300 ml/½ pint milk

1 cinnamon stick

2 tablespoons sugar

10 g/½ oz butter

3 egg yolks

25 g/1 oz diced mixed peel (optional)

225 g/8 oz apricot jam

MERINGUE

3 egg whites

75 g/3 oz sugar

Pre-heat the oven to 180°C/350°F/gas mark 4. Butter a 1.2-litre/2-pint pie dish and tip in the breadcrumbs. Bring the milk, cinnamon, sugar and butter to the boil and allow to stand for 5 minutes. Remove the cinnamon stick and pour the milk over the breadcrumbs. Leave to soak to a creamy consistency. Beat in the egg yolks with a fork and stir in the mixed peel. Stand in a roasting pan with boiling water to come half-way up the dish and bake for 20 minutes.

Spread with the jam, (raspberry is traditional but my preference is for apricot).

To make the meringue: whisk the egg whites to stiff peaks and then beat in the sugar, a tablespoon at a time.

Spoon over the custard mixture and lift into peaks with a fork. Bake for a further 10–15 minutes, until pale golden.

Carrot cake pudding with fluffy lemon sauce

SERVES 6

This will be gobbled up by all your male guests. My 'tasting testers' were two men and they demolished a great deal in a very short space of time. The lemony sauce goes really well but you can just serve it with custard, cream or both!

1 carrot cake (see page 168)

FLUFFY LEMON SAUCE

3 egg yolks

35 g/1½ oz castor sugar

juice and zest of 1 lemon

200 ml/7 fl oz water

Put the egg yolks, sugar and grated lemon in a bowl over a pan of hot water and whisk over a low heat until the sauce looks foamy. Add the lemon juice and continue whisking then pour in the water a little at a time, whisking continuously until the sauce looks fluffy. Keep warm but do not let it get hot. Just before serving, add a tablespoon of hot water and give a good whisk.

Trick of the trade

Make some custard with Birds custard powder then stir in some lemon juice, whipped cream and the stiffly beaten white of egg.

COLD PUDDINGS
Choccy pots

SERVES 6–8

Whenever consulted about the pudding choice for a dinner party, there are those whose automatic reply will be 'choccy pots', no matter how rich the preceding courses. People will never believe how simple they are to make and, when I was showing my friend Catherine the other day, she nearly fell off her chair with amazement at how easy it was.

225 g/8 oz Menier bitter chocolate
2 heaped teaspoons instant coffee, dissolved in 1 dessertspoon boiling water
25 g/1 oz unsalted butter
4 egg yolks
dash of brandy or liqueur
4 egg whites

Break up the chocolate and put it into a pudding basin, with the coffee and boiling water. Set over a pan of hot water and stir until it has melted. Beat in the egg yolks, one by one, and then the butter (this gives it a lovely sheen). Add the brandy or liqueur. I have sometimes used home-made sloe or damson gin (see page 197) and mixed in a few of the stoned fruits. Transfer to a large bowl and allow to cool.

Whisk the whites of egg stiffly and fold in. Spoon into small pots or ramekins, and chill until required. Choccy pots also freeze well.

Serve with a blob of cream on top and hand round with Mrs M's Best-ever Shortbread, see page 171

Blackberry and apple jelly

F

SERVES 6

Jelly is somehow seen as dated and conjures up visions of the bright green and other luridly coloured 'wobblies' of children's parties. However, a really tart combination of wild fruit jelly such as blackberries and crab apples, makes a wonderful summer pudding or accompaniment to a richer dish such as 'Lemon stone' crème brûlée, (see page 158).

It's impossible to say how much fruit you need to start with, in order to produce 275 ml/₁/₂ pint of juice, as the yield will vary so much; you just have to experiment. Excess juice can be frozen. You can cheat, to some extent, by using some freshly pressed apple juice from a carton.

300 ml/¹/₂ pint blackberry juice
300 ml/¹/₂ pint apple juice
300 ml/¹/₂ pint water
sugar, to taste
1 sachet of gelatine or 2 sachets of Gelozone
1 Cox's apple, peeled and chopped

Cook the blackberries and apples in 150 ml/¹/₄ pint water, until all the juice has exuded. Strain through a sieve and press to obtain the required amount of liquid. (The fruit can be puréed and the juice frozen ahead of time.) Soak the gelatine in a little liquid and then dissolve it in a bowl over hot water; in sultry weather, you may have to use 1½ sachets of gelatine. Add to the juice and pour into a glass bowl. When just beginning to set, add the uncooked, chopped apple.

Serve with thick cream.

Damson mousse

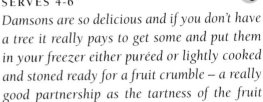

SERVES 4-6

Damsons are so delicious and if you don't have a tree it really pays to get some and put them in your freezer either puréed or lightly cooked and stoned ready for a fruit crumble – a really good partnership as the tartness of the fruit goes well with the sweetness of the topping.

300 ml/¹/₂ pint unsweetened damson purée
150 ml/¹/₄ pint cream
1 egg white
50 g/2 oz sugar
a sachet of gelatine or 2 sachets of Gelozone

Whip the egg white until stiff then add the sugar a spoonful at a time until it looks thick and glossy. Soak the gelatine in the water and dissolve over a pan of hot but not boiling water. Allow to cool then mix into the purée. Fold in the whipped cream and lastly the whipped white of egg. Spoon into ramekins and refrigerate. If you have unthawed some frozen damson purée it really is a 'QUICKIE' as all you have to do is to whip the cream and white of egg and dissolve the gelatine. Double the quantities if you want to make it in a large soufflé dish.

Serve with Swift and Speedy Sponge Cake (see page 168).

Jeanette's apple tart

SERVES 6–8

Jeanette was cook to an old friend of mine, who lived in a mouldering château in Brittany. Unfortunately, Jeanette was often drunk on the local 'Alembique' or Breton Calvados, but, when she was sober, her apple tart was ambrosial. When I finally winkled the recipe out of her, she astonished me by saying that one of the ingredients in her pastry was hard-boiled egg yolk. It is virtually impossible to roll out because there is no liquid to bind it together, so you have to press it into the flan dish with the knuckles of your hand and work it until it covers the dish.

JEANETTE'S PASTRY

225 g/8 oz plain flour

pinch of salt

75 g/3 oz granulated sugar

150 g/5 oz unsalted butter, cut in small pieces

2 hard-boiled egg yolks, sieved

MARMELADE DE POMMES

1 kg g/2 lb cooking apples, peeled and cored

1 tablespoon water

25 g/1 oz butter

150 g/6 oz sugar

TOPPING

2–3 large cooking apples, peeled and cored

1 tablespoon water

Sieve the flour and salt into the food processor, add the sugar, the butter and the egg yolks and process until it forms a ball.

Butter a 20 cm/8 in flan dish and sprinkle it with flour. Place the ball of pastry in the centre and gradually work it towards the sides, with the knuckles of your hand. Refrigerate for 1 hour.

Pre-heat the oven to 190°C/375°F/ gas mark 5. Prick the bottom of the pastry with a fork, line it with foil or greaseproof paper and fill with rice or baking beans. Bake for 6 minutes. Then remove the foil and beans and cook for a further 10–15 minutes. Take out and cool. Turn the oven up to 200°C/400°F/ gas mark 6.

To make the *marmelade de pommes*: cook the apples, water and butter in a saucepan with a tightly fitting lid until soft. Add the sugar and continue cooking over a very low heat, stirring constantly, until it begins to smell of toffee and look golden and caramelised. Allow to cool. Spread the filling over the base of the flan.

To make the topping: halve the apple, cut in wafer-thin slices and lay in concentric circles over the top of the marmelade, until it is completely covered. Bake, for about 10 minutes or until the apples are just beginning to turn brown; be careful the pastry does not burn.

Melt the redcurrant jelly or the jam in the water and brush the apples with this glaze.

Serve cold, with crème fraîche.

COLD PUDDINGS

COLD PUDDINGS

'Lemon stone' crème brûlée

SERVES 6–8

A Victorian version of this old Lancastrian recipe states that the cream should be poured into the bowl from the top of a pair of kitchen steps and I always imagine the poor kitchen maid assigned to this task wondering if she was going to miss the target. Be that as it may, this is one of the quickest and most effective recipes imaginable and it always works! To achieve the end result, it is not necessary to resort to a step-ladder; just put the bowl in the sink and pour from as high as you dare. I have taken to flavouring it with elderflower cordial (see page 191). it is widely available in supermarkets. For a really stunning effect, I usually serve this in 6 cm/2½ in diameter ramekins, accompanied by Blackberry and apple jelly (see page 156), setting both ramekins on white plates and, if it is the season, decorated with sprigs of elderflower. It is best to use cream which is nearly out of date, as it seems to set better. No idea why it's called 'Lemon Stone'.

600 ml/1 pint double cream
2 lemons
2 tablespoons white sugar
1 dessertspoon elderflower cordial (optional)
demerara sugar

Squeeze the lemon juice into a bowl and place in the sink. Bring the cream to the boil and, as it starts to come up the sides of the saucepan, pour it in a thin stream on to the juice. Add the white sugar and elderflower cordial and stir until dissolved. Pour into the ramekins, allow to cool and then refrigerate overnight.

A couple of hours before you are going to serve them, turn the grill to high. Smooth 1–2 teaspoons of demerara sugar over each ramekin and, when the grill is red hot, place them on a grill pan or similar and hold or set them as near the heat as possible. When the sugar starts to bubble and caramelise remove, cool and refrigerate. Watch like a hawk or they will burn. You can freeze crème brûlées; take them out an hour before you are going to eat them and the caramel will still be crisp. They are equally good without the topping. Made without the elderflower cordial they are perfect with wild strawberries or raspberries.

Summer pudding

SERVES 6–8

This is a wonderful standby for a summer lunch and has the added advantage that it can be frozen.

1 kg/2 lb blackcurrants, redcurrants, raspberries, strawberries and/or cherries
caster sugar
8–10 white bread slices (not steam-baked), crusts cut off

Line a 900g/2 lb loaf tin or large pudding basin with cling film and then oil it lightly. Line with slices of bread. Cook the fruit gently, with sugar to taste. Spoon half into the container and then add a layer of bread and continue with fruit, until full. Put on a final layer of bread and spoon over any remaining juice. Cover with cling film or foil and then weight down. Another 900g / 2 lb loaf tin, with some weights or tins in it, is ideal. Leave overnight.

Any juice which runs over can be used as a sauce. Serve with single cream.

Trick of the trade

If you use a 900g/2 lb loaf tin you can then freeze it. Make sure you oil it and then line with cling-film so that once frozen you can turn it out of the tin with no trouble. This also means that you don't have to mess about making the bread wedges fit a pudding basin, a most fiddly job. Another bonus is that you don't have the worry of wondering if the pudding is going to collapse when you turn it out.

When frozen you can cut the pudding in slices with a heated carving knife and wrap individual portions to store in the freezer. I make several puddings at the appropriate season, to savour during the winter.

Treacle tart

SERVES 4–6

Why, you may well ask, am I giving a recipe for something like treacle tart? Well, the answer is that the home-made variety is about as different from the bought variety as chalk is from cheese. Melting pastry, with a squidgy treacle, lemon and breadcrumb filling, is hard to beat and the fact that there is never a crumb left is evidence that this old favourite is still a winner.

PASTRY

175 g/6 oz plain flour

pinch of salt

110 g/4 oz cold butter, cut in small pieces

1 egg, beaten with 2 tablespoons water

FILLING

75 g/3 oz fresh breadcrumbs

6–8 tablespoons golden syrup

squeeze of lemon juice

Sieve the flour and salt into the food processor and drop in the butter. Switch on and process for 15 seconds. Add 1–2 tablespoons of the egg and blend until it forms a ball. Wrap in cling film and refrigerate for 30 minutes.

Pre-heat the oven to 200°C/400°F/gas mark 6. Butter a 20 cm/8 in flan dish. Roll out the pastry thinly and use it to line the flan dish. Trim the edges; roll out the trimmings and reserve.

For the filling: fill with the breadcrumbs and spoon on the syrup. Squeeze over the lemon juice.

Brush the edges of the tart with the remaining beaten egg. Cut the rolled out trimmings into lengths and place them, crisscross, on the tart. Brush with more egg and bake for 10 minutes; then reduce the oven to 180°C/350°F/gas mark 4 for a further 15–20 minutes.

Serve warm, with cream, (clotted, double or crème fraîche and calories be damned!)

Trick of the trade

Keep dipping the syrup spoon in boiling water, so that the syrup falls off easily.

COLD PUDDINGS

ICE CREAM AND SORBETS

Raspberry chranachan ice cream

SERVES 6–8

This is a very attractive sweet and even though it is made with cream it makes a nice ending to a rich meal. If you are able to gather some wild raspberries, use these instead of cultivated ones.

4 egg yolks
75 g/3 oz caster sugar
600 ml/1 pint single cream
1 tablespoon whisky
4 round coarse oatcakes
raspberries

To make the ice cream: beat the egg yolks, with the sugar, in a bowl over hot water, until light and fluffy. Bring the cream and whisky to the boil then pour the cream on to the egg and sugar mixture. Stir over the hot water until it thickens and coats the back of a spoon. Pour into a container, cover with cling film, leave to cool then refrigerate.

Place in the freezer and scrape the sides down every half-hour or so, until nearly set.

Crumble the oatcakes into coarse crumbs and crisp in the oven. When cold fold into the almost-frozen ice cream together with some raspberries and then leave to 'mature' in the freezer for 24 hours. If you have an ice-cream maker, follow the same procedure and then combine them in the ice-cream maker and freeze, following the manufacturer's instructions.

Decorate with a few raspberries and just before serving just sprinkle a few bits of oatcake on top.

Trick of the trade

If you are in a hurry or can't be bothered to make the ice cream, just use a top quality Cornish or vanilla ice cream and allow to soften slightly before stirring in the whisky and folding in the oatcakes and raspberries.

ICE CREAM

Apple sorbet or 'le trou normand'

SERVES 6–8

In Normandy, after eating something rich, such as tripes á la mode de Caen, you are given an apple sorbet with Calvados, which is supposed to dig a big enough 'hole' in the digestive system to cope with further gastronomic delights. However, it can equally well be used as a delectable ending to a heavy meal. It is as well to provide a spoon into which your guests can pour their libation, otherwise they may slurp so much that it does not go round; anyway, too great a quantity will melt the sorbet.

700 g/1½ lb Granny Smith apples, peeled and cored
600 ml/1 pint water
225 g/8 oz sugar
juice of ½ lemon
1 tablespoon stiffly whisked egg white
Calvados, to serve

Bring the water and sugar slowly to the boil, stirring until the sugar has dissolved. Then boil fast, without stirring, for 5 minutes. Cool, add the lemon juice then refrigerate.

Chop the apples roughly and put them in a food processor, with the syrup. Blend in sharp bursts, until the mixture is the consistency of porridge (not too smooth, but still with some texture). Place in a bowl in the freezer and, when it is nearly set, beat well and add the egg white; cover and leave until frozen.

Serve in glasses and hand round Calvados and a small ladle or spoon.

Iced elderberry soufflé

SERVES 8–10

An ice cream that cannot fail, never goes splintery and needs no stirring: what more could you want? You can use any fruit such as strawberries or raspberries but blackberries, elderberries, gooseberries or quince should be cooked in a minimum of water before puréeing. Pippy fruits should also be sieved.

300 ml/½ pint sieved elderberry purée
1 tablespoon lemon juice
300 ml/½ pint double cream
150 ml/¼ pint single cream
3 egg whites
175 g/6 oz caster sugar

Add the lemon juice to the purée. Whip the two creams together into soft peaks and fold into the fruit purée. Whisk the egg whites until they are really stiff; then add the sugar, a tablespoon at a time and continue whisking until the mixture is thick. Fold into the fruit and cream, spoon into a soufflé dish and freeze until firm. Take out of the freezer 1 hour before you are going to eat it. I have occasionally left it too late, the result being that my guests needed an ice pick and not a spoon to eat it! Serve with amaretti biscuits.

ICE CREAM

Blackcurrant leaf or elderflower sorbet

SERVES 6–8

Another refreshing and tangy sorbet, this will tempt the jaded appetite in hot and sultry weather. If you don't grow blackcurrants yourself, beg some leaves from a friend who does, or pick a few on your next visit to a pick-your-own fruit farm. Be provident and make a surplus to store in your freezer, as this is something which you will not find out of season. The same goes for elderflowers so that, in the depths of winter, you can remind yourself of those leafy lanes where the scent nearly knocked you back as you picked basketsful of the creamy flowers. If you are not able to pick fresh elderflowers, use 2–3 tablespoons of elderflower cordial.

1 handful (about 50 g/2 oz) young black-currant leaves or 2 fresh elderflower heads or 2–3 tablespoons elderflower cordial (see page 191)

600 ml/1 pint water

225 g/8 oz sugar

300 ml/½ pint lemon juice

2 egg whites

blackcurrant leaf sprigs, to decorate

To make the syrup, bring the water and sugar to the boil slowly, stirring to dissolve the sugar. Then boil fast for 5 minutes, without stirring. Pour on to the blackcurrant leaves or elderflower heads or cordial. Cover and leave to get cold. Strain and add the lemon juice. Pour the liquid into the container, place in the freezer and stir from time to time, until it thickens to the consistency of thick mayonnaise. Whisk the egg whites to stiff peaks. Add the whites to the frozen mixture, stir well and leave for 15 minutes.

Beat furiously with a hand- or electric-beater until very smooth. Return to the freezer until firm.

Take out before the first course, scoop out and serve in individual glasses, with a sprig of blackcurrant leaf on each.

ICE CREAM

Tangerine sorbet

SERVES 12

A glass bowl piled with whole tangerines filled with sorbet looks absolutely stunning, as does a large platter with the frosted fruits piled in a pyramid and decorated with fresh bay leaves. It is not nearly so difficult to make as you might imagine, especially if you use real tangerines, as the skin is looser and it is easier to winkle out the segments. The pips don't matter, as you only use the juice.

12 tangerines or similar citrus fruit
300 ml/½ pint tangerine juice
juice of 2 lemons
600 ml/1 pint water
225 g/8 oz sugar
2 egg whites
12 bay leaves

Cut 'hats' off the top of the tangerines and then scoop out the flesh. Freeze the tangerine 'cases' and 'hats' on a tray in the freezer. Process the tangerine segments and strain the juice, through a sieve. Add the lemon juice and, if necessary, some orange juice or water to make up the quantity to 275 ml/½ pint. Bring the water and sugar to the boil slowly, stirring to dissolve the sugar. Then boil fast, without stirring, for 5 minutes. Mix with the tangerine-juice mixture in a bowl and allow to cool. Transfer to the freezer and stir often until it thickens to the consistency of thick mayonnaise.

Whisk the egg whites to stiff peaks. Fold into the tangerine mixture and leave for 15 minutes. Beat furiously with a hand-held whisk or electric beater until very smooth. Spoon into the tangerine 'cases', cover with the 'hats' and stick a bay leaf in each one. Freeze until hard.

This makes a lovely ending to a rich Christmas dinner.

ICE CREAM

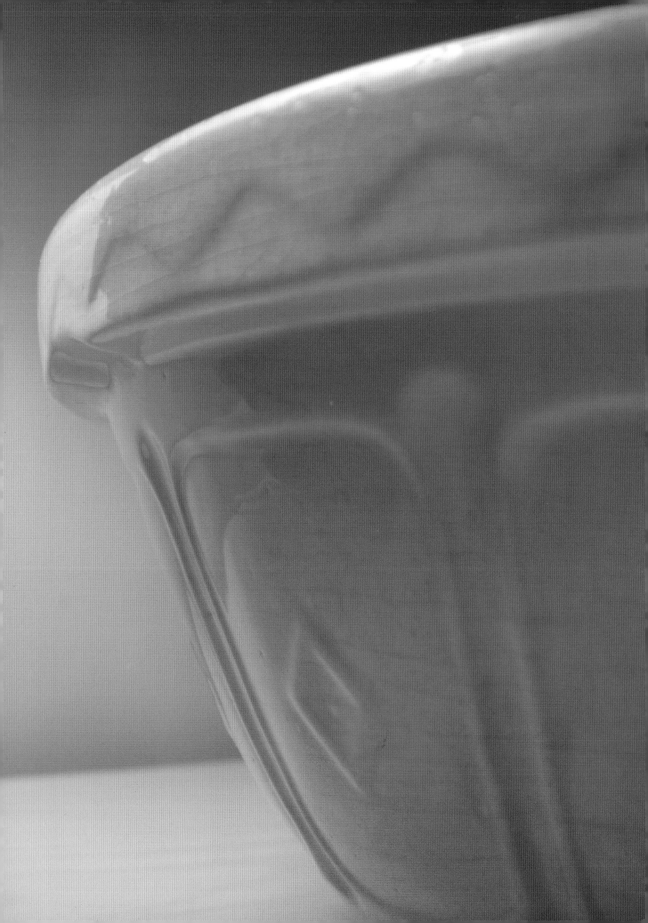

BREAD, CAKES AND BISCUITS

MAKING your own bread is one of the most therapeutic things imaginable and it is really so easy that even the busiest person can do it, especially since easy-blend dried yeast became available. The only problem is that the smell is so good, and the taste is so different from the 'plastic' sliced loaf, that it encourages calorific binges. You don't even need a loaf tin, a baking sheet will do and you can have lovely experiments with sun-dried tomato or olive topping and make a kind of ciabatta. Before the Second World War, in remote rural areas, farmers still took their wheat to the local miller to be ground and a stock of flour would be kept to last the whole winter, when farms and cottages would sometimes be cut off for weeks at a time.

It is sad that the habit of afternoon tea is slowly dying out. Not so long ago, if you called on anyone in the country you would be offered a slice of home-made cake or biscuits and, sometimes, if you were lucky, a delicious aroma would assail your nostrils and you would be the beneficiary of the weekly bake. Most country people liked to have their own chickens, so there were always eggs for baking, and even in towns there were many little backyards which boasted a hen house and pen with a few chickens scratching about. But even if teatime is nearly a thing of the past, the bread, scones, cakes and biscuits you make will all be greeted with joy. Home baking really cannot be beaten.

Hugh's quick olive oil bread

When my new kitchen was being installed, I got talking to the fitter, who said he had invented a quick and healthy bread recipe. Including the rising time, it takes 1¾ hours from start to finish and it is truly delicious. You can use dried, 'easy-blend' or fresh yeast. The following is made with 'easy-blend' but I have also given the method for using fresh yeast. If you want to be more traditional, you can let the dough rise twice, which gives a more aerated loaf, but this is not strictly necessary.

| 700 g/1½ lb strong white flour |
| 1 teaspoon salt |
| 2 tablespoons olive oil |
| 1 sachet of easy-blend dried yeast |
| 300 ml/½ pint hand-hot water |
| 1 dessertspoon honey |

Sieve the flour and salt into the food processor, sprinkle in the dried easy-blend yeast, and pour in the oil. Blend with a dough hook for a few seconds. Add the water and honey, and blend until it has stopped being sticky. You may have to do this in two batches, if the machine sounds laboured. (Otherwise, mix in a bowl.) Take out, place on a floured board and knead with the knuckles of your hand for a few minutes. Knead and pull into a rectangle, fold each end to the middle, turn over and place on a greased baking sheet. Leave to rise in a warm place, until doubled in bulk. Pre-heat the oven to 200°C/400°F/gas mark 6.

Bake the loaf for 30–35 minutes. It should sound hollow when tapped. Leave to cool on a wire rack and then restrain the ravening hordes who will try to eat it at one sitting!

Variation: Paint the loaf with basil or herb oil (see page 146) before it has 'risen', press in some pieces of sun-dried tomatoes in oil, or halved olives and sprinkle with coarse salt.

Traditional loaf: Use the same ingredients as above but replace the easy-blend yeast with 25 g/1 oz of fresh yeast. You will have to suss out a baker who bakes on the premises, or a health-food shop.

Mix the yeast with the honey and a little hand-hot water and leave in a warm place until it bubbles and foams. Add to the flour and salt, with the rest of the water and proceed as in previous recipe.

When you have kneaded it, put it back in a bowl, cover with a cloth and leave until it has doubled in bulk. Punch it down, knead for a few minutes, divide in half and knead each piece into a rectangle.

Fold each end over to the middle, turn over and place in two greased 450 g/1 lb loaf tins. Cover the tins with a cloth and leave in a warm place to double in bulk; then cook as above.

Soda bread

This has the advantage that you don't have to wait for it to rise and it is so good that you will probably want to make a weekly batch. Should you make some for your local fête or charity sale, be prepared for a stampede of fellow helpers before the official opening as both this and home-made yeast bread just vanish, and you will be lucky to have any to sell to the public. It improves with keeping, freezes well and is ideal if you run out of bread in your rented holiday cottage, as it can be cooked on an AGA hot-plate or in a heavy-based frying-pan.

625 g/1 lb 6 oz wholemeal flour

275 g/10 oz strong white flour

50 g/2 oz oatmeal

2 teaspoons salt

2 teaspoons bicarbonate soda

4 teaspoons cream of tartar

2 teaspoons sugar

900 ml/1½ pints milk and water mixed, or all semi-skimmed or skimmed milk

Pre-heat the oven to 180°C/350°F/gas mark 4. Sift all the dry ingredients into a large bowl and add enough liquid to make a soft dough. Turn on to a floured surface, shape into a large round and score into 4 with a sharp knife. Place on a greased baking sheet and bake for 20–30 minutes. It is done if it sounds hollow when tapped.

Variation: Add a handful of dried fruit, dried bilberries or cranberries on their own or combined with nuts, sesame or poppy seeds.

Nannie's scones

Archie's old nanny was a pretty hopeless cook, but, being Scottish, she was a superb baker. Her scones were always a dream, even though she never weighed anything.   One day, to her consternation, I pinned her down and we weighed everything out. The following recipe should produce exquisitely light scones that melt in the mouth, and, when eaten with clotted or whipped cream and uncooked raspberry jam (see p 178), are as near heaven as makes no odds.

225 g/8 oz self-raising flour

½ teaspoon each bicarbonate of soda and cream of tartar

pinch of salt

milk and yoghurt, to mix

Pre-heat oven to 200°C/400°F/Gas Mark 6. Sift dry ingredients into a bowl and mix to a soft dough with the milk and yogurt, or better still sour milk. Pat out gently on a floured board and cut into 7.5 cm/3 inch rounds and bake for 12 – 15 minutes, until risen and golden.

Swift and speedy sponge cake

I don't go along with all the effort of creaming together the butter and sugar, for if you have a food processor all you have to do is stick the ingredients in, switch on, whizz for 15 seconds or so and 'Hey! Presto!' there you are. Of course if you are making a true sponge with whipped white of egg, you have to adhere to the time-honoured rules. However this is another story and all you have to remember is 666 and 3 or 444 and 2: in other words, equal quantities of flour, sugar and butter and half that in eggs. I am afraid that means imperial measures, so for once I have given the imperial measures first and the metric equivalent last!

6 oz/175 g self-raising flour
1 teaspoon baking powder
6 oz/175 g caster sugar
6 oz/175 g softened butter or margarine
3 large eggs
1 pot jam of your choice

Place the flour, baking powder and sugar in the food processor and whizz for a few seconds. This saves all the messy hassle of sieving. Put in the butter or soft margarine, switch on and break in the eggs. Process for 15 – 20 seconds then switch off. Spoon into two well greased 18 cm/7inch cake tins and place in a pre-heated oven set at 175°C/350°F/Gas Mark 4 for 20 to 25 minutes. They should be firm to the touch. Turn out onto a wire rack and spread thickly with the jam of your choice. Dust with icing sugar. For a special occasion you can fill with whipped cream and strawberries, in fact it is the ideal vehicle for those wild strawberries.

Carrot cake

Once this cake is offered to guests, take no heed of 'just a small slice' for the long and short of it is that surreptitious 'large slices' will be guzzled down when your back is turned. Instead of ground ginger I have used grated fresh ginger and also coriander as this goes so well with carrot.

100 g/4 oz wholemeal flour
2 teaspoons bicarbonate of soda
1 teaspoon salt
225 g/8 oz demerara sugar
1 teaspoon ground cinnamon
1 teaspoon grated fresh ginger
1 teaspoon grated orange zest
1 teaspoon ground coriander seeds
175 ml/6 oz sunflower oil
175 g/6 oz grated carrot
2 eggs
50 g/2 oz chopped walnuts

FOR THE TOPPING
225 g/8 oz icing sugar
75 g/3 oz Philadelphia cream cheese
grated orange zest
orange juice

Place all the ingredients in a food processor and process for a few seconds until it is mixed then stir in the nuts by hand. Spoon into a 1.2 litre/2 pint cake tin and cook in a pre-heated oven at 180°C/350°F/Gas Mark 4 for 1 hour.

When cold, spread over the cream cheese topping. You can use grated lemon zest and juice instead of the orange and it will be equally delicious.

Keeper's cake

My friend, Jenny, was given this recipe by a game-keeper's wife. It is so popular that she has to make double the quantity and has learned from bitter experience not to leave it unattended in her kitchen or it vanishes into thin air, or, in other words, into her farmer husband's tummy. For some unknown reason, it is much better made with margarine than butter.

450 g/1 lb self-raising flour
pinch of salt
225 g/8 oz hard margarine, cut in little pieces
110 g/4 oz caster sugar
225 g/8 oz sultanas
2 eggs, well beaten
200 ml/7 fl oz milk

Pre-heat the oven to 180°C/350°F/gas mark 4. Sieve the flour and salt into a food processor, add the margarine, and give the mixture a few short bursts, until it resembles breadcrumbs (or put everything in a bowl and rub the fat in). Tip into a large mixing bowl, stir in the sugar and sultanas and then mix in the eggs and enough milk to give the consistency of a scone mix. Spoon it into a greased 23 cm/9 in square baking tin and bake for 45 minutes or until golden brown.

Cool on a wire rack, cut in half, eat one lot and freeze the other – that is, if your family and friends allow!

Raisin, rum and nut cake

This is as far away from a stodgy fruit cake as you can get and it is so light and delicious that you could almost serve it as a pudding. If you don't like rum, you can always use whisky instead.

175 g/6 oz raisins
75 ml/3 fl oz rum
175 g/6 oz butter
175 g/6 oz sugar
3 eggs, separated
175 g/6 oz self-raising flour
1 teaspoon grated lemon zest

FILLING
110 g/4 oz icing sugar
50 g/2 oz butter, softened
1 teaspoon grated lemon zest
25 g/1 oz walnut pieces
dash of rum

Pre-heat the oven to 180°C/350°F/gas mark 4. Soak the raisins in the rum overnight; then strain. Cream together the butter and sugar, until light and fluffy. Break in the egg yolks, one by one, and beat well. Fold in the raisins, half the flour and the strained rum. Beat the egg whites until stiff and fold in, with the remaining flour. Turn into a buttered 18 cm/7 in cake tin and bake for 1 hour. Turn out on to a wire rack to cool.

To make the filling: beat together the icing sugar and butter, until light and creamy. Add the lemon zest, walnuts and enough rum to flavour. Split the cake in half, spread with the filling and then sprinkle with icing sugar.

Spiced apple cake

If you have a glut of apples, this cake is one way of using them up. It is ideal for packed lunches or picnics, improves with keeping and freezes well. Served straight out of the oven, with custard or cream, it becomes a 'Piggy Pudding' so all in all, it is a must for your culinary repertoire.

450 g/1 lb cooking apples, peeled, cored and chopped
225 g/8 oz sultanas
150 ml/¼ pint milk
175 g/ 6 oz brown sugar
350 g/12 oz self-raising flour
2 teaspoons ground cinnamon
175 g/6 oz margarine, melted
1 egg, well beaten
25 g/1 oz demerara sugar

Pre-heat the oven to 170°C/325°F/gas mark 3. Mix together the apples, sultanas, milk and sugar. Sieve together the flour and cinnamon and then add the melted margarine, the fruit mixture and, finally, the egg. Stir well to combine thoroughly. Spoon into a greased square cake tin lined with greaseproof paper. Sprinkle with demerara sugar and bake for 1½ hours, until risen and golden brown.

Sophy's chocolate cake

Before the war, Sophy and her husband had lived in great grandeur in a big castle in Eastern Poland. After being liberated from Ravensbruck, she had to push her ailing aunt in a wheelbarrow for days on end until she reached friends. All she brought with her was the following recipe, which, she said, often filled her dreams in those hunger-ridden days. Like raisin, rum and nut cake (see page 169), you can use it as a pudding.

150 g/5 oz plain flour
1 teaspoon each baking powder and bicarbonate of soda
2 tablespoons cocoa
150 g/5 oz margarine
110 g/4 oz sugar
3 eggs, well beaten

FILLING
raspberry jam

TOPPING
2–3 tablespoons cocoa
granulated sugar
single cream

Pre-heat oven to 180°C/350°F/gas mark 4. Sieve together the flour, baking powder, bicarbonate of soda and cocoa. Cream the margarine and sugar together, until light and fluffy. Sprinkle in the flour a tablespoonful at a time. Or put everything in the food processor and blend for 15-20 seconds. Spread evenly over a buttered and floured 20 cm/10 in tin (preferably non-stick). Bake for 20–25 minutes.

Leave for a few minutes; then turn out. Split in half and spread thickly with jam; this must be done whilst the cake is still hot. Sandwich together and leave to cool.

When quite cold, cover with a thick, spreading mixture of cocoa, sugar and cream and refrigerate.

Mrs M's best shortbread ever

MAKES ABOUT 18

For over twenty years, Mrs M was cook to Archie's cousin, Constance. Her shortbread was to die for and was the downfall of many an avowed non-tea-eater. Well into her nineties, Cousin Constance was an astounding trencherwoman, which must have been the reason she lived so long. She ate a full cooked breakfast, Ovaltine for elevenses, two-course lunch and cheese, full tea, frequently with hot buttered toast or crumpets and a two-course dinner. I always had to go into culinary retreat after I had been staying there.

175 g/6 oz plain flour
50 g/2 oz ground rice
50 g/2 oz caster sugar, plus extra, to decorate
110 g/4 oz butter, softened

Pre-heat the oven to 170°C/350°F/gas mark 3. Sieve the flour, ground rice and sugar into a bowl. Rub in the butter and knead together into a ball. Roll out on a floured board to 5 mm/¼ in thick and cut into biscuits – it should make approximately 18. Prick with a fork and place on a greased baking sheet. Bake for 35–40 minutes. Cool on a wire rack and dust with caster sugar.

Eat for tea or serve with fruit mousses or ice creams.

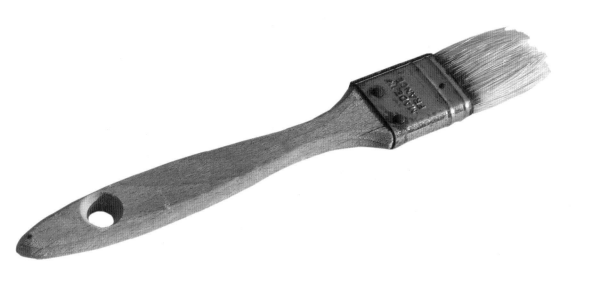

PRESERVES AND BOTTLING

I think that, in even the most modern-minded of us, there lurks a vestige of that atavistic instinct which is to hoard against a rainy day. However busy I may be with other things, the first sign of glut sends me into preserving mode. Nothing beats those rows of nicely labelled jars in your cupboard, and, every time you look at them, you feel a glow of self-righteousness. One particular delight, and for me the best, is to gather something wild. A walk along a bridle path bounded by blackthorn bushes, with their blue-black sloes, is like finding hidden treasure and, maybe, you will come across a gnarled crab apple tree whose crop has been scattered by a gale on the ground, shining like gold doubloons. This is the time to gather them, for you know they will be ripe. The heady smell of elderflowers and the winey aroma of blackberries make you want to go on picking more than you can possibly use, so the answer is jam or jelly. If you live in a town, even in the supermarkets there are times when certain fruits such as nectarines or pears are on offer and you can bottle them in an alcoholic syrup for exotic Christmas gifts; that is, if you can bear to part with them. Wild mushrooms can be threaded on string and dried, and French friends of mine who live in the country preserve game and fungi in bottles. Freezing is another option but, except for vegetables and some fruits, it somehow doesn't give me quite such a 'buzz'.

JELLIES

Jellies should be crystal clear when you hold them up to the light. That is, if you want to win a prize at the local flower show, but if they are a bit cloudy, it won't affect the taste. Kitchen shops or ironmongers should sell jelly bags, as will mail-order companies, such as Lakeland. However, a tea towel draped over a colander, or with each corner tied to an upturned kitchen stool, will do the trick quite well. For very small amounts, you can use a large saucepan but, if you are going to make jam or jelly on a regular basis, do invest in a good preserving pan, preferably with a ground base. This prevents the fruit from burning and sticking and the horrible sight of brown bits appearing as you pot up the jelly. The wide surface area helps to set the preserve, by fast reduction and dispersal of liquid by steam.

The setting agent, pectin, is present in varying quantities in all fruit. Apple, plum and quince have a high pectin content and can be used as a setting agent for fruits such as elderberry or blackberry. If desperate or unsure of yourself, use pectin-enhanced sugar or bottled commercial pectin, such as Certo.

Apple jelly, basic recipe

1.8 kg/4 lb crab, cooking or windfall apples
2.25 litres/4 pints water
granulated sugar

Wash the apples, remove any bad bits and cut up roughly. Do not peel or core. Put into a pan with the water and cook until mushy. Place in a jelly bag, hang over a bowl and leave to drip overnight. This is important, as it extracts all the magical pectin. Measure the liquid, pour into a pan and tip in 550 g/ 1¼ lb of sugar to each 570 ml/1 pint of liquid.

Place over a low heat and stir until all the sugar has dissolved; then turn up the heat and bring to a full rolling boil, periodically skimming off any scum. Place a metal plate in the freezer and, after 30 minutes, put a few drops of jelly on the plate.

When it cools, run your finger over it, and, if it wrinkles, the jelly is ready to pot up.

Warm your sterilised jam jars in a low oven and fill them right up to the top. Cover each one with a square of cling film, pulled over tightly. As the jelly cools, it will form a hollow, thus creating a vacuum which will prevent moulds entering, When quite cold, put on the screw tops and label clearly.

Elderberry and apple jelly

Elderberries are very low in pectin, so you need a high proportion of apple. They are also strongly flavoured, so a little goes a long way.

1.35 kg/3 lb apples

450 g/1 lb elderberries

sugar

Follow the method for Apple jelly, basic recipe, opposite, and cook the 2 fruits together.

Gooseberry and elderflower

Gooseberries and elderflower are a marriage made in heaven, of which this is the perfect example. The taste is delicate and much resembles a fine dessert wine.

1.8 kg/4 lb unripe gooseberries

1.75 litres/3 pints water

sugar

6–8 elderflower heads

Proceed as for Apple jelly, basic recipe, opposite. When the sugar has dissolved in the drained juice and has come to the boil, add the elderflower heads, tied up in some butter muslin. Remove when the setting point has been reached.

Redcurrant jelly

Good with lamb, venison or game. Spread over a joint before roasting and add to casseroles or gravy.

1.35 kg/3 lb redcurrants

425 ml/³/₄ pint water

sugar

Follow the method for Apple jelly, basic recipe, opposite.

Herb jellies

The most universal of these is mint jelly but you can make a number of variations, such as rosemary, parsley and bay leaf. Follow Apple jelly, basic recipe, opposite, but include 570 ml/1 pint of white-wine vinegar in the quantity of water. Stir in 2 tablespoons of your chopped fresh chosen herb when the setting point has been reached. Allow to cool slightly before potting. For the bay-leaf jelly, just insert 1 or 2 bay leaves in each jar of jelly.

Rowan and apple jelly

Rowanberries are very bitter if made into jelly on their own, so they need to be mixed with apple. This is delicious with rich game dishes and a spoonful in a casserole adds depth. Try to pick the berries at the end of the season, when they are really ripe: in England, this will be around the end of August or the beginning of September; in Scotland, it will be considerably later. You will know the right moment has arrived when the blackbirds start tucking in.

700 g/1½ lb ripe rowanberries
700 g/1½ lb crab or cooking apples
water
sugar

Put the fruit in a pan and cover with enough water so that it is just floating. Cook until soft and drip through a jelly bag or tea towel.

Measure the resulting juice and add 450 g/ 1lb sugar to each 570 ml/1 pint juice. Proceed as for Apple jelly, basic recipe, page 174.

Quince jelly

Quinces have a very high pectin content and a tangy taste. If you are short of them, just use what you have got and make up the quantity with apples. Follow the Apple jelly, basic recipe, on page 174, but include the juice of 2 lemons.

You can make a delicious paste with the strained pulp, from quince jelly, which is widely eaten in Spain with cheese and is called membrillo. You can use gooseberry pulp for the same purpose.

Membrillo

Push as much quince or gooseberry pulp as possible through a sieve and to each 450 g/ 1 lb add 450 g/ 1 lb sugar. Put the pan over a very low heat and stir constantly, to prevent it from sticking, until it becomes really thick and dark and a channel remains when you draw the spoon through it. Line a shallow tray with foil and pour in the mixture. When cold, cut into slabs, wrap in more foil and store in an airtight tin. Once opened, store in the fridge.

Membrillo goes well with cold meats and cheese. You can also cut it in little cubes, then dust with icing sugar. Packaged prettily, you can sell it at your charity fair or give away as Christmas presents.

JAMS

The method for making jam is the same as for jellies, except that you don't have to drip it through a tea towel or jelly bag. Some fruits that are low in pectin need the addition of lemon juice or plum juice to make them set and, if you are making plum jam and take out the stones, you must put them in butter muslin and boil them with the fruit. Under-ripe fruit will set better than that which is too ripe.

Plum jam

This is one of my favourites and I use it in cooking, especially to make plum sauce to go with Mick's hair drier duck (see page 90). This particular recipe is for Victoria or red plums, which can be halved and stoned. You can also use bullace (wild plums) or damsons, but it is impossible to stone these when they are uncooked, so you either have to pour the fruit into a sieve and laboriously pop out the stones before returning the pulp to the pan or skim off as many of the stones as possible when they come to the surface during cooking. In this case, warn your guests that they may break their teeth! However, the lovely, tangy jelly is well worth the risk.

1.8 kg/4 lb plums
150 ml/¼ pint water
1.3 kg/3 lb sugar

Halve the fruit and remove the stones. Crack some of these, take out the kernels and reserve. Tie the rest of the stones up in some muslin. Place the fruit in a preserving pan, with the water, and cook over a very low heat, stirring occasionally. Tip in the sugar and stir until it has dissolved. Add the kernels and bag of stones and bring to

a full rolling boil. Test for a set after 15–20 minutes. Remove the bag of stones and pot up into sterilised hot jars. Cover with cling film and put on screw tops when cold.

Strawberry jam

Strawberries don't have a lot of pectin so, if you want a stiffer jam, you will have to use some of the commercial variety. It is important to have slightly under-ripe fruit and it must be picked on a dry day. Often, pick-your-own fruit farms will sell fruits from their strawberry beds that are classed as jam fruits. This means that they are firmer and smaller as the crop is nearing the end of production. If possible, these are the ones to go for.

1.8 kg/4 lb strawberries
1.3 kg/3 lb sugar
juice of 2 lemons
10 g/½ oz unsalted butter

Crush a dozen or so strawberries, put them in the bottom of a preserving pan and cover with a layer of sugar. Continue with layers of fruit and sugar. Cover and leave overnight. Bring very slowly to the boil, stirring very gently to avoid breaking up the fruit. Add the lemon juice and boil fast for 10–15 minutes. Test for a set and, if not ready, continue for another 4–5 minutes, until a set is obtained. Add the butter, to disperse the scum, and allow to sit for 10 minutes, so that the fruit does not float to the top in the pots. Pour into sterilised, hot jars, cover with cling film and put on the screw tops when quite cold. Don't worry if it isn't very firm; overcooking takes away the colour and fresh flavour.

Uncooked raspberry jam

This is the freshest-tasting jam you will ever come across and avoids all the hassle of preserving pans and jam boiling over while you answer the telephone. The person who gave me the recipe said it would only last for 6 weeks before going mouldy but I have found it can last for up to a year and, if in doubt, you could always freeze it in small quantities. All you need are 2 bowls which will fit into your oven and equal quantities of sugar and raspberries. Heat the sugar and fruit in a very low oven set at 140°C/275°F/ gas mark 1, until they are really hot. Remove and mix both together. The sugar will dissolve easily and you will have a runny mass of fruit. Pour into sterilised, really hot jars, cover with cling film and, when cold, screw on the lids.

Seville orange marmalade

I think the following story shows the right kind of priority. During the war, I lived in London and, when there was an air raid, all the tenants trooped down to the cellar with their most treasured possessions. Two sisters lived on the top floor. One used to wear her mink coat but the other brought down 8 jars of home-made marmalade!

Even guests who normally only start the day with a bowl of cereal can't resist the smell of toast made from home-made bread and the sight of shiny slices of orange gleaming translucently against the light in a jar of marmalade. Under these circumstances, a pot doesn't last long. When I left my home in Hampshire, I discovered at least 150 jars of marmalade, jam and jelly in my cupboard. Providentially, there was a sale in aid of the local church. I bought some checked gingham, borrowed some pinking shears and made covers for all the pots. I took my kitchen trolly to the sale and arranged the jars on it with the light behind them. Every single one was sold and we raised nearly £100.

1 kg/2 lb Seville oranges
2.25 litres/4 pints water
1.8 kg/4 lb sugar
juice of 2 lemons

Squeeze the oranges and lemons and tie the pips in a piece of muslin. Cut the peel up by hand (tedious) or chop in the food processor. The latter will not give you slices but is quite good for everyday use. You can cut the squeezed oranges into 4 and then into 4 again and put them through the fine slicing attachment, which is what I do.

Put it in a preserving pan with the water, the bag of pips and the lemon juice. I include the peel from 1 of the lemons because I like the taste, but it is up to you whether you do the same. Bring slowly to the boil and cook, uncovered, until the peel is soft and it has reduced by half. Add the sugar and stir until it has dissolved. Bring to a full rolling boil. Continue until a set has been achieved, remove the bag of pips and squeeze out surplus juice. Pour into sterilised, hot jar, cover with cling film and put on the screw tops when cold.

Mighty muscovado marmalade: This is quite my favourite; it may not be to everyone's taste, as it is very strong, but I love it. Just follow the above recipe but, instead of using white sugar, use dark muscovado sugar, or demerara sugar and 1 tablespoon of black treacle if you don't fancy it quite so strong. A spoonful in a rich casserole is heavenly.

PRESERVES AND JAMS

CHUTNEY

Chutney is the English version of the Indian word chutna, which arrived in this country during the nineteenth century. In India, chutney is not generally cooked but is made with fresh ingredients and served as a side dish; in fact, it is more akin to a fresh relish. Chutneys are one of the countryman's ways of using up Nature's bounty and, for the old-time cottager or farmer's wife, were a means of 'lifting' boring cold meat out of the usual rut. You can make chutney out of almost anything, even runner beans, as you will see from one of the following recipes, provided that you use fruit, dried fruit, sugar, vinegar and spices and cook until the mixture looks really thick. A good rule of thumb as to quantities is 1.8 kg/4 lb of fruit and vegetables, 225 g/8 oz of dried fruit, and 900 ml/ 1½ pints of vinegar, with spices of your choice.

Apple and raisin chutney

This must be the easiest chutney in the world to make and, as the ingredients are available all the year round, you can just whip some up when the store-cupboard is empty. If you don't have raisins, just use sultanas or other dried fruit. You can also put in a few walnuts and some orange or lemon peel and vary the spices according to your whim.

1.3 kg/3 lb cooking apples, peeled and cored

110 g/4 oz onion, peeled and cut up

450 g/1 lb seedless raisins

600 ml/1 pint malt vinegar

450 g/1 lb muscovado sugar

2 teaspoons ground ginger

½ teaspoon ground cloves

1 teaspoon black peppercorns

2 teaspoons salt

Chop the apples, onion and raisins finely by hand or in the food processor or put through the mincing machine. Add the vinegar, sugar, spices and seasoning and cook in an uncovered pan, until thick. Spoon into sterlised heated jars, cover with cling film and put on lids when cold.

Marrow chutney

Gone are the days when every cottage garden would have a profusion of gigantic marrows, glowing in colours ranging from mottled green to cream and deepest orange. Many of these monsters were entered in the local flower show, but as a vegetable they had usually passed their 'sell-by' date and the only thing was to make them into chutney or even 'rum'. Country lore said you should hang the marrow up in a net (old tights would do), cut off the top, remove the seeds and fill with dark brown muscovado sugar. This would eventually drip through the uncut end into a bowl and the final alcoholic beverage would be bottled and drunk at Christmas time. To make the chutney, which is quite sweet, this is what you do.

1.3 kg/3 lb marrow, peeled de-seeded and cut up

675 g/1½ lb demerara sugar

2 teaspoons salt

225 g/8 oz cooking apples, peeled and cut up

225 g/8 oz onions or shallots, peeled and cut up

225 g/ 8 oz sultanas

900 ml/1½ pints malt vinegar

10 g/½ oz ground ginger

2 teaspoons mixed pickling spices, tied in muslin

Put everything in a large preserving pan and cook slowly, until thick and dark. Remove the bag of spices, pour into sterilised, heated jars and cover.

Red onion, apple and sage relish

This delicate relish goes really well with all game or with cold meats. The red onions and the red-wine vinegar give it a beautiful colour and the oil makes it translucent and shiny. It is important to use a firm-fleshed apple, such as Granny Smith, as you don't want to end up with a mush.

1 kg/2 lb red onions, peeled

450 g/1 lb Granny Smith apples, peeled

2 tablespoons olive oil

2 tablespoons sugar

pinch of salt

150 ml/¼ pint Sage vinegar (see page 144)

300 ml/½ pint red-wine vinegar

1 teaspoon chopped fresh sage leaves

1 teaspoon pink peppercorns

Cut the onion into thin rings and the apples into thin slices. Heat the oil in a saucepan and tip in the onions, apples, sugar and salt. Cook, covered, over a low heat, for about 1 hour, or until tender but not mushy. Add the two vinegars, and peppercorns and cook, uncovered, for an hour. Pot in the usual way.

Mrs Watkins' runner-bean chutney

Mrs Watkins, who kindly gave me this recipe, is a farmer's wife and lives on the Welsh Marches. When I first tasted it, I could not believe that it was made from runner beans, and it is a sure-fire winner whenever I serve it. The bean family are very annoying: one minute, there are not enough for one person, let alone two, and then you go away for the weekend and, lo and behold, there are enough for a whole regiment. There is a limit to the number you want to freeze, so make some into this delicious chutney.

1kg/2 lb runner beans, stringed and sliced

450 g/1 lb onions, peeled and chopped

450 g/1 lb demerara sugar

300 ml/1 pint spiced vinegar (see 183)

1 tablespoon cornflour

1 tablespoon mustard powder

1 tablespoon ground turmeric

1 teaspoon salt

1/2 teaspoon pepper

Cook the beans until tender and then drain. Combine with the onions, sugar and all but 2 tablespoons of the spiced vinegar in a saucepan and cook for 15 minutes.

Mix the dry ingredients to a smooth paste with the remaining vinegar, add to the saucepan and boil until thick. Pour into sterilised, heated jars, cover with cling film, and, when cold, put on screw tops.

Quince and red onion chutney

I know that not everyone has access to quinces but, if you can, do try and beg, borrow or steal some for this recipe. Even the fruits of the climbing shrub Chaenomeles japonica (flowering quince) will do or, failing all else, substitute apple for the quince and be really extravagant and add a small pot of quince jelly to the cooked mixture. It will be worth it.

1.3 kg/3 lb quinces, peeled and chopped

450 g/1 lb red onions, peeled and chopped

225 g/8 oz sultanas

1 kg/2 lb soft brown sugar

900 ml/1 1/2 pints red-wine vinegar

25 g/1 oz salt

2 cinnamon sticks or 1 dessertspoon ground cinnamon

1 teaspoon pink peppercorns

pinch of cayenne pepper

Simmer the quinces and onions in half the vinegar until soft. Add the remaining vinegar and the rest of the ingredients. Simmer until thick, about 1–1 1/2 hours. Spoon into sterilised, hot jars and cover with cling film. Screw on the tops when cold.

With nice labels, they make attractive Christmas presents. You should get about 1.8 kg/4 lb. If you want to make double the quantity and haven't enough quinces, use half quince and half apple.

Sophie's chutney

This is undoubtedly one of the best chutneys you will ever eat and, like good wine, it improves with age. Sophie was cook to Archie's cousin before the war and the recipe was handed on to his widow, the redoubtable cousin Constance, who did not believe in such things as 'sell-by' dates. In her latter years, visitors who had to fill in with the odd bit of cooking often found objects in the fridge covered in grey fur, because she could not bear to waste them. They had to be thrown away without her knowledge! This chutney was the exception and I have eaten a five-year old vintage which was really mellow. It certainly improves if kept for at least 6 months to a year.

1.3 kg/3 lb green tomatoes
1.3 kg/3 lb onions, peeled
1.8 kg/4 lb apples, peeled
450 g/1 lb sultanas
450 g/1 lb preserved ginger pieces
6 pieces of fresh root ginger, crushed
1.2 litres/2 pints malt vinegar
1.1 kg/2½ lb demerara sugar
1 teaspoon salt
1 teaspoon allspice berries
1 teaspoon peppercorns
2 dried red chillies

Chop the tomatoes, onions, apples, sultanas and stem ginger, either in the food processor or by hand. Add the vinegar and sugar and mix well. The recipe says tie up the spices in a bag but I think it is nicer not to do this, as the flavours permeate better. Boil gently for 4 hours, add the remaining sugar and boil for another 3 hours or until it looks almost black and is very thick. Heat sterilised jars and fill with the chutney. Cover with cling film and, when cold, put on the screw tops.

Basic spiced vinegar

1.2 litres/2 pints malt vinegar
25 g/1 oz pickling spice

Put the vinegar and spices in a saucepan, cover and bring slowly to the boil. Remove from heat and leave to get cold. Strain and pour into clean, sterilised bottles.

Basic sweet spiced vinegar

1.2 litres/2 pints distilled malt vinegar
25 g/1 oz mixed pickling spices
225 g/8 oz demerara sugar

Bring the vinegar and spices slowly to the boil and boil rapidly for 15 minutes. Strain and pour back into the pan, with the sugar. Stir until dissolved. Boil rapidly for a minute. Allow to cool. You can make double the quantity and put any surplus in bottles, to use when required.

Pickled spiced crab apples

This is best made with crab apples, but you can make it equally well with the ornamental garden varieties. The bright reds, deep maroons and golden yellows are very decorative, especially if you put them into tall jars, such as Libby's tomato-juice jars. Bullace plums can be treated in the same way.

crab apples

basic sweet spiced vinegar, made with 450 g/1lb demerara sugar

cinnamon sticks.

Pre-heat the oven to 150°C/300°F/gas mark 2. Make the spiced vinegar, see opposite, but using the greater quantity of sugar. Pack the crab apples into preserving jars, and put a lid on loosely. Stand on 2 or 3 thicknesses of newspaper and place in the oven until the fruit begins to split. Add a cinnamon stick to each jar and then pour on the boiling syrup. Cover when cold.

Tiny pickled beetroot in sweet spiced vinegar

If you grow them yourself, the beetroot to use for this are the thinnings. These are not much bigger than marbles and are really delicate in flavour. Otherwise, just use ordinary beetroot and cut them in chunks. Mammoth ones can be treated with a melon baller and the leftover flesh used in Beetroot and cranberry bortsch (see page 7).

beetroot

basic sweet spiced vinegar (see opposite)

Cook the beetroot in lightly salted, boiling water for 1½ hours or until tender. Rub off the skins and pack into preserving jars or ordinary jars with screw top lids. Cover with cold sweet spiced vinegar, and screw on the lids.

Pickled onions

For this recipe, use small pickling or white silverskin onions. I prefer a sweet pickle but you can, if you wish, make it with the Basic spiced vinegar (see page opposite). These are useful for casseroles, where the recipe calls for small whole onions.

pickling onions

salt

basic sweet spiced vinegar (see opposite), or basic spiced vinegar (opposite), made with white-wine vinegar

Peel off the outer skins and lay on a dish. Cover with salt and leave for 12 hours. Wipe dry and pack into jars. Pour on hot spiced vinegar and cover tightly.

Trick of the trade

Blanch peeled silverskin onions in salted, boiling water for 1 minute. Strain and spoon into small yoghurt tubs or similar. Pour over melted butter. When cold, freeze.

PRESERVES AND BOTTLING

BOTTLING

Before the advent of deep-freezes, the only way to preserve your surplus fruit and vegetables was either by drying or bottling. In old kitchens, you would see vast copper contraptions which would have gone on the kitchen range, containing many of 'Mr Fowler's' bottling jars filled with produce from vegetable garden or orchard. Nowadays, it is all too easy to just stick things in the freezer but I notice a trend for bottled fruits, expecially at Christmas time, when they are sold at inflated prices. Barring the actual outlay on the jars, you can do it yourself at a fraction of the cost. Certain fruits, such as pears, peaches and plums, don't freeze well but do lend themselves to this form of preservation. If you make a syrup with some kind of alcohol, they can then be used for dinner parties or as gifts.

There are 5 methods of bottling: slow water-bath; quick water-bath; pressure cooker; slow oven; moderate oven. The one that I use is the moderate oven method, which I find is best for pears, nectarines and plums. Soft fruits are best frozen. The only time I use the slow water-bath method is for Mauro's Marvellous Mixture (see page 186) and for fungi .

Pears in red-wine syrup

This takes care of the odds and ends of wine which seem to accumulate and the final result is a dinner-party pudding, the perfect follow-up to a rich main course. The moderate oven method is best for fruit, as covering it with syrup prevents discoloration.

pears
2–3 cloves per jar

SYRUP
225 g/8 oz sugar
600 ml/1 pint water, wine or wine and water

Pre-heat the oven to 170°C/325°F/gas mark 3.
To make the syrup: dissolve the sugar in the liquid and bring to the boil. Boil rapidly for 3 minutes **without stirring.**

Peel and halve the pears and remove the cores with a teaspoon or melon baller. Pack into heated jars, with the cloves, and pour in the boiling syrup to within 2.5 cm/1 in of the top. Put on the lid but not the clip or screw band. Line the base of a roasting tin with 3 or 4 thicknesses of newspaper and place in the oven for 60 – 70 minutes.

Remove from the oven, screw on the screw bands or fix the clips and leave until next day. As they cool, tighten the screw bands, if that is what you have used. You will probably hear a pop as the vacuum is formed. Test by undoing the clip or screwband and lift up a little way by the seal. If it doesn't come off, you have been successful.

Peaches in Madeira syrup: Follow the method for Pears in red-wine syrup, above, but use Madeira instead of red wine and insert a cinnamon stick in each jar.

Trick of the trade

To peel the peaches, just cover with boiling water for 1 minute and the skin will slip off easily. Halve the fruit and take out the stones.

Plums in white-wine syrup: Do not peel the plums but halve and stone them. Follow the method for pears in red-wine syrup, above, but put a small piece of dried root ginger in each jar.

Gooseberries in elderflower syrup: Top and tail the gooseberries. Follow the method for pears in red-wine syrup, above, but infuse 2–3 elderflower heads in the basic syrup. Remove the heads before pouring into the jars. Failing this, add 2 tablespoons of Elderflower Cordial (see page 191) or, if you have not made any yourself, use the bought variety.

Bottled fungi

Wild mushrooms, such as ceps or blewits, can be preserved in the same way but should be washed carefully beforehand and then boiled for 5 minutes in vinegar and water. The proportions should be two-thirds vinegar to one-third water, with plenty of salt. They should then be drained and packed into bottling jars, covered with olive oil and bottled by the water-bath method (see Mauro's marvellous mixture).

To freeze: Cook the fungi in a little butter and lemon juice beforehand.

To dry: Thread on to string and hang over

the AGA or in the airing cupboard. On a sunny day, they can be spread out on a tray; otherwise put them in a very low oven. Keep in airtight jars.

Mauro's marvellous mixture

My friend, Mauro Bregoli, once brought me a pot of this when he came to have lunch. It is 'ab fab' and I persuaded him to divulge how he made it. Indispensable in the store-cupboard, it can be used as a topping for pasta (see page 100), as a relish or on top of crisply baked bread, drizzled with oil and coarse salt, with or without goat's cheese. If it is to be used within a week, it can be refrigerated but, if you want to keep it, you have to bottle it by the water-bath method; for the odd jar, this is not difficult.

| 1 red pepper |
| 1 aubergine |
| 2 or more garlic cloves |
| best-quality olive oil |

Pre-heat the oven to 230°C/450°F/gas mark 8. Halve the pepper lengthways and remove the core and seeds. Wipe with oil and roast until the skin browns and begins to bubble. Remove from the oven and take off the skin. Chop into chunks and set aside.

Cut the aubergine into chunks and grill until golden. Pack the bits of pepper and aubergine and the garlic cloves into a 500 ml/18 fl oz preserving jar, cover with olive oil and close tightly. Place on folded newspaper in the bottom of a deep saucepan, place a saucer on top of the jar, with a weight on it, and fill the saucepan with cold water, which must come above the jar. Bring slowly to the boil and then simmer for 1½ hours. Remove and tighten the lid. When completely cold, test the seal, as for pears in red-wine syrup (see page 185).

Trick of the trade

To remove the skin of the roast pepper easily, put it in a plastic bag and leave for 10 minutes. The skin will then rub off without any trouble.

DRINKS

The word 'drinks' does not really evoke quite what I have in mind, which is an exultation and celebration, not to say a distillation, of the countryside. There is really virtually nothing that cannot be made into something alcoholic, from parsnips to runner beans and, of course, fruits. On many occasions, I have been offered a hospitable glass of home-made wine and have had to restrain my facial muscles from making a grimace of distaste but, at other times, the potion has been ambrosial. Liqueurs and drinks such as sloe gin are very easy to make and slurping down a glass on a gloomy winter's eve can evoke happier times, when you strolled up a hedgerow on a glowing autumn day to pick the ingredients. A glass of kir is that much more enjoyable for having been concocted from home-made blackcurrant cassis, which is a doddle to make and at a fraction the cost of a brand-named product.

A sultry summer's evening is lightened by a cool, refreshing glass of real lemonade or ginger beer. A sick child or invalid will perk up considerably after a draught of home-made lemon barley water. The great thing about all these beverages is that you know exactly what ingredients were used in making them and that they contain no additives. Remember that, as with ways of preserving perishable ingredients for long periods, it is vital to sterilise mixing containers and bottles and so on. Use sterilising tablets, such as Campden tablets, which are available from Home Brew shops, and scald utensils in boiling water, as necessary. The method for sterilising bottles is given in the recipe for lemon or elderflower cordial (see page 191).

NON-ALCHOHOLIC DRINKS

Elderflower champagne

I resolutely refuse to bow to edicts by the French champagne houses: as far as I am concerned, this has always been known as elderflower champagne and the old lady who gave me this recipe would never have called it by any other name. It is a seasonal, deliciously refreshing, non-alcoholic drink that has to be quaffed within a few days as it does not keep. This is no hardship! A word of warning: do be sure and wire on the tops. A fanatical wine-making friend of mine did not. He lived in a London flat and used to keep his fermenting jars and bottles in his wife's airing cupboard. One night there was an almighty explosion. They leapt out of bed thinking it was the IRA only to find that one of his bottles had burst. He got no 'brownie points' and had to foot the laundry bill.

6 or more elderflower heads
4.5 litres/8 pints water
700 g/1½ lb sugar
2 tablespoons cider vinegar
thinly pared zest and juice of 1 lemon

Sterilise a plastic container, such as a bucket. Steep the flower heads in the water, with the sugar, lemon zest, juice and vinegar, for 2 days. Fill 6–8 × 570 ml/1 pint sterilised bottles, leaving 2.5 cm/1in headroom. Screw on the tops and then secure them tightly with garden wire. After 10 days, take the wire off and unscrew very slightly each day. It should be ready to drink in 2 weeks. Serve ice-cold, in champagne glasses.

Lemon barley water

This is another refreshing drink and, if you have an invalid, it assuages the thirst and feeds at the same time. Once made, it should be refrigerated and used within 2 or 3 days.

juice and thinly pared zest of 2 lemons
2 tablespoons sugar
50 g/2 oz pearl barley
2.25 litres/4 pints water

Put the lemon juice, zest and sugar in a jug. Bring the barley and water to the boil and simmer for 10 minutes. Pour into the jug. Allow to get quite cold and then strain and use.

DRINKS

Ginger beer

This goes down well with young and old alike and makes a nice change to take on a picnic.

225 g/8 oz sugar

4.5 litres/8 pints water

1 tablespoon dried yeast

50 g/2 oz fresh root ginger, well bruised

juice and thinly pared zest of 1 lemon

extra sugar, for bottling

Thoroughly wash and sterilise a plastic container, such as a bucket, with sterilising tablets and do the same for 6 × 570 ml/1 pint bottles. Heat a little of the water but do not allow it to boil. Add the sugar and stir until dissolved; then pour into the container. Cool until tepid and then put in the yeast, ginger, lemon juice and zest and the rest of the water. Cover and stand in a warm place for a week. Strain the ginger beer. Pour into the bottles and screw the tops on tightly.

Drink after a week but be careful, when pouring, not to disturb the sediment at the bottom.

Elderflower cordial

This is quite the best elderflower cordial I have ever drunk and my friend Christine has kindly given me her recipe. On the dreariest winters day it brings back memories of hot summer days and the exquisite scent of the creamy elderflower.

2 kg/4¼ lbs sugar

2 lemons, sliced

30 elderflower heads, still warm from the sun

50 g/2 oz tartaric or citric acid

2 Campden sterilising tablets

2¼ litres/4 pints boiling water

Place all ingredients in a large bowl. Let the boiling water cool slightly then pour over and stir. You have to let it cool slightly as if you pour boiling water over the elderflowers they turn brown. Cover and leave for 6 days stirring twice daily. Strain twice through muslin. Bottle and store in a cool, dark cupboard. Makes 3½ litres. Dilute to taste. Tartaric acid Cnot to be confused with Cream of Tartar) and citric acid are obtainable rom Home Brew shops.

To sterilize bottles: Stand the filled bottles on a trivet or rack in a deep saucepan or preserving pan. Separate the bottles with cardboard, screw the tops on lightly and fill the pan with cold water, to come up to the level of the cordial. Bring slowly to boiling point, and then simmer for 20 minutes. Remove the bottles, tighten the caps, label and store in a cool, dry place.

If you don't want the faff of doing this, just wash the bottles well, then put a Campden tablet in each and a little hot water and swirl round before emptying.

If you are going to freeze the cordial, either use ice-cube trays or small plastic containers, such as yoghurt pots.

DRINKS

Spicy iced coffee

This is just the job for taking on an evening picnic, such as Glyndebourne, for those of your guests who have to eschew alcohol because they are driving (though you can, if you wish, add a soupçon of brandy). As a real 'quickie' for home consumption, you can make it with Camp coffee; I always keep a bottle handy in the fridge in the summer.

300 ml/½ pint extra-strong coffee

1 teaspoon cloves

1 cinnamon stick

1 dessertspoon demerara sugar

1 tablespoon brandy (optional)

milk or cream

Make the coffee with instant continental coffee granules. Stir in the sugar until it dissolves and then steep the spices for 5 minutes. Add the brandy, if using, strain, pour over ice and make up to the required strength with milk or milk and a drop of cream.

Variation: Instead of cloves and cinnamon, use crushed cardamon seeds.

ALCOHOLIC DRINKS

Blackberry whisky

This recipe was given to me by my plumber, a real countryman. I hate to think what happens when he is called out to repair a leaking pipe and sees an inviting blackberry bush on the way. This liqueur has often fooled my in-house tasting panels and, when asked to adjudicate between several brews, nine times out of ten it comes 'top of the pops'. In general, cooking blackberries seems to bring out the flavour, whilst raw ones can be a bit disappointing; marry them with whisky and sugar, however, and you have a winner. So pack a plastic bag when you wander along a leafy lane. You can, of course, use cultivated blackberries, but the wild ones do have the edge as regards flavour.

1.8 kg/4 lb blackberries

225 g/8 oz sugar

bottle of whisky

Place the fruit, sugar and whisky in a large, clean screw-top jar or plastic bottle (I sometimes use well washed 2-litre Coca Cola or lemonade bottles). Stand the bottle on a sunny windowsill and shake every 3 or 4 days, until the sugar has completely dissolved. Place in a dark cupboard for 3 months or so, until the whisky has turned a dark purple colour. Strain and bottle in sterilised bottles. Keep its whereabouts secret for as long as a year, if possible: it improves with age.

DRINKS

Breach orange vodka

MAKES 3 BOTTLES

We used to slurp this down at Breach Farm, the home of Joe, a dear neighbour, after lunch. It was so good that we drank far more than was good for us. Sadly, he has now moved north, so, Scots, beware! Joe, always thought big, so, when he gave me the recipe, it specified 4.5 litres/8 pints of vodka! I have cut it down to half, which makes 3 bottles.

4 Seville oranges
4 lemons
2.25 litres/4 pints vodka
700 g/1½ lb cane sugar

Peel the oranges and lemons very thinly, taking care not to leave any pith on the zest. Stick the zest into a 2.25- litre/4-pint jar (a wine-making jar, obtainable from Boots, is ideal). Add the sugar and vodka and cork tightly. Leave for at least 3 months in a dark cupboard, shaking occasionally to dissolve the sugar. Strain and pour into clean bottles.

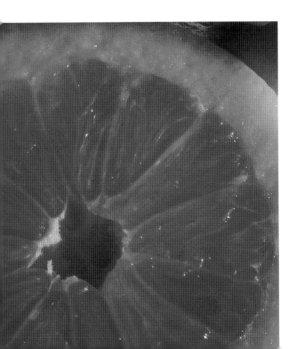

Cassis, or blackcurrant liqueur

This vital ingredient of 'kir', a cocktail of blackcurrant liqueur and white wine or kir Imperial, made with champagne or sparkling wine, is really easy to make. If possible, beg borrow or steal some young blackcurrant leaves, as the addition of these makes it taste really special.

1 kg/2 lb blackcurrants
10 blackcurrant leaves, well crushed
1.2 litres/2 pints vodka
700 g/1½ lb sugar
1 cinnamon stick
1 clove

Place the spices and the well-crushed blackcurrant leaves in the bottom of a bowl. Add the fruit and crush thoroughly. Pour in the vodka and mix well; then add the sugar and stir again. Put into a large, sterilised jar, screw on the top tightly and leave to infuse in a warm place, preferably in the sun, for a month.

Strain through a cloth and squeeze to extract all the juice. Filter through a jelly bag or through kitchen paper, laid over a colander; then put into sterilised bottles.

DRINKS

Elderflower wine

I have been most successful with this delicate of wines, which is relatively easy to make. Archie and I managed to bamboozle an old friend of ours, Ralph Cobbold, who was at the time managing director of Justerini and Brooks. We served the wine at dinner, with a napkin draped round the bottle, and asked him what he thought of it. After much snuffling and wine-taster's speak he said he thought it was a Frontignan dessert wine, but, on seeing our faces, realized he had been duped. Luckily, he took it all in good part, so much so that he took a bottle away and tried it out on the J and B partners; they too were taken in but were 'not amused'!

To make wine, you do need some basic equipment, such as a plastic bucket, a 4.5-litre/8-pint glass bottle (a demi-john), a funnel, a fermentation lock and a length of plastic tubing, all of which are obtainable from Home Brew shops.

---

600 ml/1 pint elderflowers
2 teaspoons wine yeast compound
150 ml/¼ pint tepid water
2 lemons
1.3 kg/3 lb sugar
4.5 litres/8 pints boiling water

Sterilise the plastic bucket, funnel and jars with sterilising tablets, according to the instructions on the packet. Prepare the yeast compound by mixing in the tepid water and pouring into a small bottle (I use an empty tonic-water bottle). Screw the cap on tightly, shake well, loosen cap and leave at room temperature for 6 hours.

Pick the elderflowers on a dry sunny day, snip the florets off with a pair of scissors, press them down into a 570 ml/1 pint jug and then empty into the sterilised bucket. Pare the lemons thinly and add the zest to the flowers, with the sugar. Pour on the boiling water and stir until the sugar has dissolved. Then add the juice of the 2 lemons and leave until it has reached 'blood heat', or when it feels tepid on the back of the hand. Now add the yeast, cover with a clean towel and leave for 3 days, stirring twice daily.

Strain the wine and pour through the funnel into the glass demi-john. Insert the fermentation lock, half-fill with water and leave the wine to ferment at room temperature until the air lock has stopped making rude sounds, about 6 weeks. Take out the airlock and siphon off the wine through the plastic tubing into the bucket. Place the glass bottle on a table, and insert the tubing so that an end hangs down lower than the level of the bottom of the jar. Contort yourself so that you can take a suck at the tube and, with any luck, the wine will then dribble into the bucket on the floor. When you have siphoned off all the wine, except the sediment, wash out the jar and pour back the wine. Cork tightly with a cork, which you have sterilised in boiling water for 10 minutes. Place in a cool, dark place until it has become clear and then pour into clean, sterilised bottles. Keep for a year or as long as willpower allows!

If you are making more than this, it is worth investing in a filter kit and fining crystals. All the technology is obtainable at Boots but I don't understand the intricacies of specific gravity so it is really up to you if you want to do it the hard way. In the beginning, I used to make it with baker's yeast on a piece of toast, the old cottager's way, and it seemed to work just as well.

Hot bullshot

SERVES 6–8

This is an excellent beverage to take to a sporting event, such as a rugger/football match or on a cold day's fishing or shooting. Served ice-cold, it makes a good cocktail.

1 carton tomato juice
1 tin beef consommé
squeeze of lemon juice
$\frac{1}{2}$ teaspoon oregano
$\frac{1}{2}$ teaspoon celery salt
Lea & Perrins Worcestershire Sauce, to taste
sloshes of vodka or sherry, to taste
(be generous!)

Mix the tomato juice and consommé and heat gently but do not boil. Add the seasonings and, lastly, the vodka or sherry. Put in a warmed thermos flask.

Lemon vodka

Jamie Illingworth's wife, Tania, who gave me this recipe, is Russian. Luckily, the first time Archie and I imbibed it at one of their dinner parties when we were staying with them. Had we been breathalysed, we should have been way over the limit. We consumed large quantities with the smoked-salmon first course and, as is the custom in Russia, each glassful was drunk in one go. They were, admittedly, small liqueur glasses, but they kept being re-filled and the vodka Tania had used was high strength Stolychnya.

Lemon vodka is very easy to make. Just pare 1 or 2 lemons very thinly, stuff the zest into a bottle of vodka, screw on the top and place in the freezer. It will be ready to drink in 2 days and should be kept in the deep-freeze.

It goes well with fishy first courses and, if you are lucky enough to be given some, caviar. Cream cheese and jellied consommé blended, put into ramekins and covered with lumpfish roe (fake caviar) goes very well with this potion.

Lucy's raspberry brandy

This creation of my daughter, Lucy, has the great advantage, unlike most home-made liqueurs, of being drinkable within a fortnight, though it is even better if kept. It is equally good made with loganberries or mulberries and the latter's unusual taste will certainly puzzle your guests.

2 small punnets of raspberries
225 g/8 oz sugar
bottle of brandy

Put the raspberries into a sterilised screw-top jar or a bottle large enough to take all the ingredients. If it is too small, the principle of Archimedes will apply and the juice will overflow. Add the sugar and brandy, stopper tightly and place in a dark cupboard. Turn upside-down every so often. Strain and bottle in sterilised bottles after 2 months, that is, if there is any left.

Use the fruit for an alcoholic ice cream or mousse.

DRINKS

Prue's hot Christmas punch

When the carol singers called at Christmas time, we always used to give them hot punch and mince pies. Amongst them was my friend, Gladys, who never normally touches a drop of alcohol. The evening was not complete unless we could send Glad on her way giggling and slightly unsteady on her feet. I may say she was not the only one to be affected by the cold night air.

2 bottles red cooking wine

1 wine glass brandy

juice of 2 lemons

juice of 2 oranges

1 cinnamon stick

1 apple, stuck with cloves

1 pinch grated nutmeg

sugar, to taste

slices of lemon or orange, to garnish

Heat everything up in a large saucepan *but do not allow to boil*. Allow to steep. The punch can be made the day before but, when, re-heating, I reiterate, do not allow to boil, as otherwise the alcohol will evaporate!

Quince brandy

This liqueur is one of the most delicate and delicious home-made liqueurs that I know and, of all the ones I make, it is my favourite. I realize that very few people have a quince tree but it is likely that someone in your neighbourhood has, so you can beg a couple of the exquisite, golden, pear-shaped fruits. In Spain, they are quite common and, in the rural outback, you will commonly see them hanging from the ceiling, beside peppers and strings of garlic. A quince tree – Cydonia oblonga 'Lusitanica', was one of the first things I planted in my previous home and every year it produced masses of fruit – it must have known how much I loved it!

4 large quinces

caster sugar

brandy

Rub the down off the quinces and rinse under the tap. Cut into chunks, without peeling or coring. Put into a well washed 1.2-litre/2-pint bottling jar or similar. Pour in sugar, to come one-third of the way up the jar, and fill with brandy. Place on a sunny window sill and shake every 3 or 4 days, until the sugar is dissolved.

Place in a cool, dark cupboard. Keep for as long as possible before straining into clean, sterilised bottles and try not to drink it too soon. If you become as hooked as I am you will have to double or even treble the quantity. On a hot summer evening, it is nice *frappé*, that is, poured over ice.

DRINKS

Sangría

Many is the time I have drunk this delicious drink at shooting lunches in Spain and even more copious quantities of '103' Spanish brandy and Cointreau in the evening. I often wondered how we managed to stagger out of bed at 6 o'clock the next morning.

| 1 bottle of Spanish red wine |
| juice of 1 lemon |
| juice of 2 oranges |
| 1 small sherry glass brandy |
| 1 small sherry glass Cointreau |
| sugar |

TO SERVE
| 500 ml bottle of soda water |
| ice cubes |
| slices of orange and lemon or lime |

Mix together the wine, fruit juice, brandy, Cointreau and sugar, to taste. At the last minute, add the soda water and ice. Place a slice of lemon or orange in each glass.

Sloe, damson or wild plum gin

The method for making all these liqueurs is the same and you can, if you wish, substitute vodka for the gin. Mentally marking down a blackthorn bush covered in sloes in early autumn is a good idea, for they should be picked when the first frost has been on them. If you don't know anyone with a damson tree, your greengrocer will probably be able to get you some but the gastronomic queen of fruits for quaffers is the wild plum. In Hampshire, there is a certain windbreak planted by Lord Rank where, once in a blue moon, there is one of Nature's extravaganzas. The tall bushes can be laden with the translucent little plums, ranging from deepest burgundy and ruby red to amber. One year, there were so many fermenting fruits on the ground that I actually saw drunken pheasants reeling about. In the old days, poachers sometimes put out raisins soaked in alcohol to catch their quarry; on this occasion, it wouldn't have been necessary. The best fruit always seemed to grow high up so I used to stand on the bonnet of the Land Rover to pick them.

| 2.3 kg/ 5 lb fruit of your choice |
| 700 g/ 1½ lb sugar |
| 3–4 drops almond essence (optional) |
| bottle of gin or vodka |

You can avoid the tedious chore of pricking the fruit by freezing and then thawing it. It should then split. Put the split or pricked fruit into a clean container with a screw top. (A plastic sweet jar, begged from your village shop, is ideal.) Add the sugar and almond essence, if using, and top up with your preferred alcohol. Cover tightly and place in a dark cupboard. Shake occasionally, to dissolve the sugar. Leave for at least 2 months.

Strain into sterilised bottles. The alcoholic fruit can be stoned and covered in melted chocolate for Christmas presents or you can stir it into vanilla ice cream for a delectable pudding.

DRINKS

Spiked South Seas tea

My daughter, Lucy, picked this recipe up on her honeymoon in Bali. It contains a ferocious amount of rum. I have given the full amount of rum but I think half would probably be sufficient.

1.2 litres/2 pints strong tea
110 g/4 oz caster sugar
juice of 1 lemon
275 ml/½ pint Lamb's Navy Rum
ice cubes
lemon slices

Make the tea, strain into a jug and add the sugar, lemon juice and rum. Stir well, until the sugar has completely dissolved. Cool, add plenty of ice and serve with a slice of lemon in each glass. The tea can also be drunk hot.

Archie's Bloody Mary

SERVES 3–4

In memory of Archie, the last recipe in this book is his very special Bloody Mary. These are knock-out drops, which appear to be perfectly harmless but in fact are fairly lethal, yet, nonetheless, quite delicious. He used to make it the evening before it was to be drunk, usually just as I was doing some complicated cookery, all of which had to stop as he issued a list of requirements (he was disabled). He used to make it in a preserving pan and then pour it into tomato-juice jars for storage in the refrigerator. The following recipe has been scaled down for 3 or 4 people. It is much better made the day before, to allow the flavours to develop. Taste as you go but don't drive afterwards!

1 teaspoon Lawry's or other seasoned or ground black pepper
1½ teaspoons dried oregano
2 teaspoons sugar
½ teaspoon celery salt
1 jar tomato juice
150 ml/¼ pint vodka
1 tablespoon lemon juice
Lea & Perrins Worcestershire Sauce, to taste
4 shakes of Tabasco sauce

Mix the dry ingredients in a jug and then pour in the tomato juice and stir well. Add the vodka and stir again.

Finally, add the Worcestershire and Tabasco sauces, mix well and pour into a jug. Cover with cling film and refrigerate. Lucy likes to add a dash of sherry, but this is optional. Add ice cubes just before serving.

Variation: For a 'Virgin Mary', also known as a 'Bloody Shame', omit the alcohol.

DRINKS

LIST OF USEFUL MAIL-ORDER ADDRESSES

This is just a sample of my personal favourites.

Smoked food

FORMAN & FIELD. One of the oldest fish smokers. Smoked organically-farmed salmon, wild smoked Scottish salmon and smoked eel. Also do boxes for freezer of Welsh lamb, naturally reared in Snowdonia and many other goodies.
Telephone: **020 8221 3939**
Website: **www.formanandfield.com** E-mail: **info@formanandfield.com**

BLACK MOUNTAINS SMOKERY LTD. Traditional smoked foods, salmon, trout and in season, local eels.
Telephone: **01873 811566**
Website: **www.smoked-foods.co.uk** E-mail: **sales@smoked-foods.co.uk**

Organic meat

EASTBROOK FARMS ORGANIC MEAT. Organic fresh free-range lamb and beef and poultry, honey-cured ham, green and smoked bacon.
Telephone: **01793 790460**
Website: **www.helenbrowningorganics.co.uk** E-mail: **info@helenbrowningorganics.co.uk**

SWADDLES GREEN FARM. Complete range of award-winning organically produced meats, poultry, bacon etc.
Telephone: **01460 234387**
Website: **www.swaddles.co.uk** E-mail: **information@swaddles.co.uk**

Air-dried ham

DENHAY FARMS LTD. Air-dried Parma type ham from whey-fed pigs cured in apple-juice, honey, salt and local herbs. Also other farm products.
Telephone: **01308 458963**
Website: **wwwdenhay.co.uk** E-mail: **sales@denhay.co.uk**

Game

WILLO GAME. All game. Woodcock, teal and widgeon in limited supplies.
Telephone: **01588 650539**
Website: **www.willogame.co.uk** E-mail: **enquiries@willogame.co.uk**

YORKSHIRE GAME. All game plus heather-bred Scottish black-faced lamb and Iron-age pork (Tamworth/wild boar).
Telephone: **01387 730326**
Website: **www.blackface.co.uk** E-mail: **ben@blackface.co.uk**

Cheeses

NEAL'S YARD DAIRY. Specialist cheese-mongers who sell a huge selection of cheeses, mostly hand-made from raw milk and ripened in the Dairy's cellars.
Telephone: **0207 6453555**
Website: **www.nealsyarddairy.co.uk** E-mail: **mailorder@nealsyarddairy.co.uk**

THE CHEESE SOCIETY. Over 200 cheeses available.
Telephone: **01522 511003**
Website: **www.thecheesesociety.co.uk** E-mail: **cheese@thecheesesociety.co.uk**

Vegetables and Fruit

FARM SHOPS and FARMER'S MARKETS are an invaluable source of fresh fruit and veg. If you don't know where your nearest market takes place get in touch with THE FARMER'S MARKET ASSOCIATION.
Telephone: **0845 2302150**
Website: **www.farmersmarkets.net** E-mail: **info@farmersmarkets.net**

WFU, WOMEN'S FOOD AND FARMING UNION is a voluntary organization devoted to promoting an understanding between British producers and consumers. Amongst their other activities, they monitor production methods and scientific developments.
Telephone: **01203 693171**
Website: **www.wfu.org.uk** E-mail: **admin@wfu.org.uk**

Kitchen Equipment

LAKELAND LTD. 'Must-have' mail order outlet for all kitchen equipment. Now stocks foil bags for smoking. Listens to customers and often brings back out-of-production items on request, not to mention new inventions. Friendly staff make you feel special.
Telephone: **01539 488100**
Website: **www.lakelandlimited.com** E-mail: **net.shop@lakelandlimited.co.uk**

USEFUL ADDRESSES

CHEESE

British Cheeses and their European counterparts

The number of British cheesemakers has grown beyond all recognition and gone are the days when to most people 'British' meant Cheddar, Stilton and Philadelphia cream cheese. Connoisseurs probably knew about Dorset Blue Vinney and other more unusual varieties but for those who wished for exotic cheeses there were an increasing number of imports such as Camembert, Brie and Gorgonzola. Now you don't need to buy foreign, for our homegrown products are so diverse and wonderful that I would never have room to list them all. What I have done however is to list a few of our own cheeses (left) that are similar to the most well-known European varieties.

Buffalo Blue   Dolcelatte
Lanark Blue   Roquefort
Oxford Blue   Fourme d'ambert

Sussex Weald Feta   Fetta
Sussex Weal Halloumi   Halloumi

Buffalo mozarella   Mozarella

Somerset Brie   Brie
Cricket Organic Brie   Brie

Howgate camembert (Scotland)   Camembert

Ardrahan   Buttery and fruity like a young gruyère
Oxford Isis   Munster

Coquetdale   Tomme type

Twineham Grange   Parmesan

Cerney goat   St Chevrier d'ash
Cotswold crottin   Crottin chavignol
Golden Cross and Ragstone   St Maure log

American chicken salad, 118,

apple and raisin chutney, 180,

apple cake, spiced, 170

apple jelly, basic recipe, 174

apple sorbet or 'le trou normand', 161,

apple tart, Jeanette's, 157

apricot and almond stuffing, 66,

apricot bread and butter pudding, 150,

Archie's Bloody Mary, 198,

Archie's curry, 98,

Archie's mustard, 147,

asparagus sauce, Lucy's 131,

asparagus with Lucy's sauce, 24,

avocados sauce gribiche, 20,

avocado with feta cheese and salami, in raspberry
    vinaigrette, 20

'bag o' nails' potatoes, 106

baby broad beans in cream sauce, 104

bank-side barbecued trout with 'freebies', 43

basic brown sauce, 128

basic smoked haddock mousse and variations, 22

basic spiced vinegar, 183

basic sweet spiced vinegar, 183

basil oil, 146

bean soup, Tuscan, 14

bean, white, fennel and Pernod soup, 8

beans, broad, see broad beans

beans, french

    french bean and tomato salad, 121

    french beans with bacon and cheese, 106

béarnaise sauce, classic, 132

béarnaise, blender, 132

béchamel sauce, 126

beef

    beef in beer, with crisp bread topping, 72

    roast fore-rib of beef, 70

    Scotch minced beef collops 73

beetroot and cranberry bortsch, 7

beetroot, tiny pickled, in sweet spiced vinegar, 184

bercy sauce, 129

beurre manié, 15

beurre noir with capers, 60

biscuits see also Bread, cakes and biscuits

bisque, salmon, with diced fennel, 11

blackberry and apple jelly, 156

blackberry whisky, 192

blackcurrant leaf or elderflower sorbet, 162

blackcurrant, cassis or, liqueur, 193

blender béarnaise, 132

blender hollandaise, 133

blender mayonnaise, whole-egg, 134

Bloody Mary, Archie's, 198

boiled chicken and parsley sauce, 87

boned, stuffed duck, with truffles, 28

bortsch, beetroot and cranberry, 7

bottled fungi, 186

bottling see preserves and bottling

braised florence fennel, 104

braised lettuce, 42

brandy, Lucy's raspberry, 195

brandy, quince, 196

Breach orange vodka, 193

Bread, cakes and biscuits, 165-71

Bread

    Hugh's quick olive oil bread, 166

    soda bread, 167

bread and butter pudding, apricots, 150

bread sauce, 130

broad bean soup, with herbs and diced ham, 5

broad beans, baby, in cream sauce, 104

broth, chicken and barley, 2

broth, lamb, 12

brown sauce, basic, 128

brown stock, 15

bubble and squeak, with bacon, 99

buttered carrots, 104

butternut squash risotto, 100

INDEX

cabbage, red, see red cabbage, Lucy's
cakes see also Bread, cakes and biscuits
  carrot cake, 168
  keeper's cake, 169
  raisin, rum and nut cake, 169
  Sophy's chocolate cake, 170
  spiced apple cake, 170
caper sauce, 126
carrot cake, 168
carrot cake pudding with fluffy lemon sauce, 154
carrots, buttered, 104
carrot, coriander seed and orange soup, 10
casseroles
  beef in beer, with crisp bread topping, 72
  duck and bean casserole, 88
  hare and chestnut casserole, 63
  mixed wild mushroom and lentil stew, 114
  oxtail stew and dumplings, 74
  pigeon and tangerine casserole, 59
  venison casserole, with chipolatas, 64
cassis or blackcurrant liqueur, 193
castle puddings, with treacle, 151
celeriac
  celeriac, apple and walnut, 5
  celeriac mashed with coriander, 105
  celeriac salad, with rémoulade sauce, 188
chanterelle tart, with hazelnut pastry, 122
cheese mousse, 23
cheese sauce, 126
chervil-stuffed eggs, with lemon mayonnaise, 20
chestnut stuffing, 92
chicken
  boiled chicken and parsley sauce, 87
  chicken and barley broth, 2
  chicken, American salad, 118
  claypot roast chicken, with lemon and parsley
    stuffing, 86
  creamy walnut sauce, with, 89
  fricassée of, 88
  tarragon and star anise chicken breast, 119

chicken livers
  chicken-liver pâté, with paprika or with green
    peppercorns, 29
  Iris's spicy chicken-liver pâté, 30
  Kosher Jewish chopped chicken livers, 28
chilli sherry, 146
chilli vinegar, 146
choccy pots, 155
chocolate cake, Sophy's, 170
chowder, smoked haddock, 11
Christmas soup, 12
Christmas turkey, with three stuffings, 92
chutneys, 180–3
classic béarnaise sauce, 132
classic mayonnaise, 134
claypot roast chicken, with lemon and parsley
  stuffing, 86
Coats salad dressing, 135
coffee, spicy iced, 192
consommé, game, 3
cooked salad dressing, 118
coquilles St Jacques mornay, 40
cordial, elderflower, 191
courgette and dill soup, with fromage frais, 8
court bouillon, 16
crab apples, pickled spiced, 184
cranberry sauce, 136
creamy fresh tomato soup, with diced onion and
  basil, 10
creamy smoked haddock kedgeree, 101
crème brûlée, 'lemon stone', 158
crevettes Theodor, 40
croquettes, turkey and ham, 94
croûtons, nutmeg, 6
crumble, fruit and nut, 152
Cumberland sauce, 136
curly kale, puréed with crème fraîche, 105
curry, Archie's, 98

damson mouse, 156

damson sauce, 90

dressings

    classic mayonnaise, 134

    Coats salad dressing, 135

    cooked salad dressing, 118

    hazelnut oil dressing, 20

    raspberry vinaigrette, 20

    vinaigrette sauce, 135

drinks, alcoholic and non-alcoholic, 189-98

duck

    boned, stuffed with truffles, 28

    duck and bean casserole, 88

    duck soup, with wild mushrooms and
      Madeira, 2

    Mick's hair drier duck, with damson sauce, 90

    warm smoked duck breast, with quince and red
      onion chutney, 27

dumplings, Tread's, 74

easy grouse pâté, 30

egg sauce, 126

eggs, chervil-stuffed, with lemon mayonnaise, 20

eggs and Swiss chard with cream, 24

elderberry and apple jelly, 175

elderberry, iced soufflé, 161

elderflowers

    elderflower champagne, 190

    elderflower cordial, 191

    elderflower fritters, 'freebie', 151

    elderflower or blackcurrant leaf sorbet, 162

    elderflower wine, 194

family fare, 97-101

fennel, florence, braised, 104

fennel, Lucy's red cabbage, apple and, 108

fennel, white bean and Pernod soup, 8

fish, 39-47

    pie, with crunchy topping, 41

    stock or fumet, 16

fishcakes, oriental, 44

flash-fried fillets of sea trout, with lemon butter
    sauce and braised lettuce, 42

french bean and tomato salad, 121

french beans, with bacon and cheese, 106

fricassée of chicken, 88

fritters, elderflower, 151

fruit and nut crumble, 152

fumet or fish stock, 16

fungi, 111-4

fungi, bottled, 186

game, 49-67

    brawn, 31

    consommé, 3

    pie, hot, 66

    pie, rich raised, 33

garlic vinegar, 144

gin, sloe, damson or wild plum, 197

ginger beer, 191

goats cheese and toasted walnut salad, 27

gooseberries

    gooseberries in elderflower syrup, 186

    gooseberry and elderflower jelly, 175

    gooseberry sauce, green, 136

gravy, 93

    onion, 127

Greek mushroom salad, 121

green gooseberry sauce, 136

green sauce, 134

green tomato, Sophie's, chutney, 183

grouse, old, braised in raspberry vinegar, 52

grouse pâté, easy, 30

guards pudding, 152

Gudrun's honeyed potatoes, 107

guinea fowl, pot-roast, with spiced crab apples, 94

haddock, smoked, see smoked haddock

halibut with a dill sauce, 47

ham

   chicken and, American salad dressing, 118

   ham and cheese mousse, with spinach, 23

   triple tricolor salad, 120

   whole boiled ham, 80

hare and chestnut casserole, 63

hare medallions, with cassis, 62

hazelnut oil dressing 20

hazelnut pastry, 112

Heather's preserved mint, 147

hedgehog mushrooms sautéed with garlic, 112

Henry VIII poached eggs, 25

herbs, 139-47

herb jellies, 175

herb oil, Provençal, 146

hollandaise, blender, 133

hollandaise sauce, 133

honey and walnut pancakes, 153

horseradish sauce, 135

hot bullshot, 195

hot game pie, 66

hot-water crust pastry, 33

Hugh's quick olive oil bread, 166

ice creams, 160–4

iced coffee, spiced, 192

iced elderberry soufflé, 161

Iris's spicy chicken-liver pâté, 30

jams, 177–9

Jeanette's apple tart, 157

jellies, 174–6

   blackberry and apple jelly, 156

kale, curly, puréed with crème fraîche, 105

kedgeree, creamy smoked haddock, 101

keeper's cake, 169

kidneys, shootable stag, 81

Lady Durham's sauce, 128

lamb

   braised lamb shanks, with white wine and
     rosemary, 76

   lamb broth, 12

   roast leg of lamb, 75

   shepherd's pie, 76

lawyer's wig, with cream and mace, 113

leek and lemon sauce, 56

lemon and parsley stuffing, 86

lemon barley water, 190

lemon butter sauce, 129

'lemon stone' crème brûlée, 158

lemon vodka, 195

lentil stew, mixed wild mushroom and, 114

lettuce, braised, 42

lettuce and sorrel soup, 9

liqueur, blackcurrant or cassis, 193

liver, Sante's, with fried sage, 82

Lucy's asparagus sauce, 131

Lucy's raspberry brandy, 195

Lucy's red cabbage, fennel and apple, 108

MMMM or mighty muscovado marmalade

mallard, 54

mackerel with green gooseberry sauce, 42

main-course minestrone, 13

marmalade, mighty muscovado, 179

marmalade, Seville orange, 179

marrow chutney, 181

Mauro's marvellous mixture, pasta with, 100

mayonnaise, classic, 134

mayonnaise, whole-egg blender, 134

meat, 69-82

membrillo, 176

Mick's hair drier duck, with damson sauce, 90

mighty muscovado marmalade, 179

mighty muscovado marmalade mallard, MMMM
   or, 54

minestrone, main-course, 13

mint and apple vinegar, 144

mint, Heather's preserved, 147

mixed wild mushroom and lentil stew, 114

mornay, coquilles St Jacques, 40

mousses

  basic smoked haddock mousse and
    variations, 22

  cheese mousse, 23

  salmon or smoked salmon mousse, 23

  spinach, ham and cheese mousse, 23

Mrs M's best shortbread ever, 171

Mrs Watkins' runner-bean chutney, 182

mushrooms, 111-4

  chanterelle tart, with hazelnut pastry, 112

  duck soup, with wild mushrooms and
    Madeira, 2

  Greek mushroom salad, 121

  hedgehog mushrooms, sautéed with garlic, 112

  lawyer's wig, with cream and mace, 113

  puffball slices, fried with egg and
    breadcrumbs, 114

  roast snipe on mushrooms, 57

mussels in white wine and cream, 45

mustard, Archie's, 147

Nannie's scones, 167

nettle soup, 9

nutmeg croûtons, 6

oil, basil, 146

oil, herb see herbs

oil, Provençal herb, 146

old grouse, braised in raspberry vinegar, 52

olive oil bread, Hugh's quick, 166

omelette, Spanish, 100

onion gravy, 127

onion sauce, rich, 127

onions, pickled, 184

orange marmalade, Seville, 179

orange vodka, Breach, 193

oriental fishcakes, 44

oxtail soup, 4

oxtail stew and dumplings, 74

pancakes, honey and walnut, 153

parsley sauce, 126

parsnip patties, 107

partridge, poached, poulette, 53

pasta with Mauro's marvellous mixture, 100

pastry

  hazelnut pastry, 112

  hot-water crust pastry, 33

  Jeanette's pastry, 157

  suet crust pastry, 72

pâtés 29–36

peaches in Madeira syrup, 185

pears in red-wine syrup, 185

Peta's tuna fish salad, 123

pheasant

  pheasant 'Guidwife', 54

  pheasant sausage, with leek and
  lemon sauce, 56

  pheasant terrine, with Calvados, apple and
    mushroom, 32

pickles 184–5

  pickled onions, 184

  pickled spiced crab apples, 184

pies

  fish pie, with crunchy topping, 41

  hot game pie, 66

  rich raised game pie, 33

pigeon

  pigeon bangers and mash, 60

  pigeon and tangerine casserole, 59

  pigeon, grilled breasts, stuffed with garlic
    cheese, 58

  pigeon, grilled breasts with redcurrant jelly and
    cream, 58

  smoked pigeon pâté, 34

plum jam, 177

plums in white-wine syrup, 186

poached partridge poulette, 53

pork

   roast pork, with crunchy crackling, 78

   pork stir-fry, with lime and mushrooms, 79

pot-roast guinea fowl, with spiced crab apples, 94

potatoes

   'bag o' nails' potatoes, 106

   bubble and squeak, with bacon, 99

   Gudrun's honeyed potatoes, 107

   potato purée, with diced root vegetables, 108

   potato salad, 122

poultry, 85-95

prawns

   crevettes Theodor, 40

preserves and bottling, 173-87

Provençal herb oil, 146

Prue's hot Christmas punch, 196

Prue's perfect rice, 98

puddings, 149-163

puffball slices, fried in egg and breadcrumbs, 114

pumpkin, tomato and basil soup, 6

punch, Prue's hot Christmas, 196

purple-sprouting broccoli, with hazelnut oil
   dressing, 20

quail's eggs in poppaddums, salmon and, with
   potato salad, 122

queen of puddings, 154

quinces

   membrillo, 176

   quince and red onion chutney, 182

   quince brandy, 196

   quince jelly, 176

rabbit

   rabbit fried with almonds and creamy sauce, 61

   rabbit risotto with ramsons pesto, 62

raisin, rum and nut cake, 169

raspberry brandy, Lucy's, 195

raspberry chranachan ice cream, 160

raspberry jam, uncooked, 178

raspberry vinegar, 144

red cabbage, fennel and apple, Lucy's, 108

red onion, apple and sage relish, 181

redcurrant jelly, 175

relish, red onion, apple and sage, 181

rémoulade sauce, 118

rice, Prue's perfect, 98

rice, pudding, 150

rich onion sauce, 127

rich raised game pie, 33

roast fore-rib of beef, 70

roast leg of lamb, 75

roast pork, with crunchy crackling, 78

roast roe haunch, stuffed with apricots and
   almonds, 66

roast snipe on mushrooms, 57

roe haunch, roast, stuffed with apricots and
   almonds, 66

rowan and apple jelly, 176

runner-bean chutney, Mrs Watkins', 182

sage and shallot vinegar, 144

sage, apple and celery stuffing, 78

salads, 117-23

   celeriac, apple and walnut salad, 5

salmon

   barbecued salmon, 47

   poached or baked salmon, 46

   salmon and caper terrine, 35

   salmon and quail's eggs in poppadums, with
     potato salad, 122

   salmon bisque, with diced fennel, 11

   salmon or smoked salmon mousse, 23

   spicy 'hot-smoked' salmon moulds, 22

salmon, smoked, see smoked salmon

samphire with melted butter, 24

sangría, 197

Sante's liver, with fried sage, 82

sauces 125–136

   creamy sauce, 61

   damson sauce, 90

   leek and lemon sauce, 56

   rémoulade sauce, 118

   sauce poulette, 53

   smoked eel with dill and gherkin sauce, 21

sausagemeat

   sausagemeat stuffing, 92

   toad in the hole, 99

scallops

   coquilles St Jacques mornay, 40

scones, Nannie's, 167

Scotch minced-beef collops, 73

sea trout, flash-fried fillets of, with lemon butter

   and braised lettuce, 42

Seville orange marmalade, 179

shepherd's pie, 76

sherry, chilli, 146

'shootable. stag' kidneys, 81

shortbread, Mrs M's best ever, 171

sloe, damson or wild plum gin, 197

smoked duck breast, warm, with quince and red

   onion chutney, 27

smoked eel with dill and gherkin sauce, 21

smoked haddock

   basic smoked haddock mousse,

    and variations, 22

   creamy smoked haddock kedgeree, 101

   smoked haddock chowder, 11

smoked pigeon pâté, 34

smoked salmon mousse, 23

smoked trout and fried almond pâté, 35

snipe, roast, on mushrooms, 57

snipe, 'Butcher's treat', 57

soda bread, 167

Sophie's chutney, 183

Sophy's chocolate cake, 170

sorbets, 162- 3

sorrel, see soups

soups 1–16

Spanish omelette, 100

spiced apple cake, 170

spiced crab apples, pickled 184

spiced vinegar, basic, 183

spiced vinegar, basic sweet, 183

spicy 'hot-smoked' salmon moulds, 22

spicy iced coffee, 192

spiked South Seas tea, 198

spinach, ham and cheese mousse, 23

starters, 19-36

steak and kidney pudding, 72

stew, mixed wild mushroom and lentil, 114

stew, oxtail, and dumplings, 74

strawberry jam, 178

stock see brown, white

stuffings

   apricot and almond stuffing, 66

   chestnut stuffing, 92

   lemon and parsley stuffing, 86

   sage, apple and celery stuffing, 78

   sausagemeat stuffing, 92

   sweetcorn and cranberry stuffing, 92

suet crust pastry, 72

summer garden salad, with snipped herbs, 122

summer pudding, 158

swede soup, with nutmeg croûtons, 6

sweetcorn and cranberry stuffing, 92

swift and speedy sponge cake, 168

tangerine sorbet, 163

tarragon and star anise chicken breast, 119

tarragon sauce, 126

tarragon vinegar, 144

tart, Jeanette's apple, 157

tart, treacle, 159

tartare sauce, 134

tea, spiked South Seas, 198

ten minute mackerel mousse, 23

terrine, pheasant, with Calvados, apple and
    mushroom, 32

terrine, salmon and caper, 35

thickeners for soups, 15

tiny pickled beetroot in sweet spiced vinegar, 184

toad in the hole, 99

tomato and basil soup, with pumpkin, 6

tomato, green chutney, 183

tomato sauce, 130

tomato soup, creamy fresh, with diced onion and
    basil, 10

tomato tart with crème fraîche and basil, 26

treacle tart, 159

Tread's dumplings, 74

triple tricolor salad, 120

trout, bank-side barbecued with 'freebies', 43

trout fillets, with bacon and oatmeal, 44

trout, sea, see sea trout

trout, smoked, see smoked trout

tuna fish salad, Peta's, 123

turkey and ham croquettes, 94

turkey, Christmas, with three stuffings, 92

uncooked raspberry jam, 178

vegetables, 101-8

velvety venison casserole agro dolce, 65

velouté sauce, 126

venison casserole, with chipolatas, 64

vinaigrette sauce, 135

vinegar, raspberry, 144

vinegars, herb see herbs
  basic spiced vinegar, 183
  basic sweet spiced vinegar, 183

vodka, Breach orange, 193

vodka, lemon, 195

warm chargrilled vegetable salad with goats
    cheese and air-dried ham, 26

warm smoked duck breast, with quince and red
    onion chutney, 27

watercress and pine nut vegetarian pâté, 36

whisky, blackberry, 192

white stock, 15

whole boiled ham, 80

whole-egg blender mayonnaise, 134

wild mushroom and lentil stew, mixed, 114

wild mushrooms (fungi), 111–4

wild mushrooms, duck soup with, and Madeira, 2

woodcock with beurre noir and capers, 60

Yorkshire pudding, 71

Index of Vegetarian Dishes

'bag o' nails' potatoes, 106

asparagus with Lucy's sauce, 24

avocados sauce gribiche, 20

baby broad beans in cream sauce, 104

beetroot and cranberry bortsch, 7

braised florence fennel, 104

buttered carrots, 104

butternut squash risotto, 100

carrot, coriander seed and orange soup, 10

celeriac mashed with coriander, 105

celeriac salad, with rémoulade sauce, 188

celeriac, apple and walnut soup, 5

chanterelle tart, with hazelnut pastry, 112

cheese mousse, 23

chervil-stuffed eggs, with lemon mayonnaise, 20

chestnut stuffing, 92

Coats salad dressing, 135

courgette and dill soup, with fromage frais, 8

court bouillon, 16

creamy fresh tomato soup, with diced onion and
    basil, 10

curly kale, puréed with crème fraîche, 105

eggs and Swiss chard with cream, 24

fennel, white bean and Pernod soup, 8

French bean and tomato salad, 121

goats cheese and toasted walnut salad, 27

Greek mushroom salad, 121

Gudrun's honeyed potatoes, 107

hazelnut oil dressing, 20

hazelnut pastry, 112

hedgehog mushrooms sautéed with garlic, 112

Henry VIII's poached eggs, 25

honey and walnut pancakes, 153

Hugh's quick olive oil bread, 166

lawyer's wig, with cream and mace, 113

lemon and parsley stuffing, 86

lettuce and sorrel soup, 9

Lucy's red cabbage, fennel and apple, 108

main-course minestrone, 13

mixed wild mushroom and lentil stew, 114

nettle soup, 9

parsnip patties, 107

pasta with Mauro's marvellous mixture, 100

potato purée, with diced root vegetables, 108

Prue's perfect rice, 98

purple-sprouting broccoli with hazelnut oil
    dressing, 20

sage, apple and celery stuffing, 78

samphire with melted butter, 24

soda bread, 167

Spanish omelette, 100

summer garden salad, with snipped herbs, 122

swede soup, with nutmeg croûtons, 6

sweetcorn and cranberry stuffing, 92

tomato tart with crème fraîche and basil, 26

Tuscan bean soup, 14

watercress and pine nut vegetarian pâté, 36

Yorkshire pudding, 71

VEGETARIAN INDEX

Quickies Index

avocado with feta cheese and salami, in raspberry vinaigrette, 20

beetroot and cranberry bortsch, 7

broad bean soup, with herbs and diced ham, 5

carrot, coriander seed and orange soup, 10

celeriac, apple and walnut soup, 5

chicken-liver pâte, with paprika or with green peppercorns, 29

courgette and dill soup, with fromage frais, 8

creamy fresh tomato soup, with diced onion and basil, 10

crevettes Theodor, 40

damson mousse, 156

eggs and Swiss chard with cream, 24

fricassée of chicken, 88

goats cheese and toasted walnut salad, 27

grilled pigeon breasts stuffed with garlic cheese, 58

grilled pigeon breasts with redcurrant jelly and cream, 58

halibut with a dill sauce, 47

Henry VIII's poached eggs, 25

Iris's spicy chicken-liver pâte, 30

Kosher Jewish chopped chicken livers, 28

lettuce and sorrell soup, 9

nettle soup, 9

oxtail soup, 4

pork stir-fry, with lime and mushrooms, 79

purple-sprouting broccoli with hazlenut oil dressing, 20

'shootable stag' kidneys, 81

smoked eel with dill and gherkin sauce, 21

Spanish omelette, 100

swede soup, with nutmeg croûtons, 6

ten minute mackerel mousse, 23

triple tricolour salad, 120

Useful Information Index

basic kitchen equipment, 137

cheese, 201

list of useful mail-order addresses, 199

store cupboard flavourings, 138

Also published by Merlin Unwin Books
7 Corve Street, Ludlow, Shropshire, SY8 1DB, UK
Telephone Orders: 01584 877456
Website: www.countrybooksdirect.com

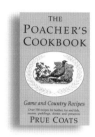

THE POACHERS COOKBOOK
Game and country recipes
Prue Coats
£11.99 Paperback

SIMPLY SALMON AND OTHER GOURMET FOOD
Over 70 delicious recipes for salmon and other gourmet food
Prue Coats
£4.99 Paperback

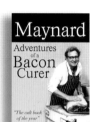

MAYNARD, ADVENTURES OF A BACON CURER
Maynard Davies
£9.99 Hardback

THE TOWNIES GUIDE TO THE COUNTRYSIDE
Jill Mason
£20.00 Hardback

CONFESSIONS OF A SHOOTING FISHING MAN
Laurence Catlow
£14.99 Hardback

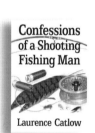

THE BEDSIDE BOOK SERIES:
THE FISHERMAN'S BEDSIDE BOOK
Compiled by 'BB'
£18.95 Hardback

THE SHOOTING MAN'S BEDSIDE BOOK
Compiled by 'BB'
£18.95 Hardback

THE RACING MAN'S BEDISDE BOOK
Compiled by Julian Bedford
£18.95Hardback